Foxe's Book of Martyrs and the Elect Nation

JOHN FOXE 1587

FOXE'S
BOOK OF MARTYRS
AND THE
ELECT NATION

WILLIAM HALLER

JONATHAN CAPE
Thirty Bedford Square London

First published 1963

© 1963 by William Haller

PRINTED IN GREAT BRITAIN BY
EBENEZER BAYLIS AND SON LIMITED,
THE TRINITY PRESS, WORCESTER, AND LONDON
ON PAPER MADE BY JOHN DICKINSON AND CO., LTD.
BOUND BY A. W. BAIN AND CO., LTD., LONDON

Contents

Illustrations

*(Illustrations are from copies of the original
editions in the Folger Shakespeare Library)*

Preface

〜※〜

M Y intention in these pages is to offer an account of the
content and purport of John Foxe's *Actes and Monumentes*,
usually referred to as 'The Book of Martyrs', in what I
conceive to be the context of its own time. The account is based
primarily on a study of that book in the successive versions and
editions published by the author in his lifetime and of the relevant
contemporary literature of Protestant edification and propaganda.
Foxe published two preliminary versions of his book on the
Continent in 1554 and 1559, the first English version in 1563,
a much revised and greatly enlarged version in 1570, and two
editions in 1576 and 1583 with some further revisions and additions but no significant changes. In the century after his death
five more editions, based on the text of 1583, appeared in 1596,
1610, 1631–2, 1641 and 1684. The same text, slightly bowdlerized
and at certain points somewhat awkwardly conflated with the
text of 1563, was again reproduced in an edition in eight volumes
issued by S. R. Cattley in 1837, later revised by Josiah Pratt, and
reissued with pagination unchanged in 1843–9, 1870 and 1877.

Quotations from the book in the following pages correspond
to the text as it appears in the Cattley-Pratt edition, corrected as
may be necessary according to the original. Spelling and punctua-
tion have been regulated according to present usage. Of the
numerous other editions or versions of Foxe's book published
subsequently to 1684, I have examined a considerable number but
not all, and have found none to be complete and many to be
grossly corrupt.

Most of the stories of the Marian martyrs appeared for the first
time in print in the pages of Foxe's book, but some were published

9

Preface

separately on the Continent during Mary's reign or directly afterwards in England. Other writings of the martyrs and many tracts, sermons, reports and treatises by returned exiles and other survivors of the Marian persecution were put into print after Elizabeth's accession. Additional information concerning the martyrs and their associates is to be found in Foxe's notes and manuscripts which, after passing through the hands of John Strype, are now preserved in the British Museum. Much material from all these sources was incorporated by Strype in his voluminous and rather ill-ordered compilations relating to the English Reformation. Many of the writings of the martyrs, exiles and other reformers drawn from Foxe and other sources were reprinted in the nineteenth century in the publications of the Parker Society.

I am much indebted throughout these pages to J. F. Mozley's informing and judicious account of Foxe's career and accomplishment in his *John Foxe and his Book* (1940). Other recent works dealing with the martyrs and their contemporaries which I have found particularly useful are as follows: A. J. Muller, *Stephen Gardiner and the Tudor Reaction* (1926); A. G. Chester, *Hugh Latimer* (1954); J. G. Ridley, *Nicholas Ridley* (1957); W. T. Davies, *Bibliography of John Bale* (Oxford Bibliographical Society, 1940); Philip Hughes, *Reformation in England* (1950-4), especially vol. II; and, disregarding its obvious bias, C. H. Garrett, *The Marian Exiles* (1938). I regret that V. J. K. Brook's *Life of Archbishop Parker* (1962) and Jasper Ridley's *Thomas Cranmer* (1962) reached me too late for me to make use of them.

A preliminary essay on the subject of the present book appeared in *The Seventeenth Century*, a volume of essays by various writers published in 1951 in honour of Richard Foster Jones. The substance of certain chapters was presented at Cornell University in 1961 as the Messenger Lectures on the Evolution of Civilization. In 1962, while preparing the book for publication, I had the privilege of serving as the Visiting Research Scholar of the William Andrews Clark Memorial Library of the University of California at Los Angeles. For the leisure which has made my studies possible, I am deeply indebted to the Folger Shakespeare Library and the

Preface

John Simon Guggenheim Memorial Foundation. The members of the staff of the Folger Library have given me their constant cheerful assistance. Miss Megan Lloyd has been of help in preparing the manuscript. I am more deeply obliged than I can say to Louis B. Wright and Sir John Neale for friendly encouragement and wise counsel.

WILLIAM HALLER

Folger Shakespeare Library

Introduction

꧁ᳩ꧂

PROFESSOR TREVELYAN has told us that the 'most influential writer in the age of Shakespeare, if it was not Foxe the Martyrologist, was Hakluyt, author of *The Principall Navigations Voiages and Discoveries of the English Nation*'. By the time, however, that Hakluyt's book was published in 1589, Foxe's book had been circulating in print for at least thirty years, Shakespeare was twenty-five years old, and the queen's reign was more than half over. Foxe had begun in 1554 as a Protestant refugee in Strasbourg by publishing the stories of certain fifteenth- and early sixteenth-century victims of persecution in a small Latin octavo of 212 leaves. At Basle in 1559 he had published a folio of over 700 pages in which to these earlier stories he added the reports that had so far reached him of victims of persecution in the reign of Mary, which had just come to an end. In 1563, back in England, he published an English version of his book, a folio of over 1,471 pages, enlarged by the addition of more stories of recent victims of persecution, illustrated with over fifty woodcuts, and dedicated to the new queen. In 1570, at the time of the revolt of the northern earls and the Pope's bull excommunicating Elizabeth, Foxe issued a second edition, a folio of over 2,314 pages, enlarged by the addition of still more martyr stories and an extended account of ecclesiastical and national history. The work was now ordered to be set up along with the Bible for all to read in churches and other public places, where in some instances it remained until quite recent times. Two more editions appeared before the year of the Armada, another in 1596 after the author's death, and four more in the following century, the ninth and last in 1684. Thus by the end of the seventeenth century something like ten thousand copies of the work, which from the beginning was commonly referred to as 'The Book of Martyrs', had been set in circulation in English print over a period of a hundred and twenty-one years – more, it is safe to say, than any other book of similar scope except the Bible. There had also been published various abridgements and abstracts, and much material drawn from the book had appeared with or without acknowledgment in other publications, such as Holinshed's *Chronicles* in 1577. Echoes of the Book of Martyrs were to be heard throughout the period from countless pulpits.

Whether Foxe's view of religion and the Church was right and his report of the facts of history true has always been a subject of disagreement, but there has never been any doubt as to the historical importance of a book which the shapers of opinion, the masters of policy, and – except for adherents of the old religion – Englishmen in general in the reign of Elizabeth accepted as an expression of the national faith second in authority only to the Bible and as an unanswerable defence of England's ideological position in the contemporary struggle for national independence and power. As Mr Gordon Rupp says, 'Foxe's *Book* counted in English history as much as Drake's drum.' It counted immediately because it gave the subjects of Elizabeth I a circumstantial report of the very striking events which led to the queen's accession, featuring the personal stories of many of the participants, including the queen herself. It counted also in the long run because, together with these stories of persons still remembered or still alive, it supplied a history of the Church and the nation, seen by the light of what was taken to be the truth of revelation: that is to say, of a conception of the meaning of history which almost everybody who thought about the matter at all took for granted. Thus the Book of Martyrs set moving in English life a body of legend which was thought to make clear how and why the situation in which the nation presently found itself had come about, and so to justify whatever course the nation, as represented by the queen, might take in its own defence and for the accomplishment of its destiny. Historians and antiquaries coming after Foxe, and better informed if not always freer from national prejudice than he, would before long express their doubts concerning this or that element of the stream of fable which took its rise in his book. People in general, however, would be slow to look critically at any part of the stream, and scholars themselves would be unable to disregard it or criticize it unopposed. The stories told in Foxe's book became, along with the stories that came from the Bible, especially the Old Testament, an essential part of that familiar code of reference and expression which no one sharing in the life of that dynamic age could do without.

Consequently the intention in the following pages is not to inquire whether Foxe told the truth about the past or whether his beliefs and opinions about religion and the Church are correct and just. The intention is rather to relate the human circumstances which led to the composition and publication of his book, to explain what the book appears to have conveyed to the people of its own time, and to suggest what seems to have been its effect on the public mind in that and the immediately succeeding age.

First, however, it is necessary to recall the historical situation which gave occasion for the stories which were the book's reason for being and which prompted its publication. Queen Mary, daughter of Henry VIII and Catherine of Aragon and wife of King Philip II of Spain, had hoped to lead her people back to the faith of their fathers and restore the realm to its ancient place in the universal order of Christendom. Her government, beginning with a degree of moderation, allowed, in some cases probably encouraged, about eight hundred persons whom there was no hope of reconciling to the restoration of the old religion to leave the country. But there were others, a score or so of conspicuous and intransigent spokesmen of the new faith, who were not permitted or who refused the opportunity to escape. These were presently arrested, imprisoned, and after a delay of months prosecuted and executed for the crime of heresy. By making an example of these few the government apparently hoped to discourage others from following the same course. The effect, however, seems to have been to stir up more apprehension against more and more persons suspected of subversive ideas, practices and associations, and so to bring on more and more prosecutions. In somewhat less than five years something like two hundred and seventy-five men and women of all ranks had been executed for heresy in the customary manner, an unprecedented number to have suffered for that offence in so brief a time.

Queen Mary died on November 17th, 1558, and was immediately succeeded by her half-sister Elizabeth; but no one could have anticipated that the new queen was destined to reign for forty-four years. The two great ruling powers of the Continent were engaged in an effort to suppress Protestant revolt among their subjects against the Catholic Church while contending at the same time with one another for the mastery of Europe, and to each the control of the English Crown seemed essential to the accomplishment of both purposes. Elizabeth's cousin Mary Stuart, granddaughter of Henry VII, daughter on her mother's side of the great French house of Guise and wife to the Valois heir to the French monarchy, at once impugned the legitimacy of Elizabeth's birth and claimed the English throne for herself and her heirs. Elizabeth's obvious course in the face of this challenge was to seek the protection of her brother-in-law, Philip of Spain, master of the Low Countries, of the wealth of the New World, and of the mightiest army in Europe. Philip for reasons of his own had stood by her during her sister's reign and was now prepared to marry her. Yet whether she put herself in his hands or was forced to submit to the Queen of Scots and the French, she was likely to lose her freedom of action as ruler of England, the English monarchy was likely to be engulfed in an alien dynasty, the interests of England were likely to be sacrificed to the needs and ambitions of one or other of the rival powers of the Continent, and the English Church was likely to be reduced once more to the domination of the Roman hierarchy.

Elizabeth neither quailed before the Queen of Scots and her French relations nor put herself in the power of Philip of Spain. At the risk of taking the Protestant side in the struggle over the Church, she clung to her freedom of action and trusted to luck and her own wits to see her through the long struggle which

Introduction

then ensued with the Catholic powers. For at least thirty years the outcome would remain extremely doubtful, but she was favoured from the start by two incalculable factors which in the event outweighed the resources of her adversaries. One was the unforeseen skill and nerve with which she was able to play the dangerous game of politics, diplomacy and undeclared war to which she had committed her own and her people's future. The other was the unprecedented outburst of personal devotion with which her Protestant subjects greeted her accession and which they continued to lavish upon her through all the vicissitudes of her long reign. It was imperative, if she was to keep clear of foreign entanglements, that she see to the establishment of a national Church order under the authority of the Crown. But this did not mean that on the crucial issue of the new religion as opposed to the old her subjects were any less divided and confused than the other peoples of Europe, and there was no telling how many of them might rally at a pinch to the side of her Catholic rival. It was therefore also imperative that as many of Elizabeth's subjects as possible should be moved as promptly as possible to embrace the faith to which the queen was presumed to have committed the Church and herself. Or so it seemed, naturally enough, to the remarkable group of reformers who, having been made to feel the sting of persecution under the late Catholic regime, came back from exile or out of hiding at Elizabeth's accession, eager to resume the preaching of the Protestant Word in her support. Knowing that they had everything to lose if she failed them, they began to prophesy triumph for her and her cause from the moment of her coming to the throne. They exploited all the available resources of pulpit and press to convert her subjects to the new religion, and also to instil in them a conception of England, of themselves as Englishmen, and of her as an English ruler which did much in the long run to bring that triumph about and give it its distinctively English character.

Yet the devotion so deeply interfused with religious and patriotic feeling which Elizabeth evoked from her Protestant subjects was to be a cause of constant embarrassment to her. In the successive parliaments which she was obliged to call to her assistance she was continually having to deal with men professing the utmost loyalty to her position and her person, but convinced that they understood better than she and were bound in conscience to let her know how God intended the nation's, the Church's and her own affairs to be governed. She was not of a temperament to welcome such instruction, and yet she was of no mind, certainly in no position, to repudiate their devotion or rebuff all that they might propose. While they could not accomplish what they wished without her, she might not be able to survive without them. This she realized to be the case even though she soon learned that no matter how far she might go in yielding to their demands for further reform in the Church, there would always be some among them who would press her to go still further, much further than she deemed either proper or safe. Her problem was not a simple one. Faced by an undetermined but formidable measure of Catholic opposition, she must maintain her hold on the loyalty of her Protestant subjects and at the same time prevent the extremists who kept springing up among them from forcing her into any action which could upset the always precarious balance of conflicting forces at home and abroad.

How the queen dealt with this problem over the years Sir John Neale has described in a masterly account which evokes admiration for the fascinating woman who is its central figure, but something less than full sympathy for those over-fearful but devoted subjects of hers who, not knowing as we do how things were going to turn out in the end, often trusted her judgment less than their own. For they knew that God had appointed England to consummate the reformation of His Church, that He had appointed Elizabeth to lead England in that work, and that He had appointed preachers of His Word to make His will known to her and her subjects. On these themes many speeches were to be made, many sermons preached, many books printed before the reign was over. But all propaganda on behalf of that national settlement of the Church which Elizabeth's long and successful tenure of the throne made possible began with the martyrs of Queen Mary's time, whose stories found their way into John Foxe's book.

CHAPTER I

The Martyrs

⟨✵⟩

CARDINAL POLE, arriving in England as papal legate
in 1554, assured Queen Mary, her recently married husband
King Philip, and parliament that God had given England
prerogative over all other realms. History testified, he said, that
England was *prima provinciarum quae amplexa est fidem Christi*. The
ancient Britons had been the first nation in the world to embrace
the Christian faith, and when they were overwhelmed by the
heathen Saxons, 'God of His goodness not leaving where He once
loved' had so moved and enlightened the hearts of their conquerors that they also embraced the faith. And after that 'the
greatest part of the world fetched the light of religion from England'. Of late, to be sure, the faith had been betrayed in England
as elsewhere, but God had kept the light alive in the breast of the
queen, had preserved her 'a virgin helpless, naked and unarmed',
and given her victory over all her enemies. 'Here you see Her
Grace established in her estate, being your lawful queen and
governess, born among you, whom God hath appointed to reign
over you for the restitution of true religion and extirpation of all
errors and sects.' By restitution of true religion Pole meant the
restoration of England to its relationship with the Church universal, which had been abrogated by the queen's father Henry VIII.
By the extirpation of errors and sects he meant the suppression of
those doctrines and practices which had been introduced into the
Church under her brother Edward VI.[1]

Yet in five years both Mary and Pole were dead, the expectations they had shared had come to nothing, and the survivors of
the party which had ruled the Church under Edward and been

[1] John Elder, *Copie of a letter* (1555); Foxe, *Actes and Monumentes*, VI, 568–71.

expelled under Mary were to all appearances on their way back to power. These latter believed as strongly as Pole had done that England held a special place in the designs of providence, and that God had miraculously preserved the virgin then on the throne for the promotion and defence of true religion. However, their conception of true religion was a very different thing, and Elizabeth was a very different virgin. The men who came back from exile at Mary's death seized upon the mistakes and misfortunes of her brief unhappy reign in order to impress upon her successor and their fellow-subjects their own idea of what God required of English rulers and their people.

The success of that undertaking was by no means a foregone conclusion. The life of faith had centred in the preceding ages on the great dramatic rite in which the body and blood of the Lord, once sacrificed on the Cross for the sins of men, were offered up again in the guise of the bread and wine of the sacrament of the altar. For the performance over and over again of that act of propitiation, the Church was believed to have been instituted. For that the churches which still lift their spires to the sky in English villages had been built, rebuilt, enlarged, enriched and adorned by generations of the faithful. For that cathedrals and monasteries had been founded and endowed. This is not to say that knowledge of the Scriptures was kept from the people or the gospel left unpreached. Yet the be-all and end-all of the Church was the continuous administration of the sacrament by an apostolic priesthood, and the high point of individual religious experience was participation in the Mass.

The question why, after all that had gone before, not merely the power of the Church as an institution but its command over the imagination and devotion of the people collapsed to the degree that it did under the attack of Henry VIII, admits of no simple or single answer, but certain things are clear enough. The idea of the Church universal lost power to convince as the institution which was supposed to be its visible manifestation on earth shrank into an Italian state differing from its rivals chiefly in the pretensions and exactions which it sought with diminishing success to impose upon them. The priesthood and the monastic life were taken up more and more by men who were looking for a public career or simply a livelihood rather than a life of devotion. The administration of the central rite of religion became a trade like any other, and, as its practitioners grew slack and incompetent, performance grew perfunctory and meaningless. Thus old habits of belief and worship came in time to lose their appeal, and the Church lost both the power and the will to resist its demolition. But all this, if it explains anything, explains why Henry was able to do what he did with so little effort and at so great advantage to himself. It does not explain how, in spite of all this, the religious spirit revived among the people, or why it revived in the way it did.

The so-called reformation set in motion by Henry VIII sprang from personal, dynastic, secular motives, not from any stirring of the religious spirit in either king or people. Henry had interests, scruples and prejudices with religious colouration, but no firm religious principles. He cleared the ground for reformers to attack what seemed the empty ritual of the Mass, the ignorance of the common clergy, the corruption of the monastic and mendicant orders, the worldliness of the hierarchy. Yet the effect of the changes he introduced was not to revive religion but to give free play to secular ambition and self-seeking. Towards the end of his reign, he made as though to arrest the revolutionary process he had started, and better men than he in his entourage tried to maintain the old stabilizing doctrines and practices; but it was too late, and under his son the dissolution of the old order proceeded at a still faster rate. It suited the interests of the men who then seized power to allow reformers a free hand, but the iconoclasm to which they resorted did no more to promote either religion or moral reform than persecution was to do in the next reign.

When after this Mary came to the throne, hoping to restore religion, she had every personal reason for wishing to go back to the order of things she had known in childhood before her father repudiated his marriage to her mother and embarked on the sequence of changes which brought both women nothing but humiliation and grief. Mary remained to the end a devout

Catholic of simple, intense, unquestioning faith, emotionally dependent on her mother's kindred and Spanish countrymen. The movement for religious reform and revival as it affected her had served simply as occasion and excuse for the oppression practised against her under the child-king her brother. At Edward's death, thanks to her own courage, to the people's devotion to her as her father's lineal successor, but above all, she believed, to the special favour of God, she had frustrated the schemes of her enemies and the enemies of her faith to bar her from her inheritance. Thus, suddenly, as if by a miracle, she found herself possessed, as she thought, of power to restore the English people to their ancient religion and so redress all the evils of the time.

But while she had been kept away from the main current of national life, times had changed. The Church of which she found herself the unwilling, anomalous head was not the Church of her mother as she imagined it to have been, but the Church which had submitted to her father. Much of its property had gone to the enrichment of laymen very much on the make and not at all inclined to restore what they had gained at the Church's expense. The men who had tried to bar her succession to the throne were of this type, and there were many more such ready to impede the fulfilment of her desires. As for churchmen, the monastic and the preaching orders had been wiped out, and of the rest few of any rank had refused to accommodate their consciences to the demands made upon them first by her father's and then by her brother's regime. There was her cousin Reginald Pole, but after nineteen years of exile he was more remote even than herself from the actualities of the English situation. There were a few men like Stephen Gardiner, the restored Bishop of Winchester, and Edmund Bonner, the restored Bishop of London, who after yielding to her father had given earnest of a change of heart by refusing to go along with the reformers under her brother. Gardiner was now taken into the privy council as Lord Chancellor, but he had earlier published a defence of royal supremacy in the Church and the queen never gave him her complete confidence. He was one of the new type of cleric which had come to the fore in the Church since the invention of printing, the advance of a vernacular-reading public, and the rise of the book trade.

Men of this class had grown up together in the intimacy of Oxford and Cambridge colleges, where they had been trained in the traditional dialectic of the schools, but where they had also been exposed to the ideas coming from Erasmus and the German and Swiss reformers. All had at least some knowledge of the ancient languages and were committed in some measure to making the Bible more widely known to the people by translation, preaching and printing. With the logic and rhetoric of the schools at their command, with the Scriptures and the fathers at their tongues' ends, with at least a smattering of other literature, they were a corps of professional intellectuals prepared not only to fill the pulpits but to keep the printers and booksellers of the coming age busy. They were also prepared to supply aid and comfort, spiritual and other, to the gentry who had taken over control of church livings along with the other property of the Church and who now more and more filled the benches of parliament. The emergence of such a corps of articulate intellectuals bent upon exploiting the techniques and the occasions now open to them for expression, communication and influence was a principal obstacle to the realization of Mary's dream of leading the realm back to its ancient obedience.

As soon as she seemed safely established in her authority, she issued a proclamation declaring that she could not 'now hide that religion which God and the world knoweth she hath ever professed from her infancy hitherto'. She wished that her subjects might embrace the same religion, but she was not minded to compel any of them to do so until 'such time as further order by common consent may be taken'. So in the meanwhile she enjoined them 'to live together in quiet sort and Christian charity, leaving those new found devilish terms of papist or heretic'. This was all very well, but the proclamation went on to say that sedition had been nourished in the realm by persons who took it upon themselves to preach and to interpret the word of God after their own brain in churches and other places both public and private, and also by playing of interludes, and printing of false-found books, ballads, rhymes, and other lewd treatises in the English tongue ... touching the high points and mysteries of Christian religion, which ... are chiefly by the printers and stationers set out to sale to her grace's subjects of an evil zeal for lucre and covetous of vile gain.[1]

All such persons were ordered to cease their activities and all public officers were ordered to see that the queen's commands were obeyed and offenders punished. The inhibition thus placed upon the voices and the implements of impending change was nothing if not comprehensive. Yet there was no concealing the dilemma upon which, in spite of herself, the single-minded queen found herself impaled. Her conscience told her that her people were living in schism, subject to the imputation of heresy. However, they were doing so according to the laws of the realm imposed upon them under her predecessor, whose authority she could not impugn without impugning her own. Therefore she could not legally require them to do all that her conscience told her they should do, unless and until parliament could be called together and induced to agree to a change in the law. And even so, until the realm became reconciled with the consent of parliament to the jurisdiction of the universal Holy Father, the authority of the Church to prosecute and of the Crown to punish anyone for heresy was at best open to challenge.

Yet there could be no doubt as to the Crown's authority to prosecute and punish for treason, and Mary's regime got round its dilemma for the time being by proceeding on that ground against men who, as soon as proper authorization had been secured, were also to be prosecuted for heresy. That this was in fact no answer to the fundamental constitutional question concerning the limits

[1] Foxe, VI, 390–91.

(References to Foxe's *Actes and Monumentes* are by volume and page to the edition in eight volumes published by S. R. Cattley in 1837 and later revised by Josiah Pratt with the same pagination.)

AT LONDON.

Printed by Iohn Daye, dwelling
ouer Aldersgate beneath Saint Martins.

¶ Anno. 1570.

Cum gratia & Priuilegio Regiæ Maiestatis.

JOHN DAY 1562

(Colophon Page *Actes and Monuments* 1570)

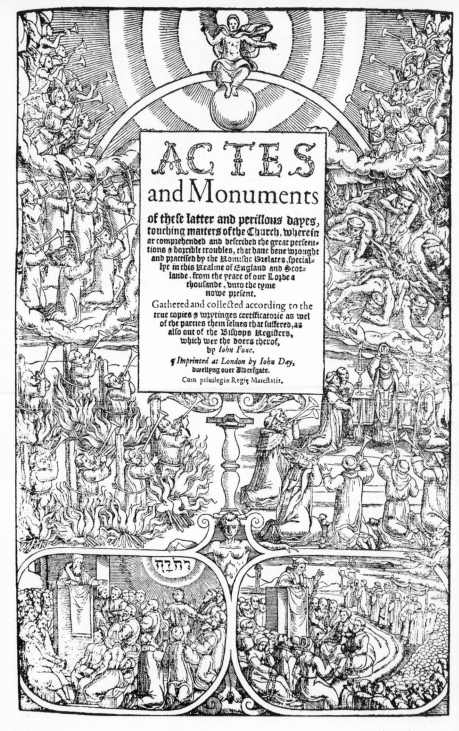

TITLE-PAGE *Actes and Monuments* 1563

of authority in either religion or civil government, the event would show. Meanwhile, the highest ranking personage prosecuted by Mary's government for treason in the early months of her reign, later to be condemned for heresy, was the Archbishop of Canterbury, Thomas Cranmer, the man chiefly responsible for the English liturgy which had replaced the Latin Mass and the author of a work, published three years before, rejecting the doctrine on which the Mass was supposed to rest.[1]

Now, provoked by a rumour that he had reversed himself and said Mass at the late king's funeral, and that he had reinstituted the Mass at Canterbury, he impulsively issued a statement reiterating his former position and offering to defend it in public debate, on condition that decision should be according to God's Word and that the arguments on both sides should be set out in writing. Soon, it was said, every scrivener's shop was occupied in copying out this challenge to the queen and the men now in power.[2] It was, of course, nothing less than a declaration of ideological war against the defenders of orthodox doctrine, particularly Cranmer's long-standing rival, Stephen Gardiner, author of a reply to his treatise of three years before.[3] But it was not especially because of his ideas concerning the sacrament that the government proceeded against Cranmer at this time. He had also put his name – reluctantly, he professed – to the will in which Edward VI had been induced to disinherit Mary and name Lady Jane Grey as his successor. On that ground Cranmer was convicted of treason and in November 1553 sent to the Tower.

Nicholas Ridley, Bishop of London, was in the Tower before him for the same reason. Younger than Cranmer by ten years, Ridley was a Cambridge man who, after three additional years at the Sorbonne, had returned to Cambridge to become Fellow and then Master of Pembroke Hall. His religious convictions had moved steadily away from the orthodox view of the sacrament, but not so precipitately as to impede the early stages of his advance-

[1] Cranmer, *Defence of the true and catholike doctrine* (1550).
[2] Foxe, VIII, 37–8.
[3] Gardiner, *An explication and assertion of the true Catholike faith* (1551).

ment in the Church. He rose to be Bishop of Rochester under Henry and Bishop of London under Edward. He took his first clear stand on the question of the sacrament in 1549 while presiding at a disputation at Cambridge. As Bishop of London, displacing Edmund Bonner, he had gone energetically about getting rid of the Mass with all its appurtenances and introducing the new English liturgy. In the course of his episcopal duties he had called on Mary in Hertfordshire and offered to preach to her and her household. She would have none of him, saying that he would not 'for his ears' have dared avouch that for God's word in her father's days that now he did. 'And as for your new books,' meaning doubtless the English Bible and prayer book, 'I thank God I never read none of them; never did, nor never will do.'[1] But in due time Ridley put his name to her brother's will, and upon the proclamation of Lady Jane Grey in her stead, he preached a sermon at Paul's Cross describing how she had repulsed him and warning the people that, if she were admitted to rule, she would bring in a foreign power and subvert the reformed religion. Naturally enough, as soon as Mary made good her claim to the throne, Ridley found himself in the Tower charged with treason.

The queen and her government, committed to the restraint of preaching and printing as conducive to heresy and sedition, could not at the same time avoid taking action to silence Hugh Latimer, the patriarch of the new religion and its most famous and influential preacher. He had been converted to the new faith in the early days of the reform movement at Cambridge by Thomas Bilney, its protomartyr, and his account of that experience became a classic example of the reorientation of a man's whole view of life under the influence of the Bible. For the essence of Latimer's conversion lay in his awakening to the imaginative appeal of that book and so to the power it gave him to sway other men from the pulpit.

The effect was to make him the prime evangelist of the book. Under Henry VIII he preached like an ancient prophet against the spiritual deadness and moral backsliding which he saw as the cause

[1] Foxe, VI, 354–5.

of the current decline of ancient ways and standards. His boldness exposed him to a charge of heresy, and in order to avoid worse punishment he withdrew into silence. But, freed from imprisonment upon Edward's accession, he went to live with Cranmer at Lambeth and preached a series of famous sermons at court in which he said a great deal about the duty of subjects to obey the ruler God put over them, but also a great deal about the duty of rulers to obey God, and of preachers to instruct both rulers and subjects in their obedience by the light of God's Word. Finally, though relatively late in his career, Latimer took the crucial step of attacking the doctrine of the sacrament. But this was not all that made him potentially a dangerous opponent of the queen's purpose. His recent sermons had been put into print by John Day, and there was thus additional reason to expect that, if any one was likely to speak out against the queen's orders, it would be Latimer. Hence the government felt obliged to order him up to London to answer for his doings before the privy council, and presently sent him to join Cranmer and Ridley in the Tower.

But on the question of what in general to do with men likely to oppose the queen's commands, Gardiner, as the queen's principal minister and the man in the government who best knew their capabilities, found it difficult to decide. The best that could be hoped for was that the leaders would be induced to set an example to others by returning to their former obedience or by submitting quietly to its restoration. Next best was to permit or even encourage as many as possible to take themselves off to the Continent, whence, it was hoped, they would be heard from no more. The evidence is clear that a good many, including Latimer, were given the chance thus to take their leave. The result was that a certain number of persons who had adhered to the late regime, now displaced, submitted and came back into the fold; but a considerable number chose exile, and a small but extremely influential group chose to stand fast, face the possibility of martyrdom, and make what they could of it for their purposes. The government's most difficult problem was to deal with this latter group – devotees of the Word, some of them capable, perhaps wishful, as such men have it in them to be, of dying for their convictions, however mistaken. They could, of course, still be argued with, and, if they persisted in arguing back, they could be threatened with punishment; but if threats were of no effect, there would be nothing to do but take the risk of making martyrs of them.

The kind of stiff-necked, contentious, sophistical, irrepressible character Mary's government had on its hands was exemplified early in the reign by the case of John Philpot. A fortnight after Cranmer's arrival in the Tower, Mary was crowned. Parliament met directly afterwards and began repealing the legislation of the preceding reign which had established royal supremacy over the Church and required the use of the Bible and prayer book. The convocation of the clergy met at the same time with instructions to draft canons for the restoration of the Mass. This was to raise the vexed issue of the sacrament, and the men in charge attempted at the start to head off discussion by general agreement. But a handful of objectors would not have it so, and there followed a debate, conducted, as such things were, according to scholastic rules and ending in confusion worse confounded by acrimony on both sides. The champions of the Word were of course overridden, but the champions of the Mass gained only a dubious advantage. For in John Philpot, Archdeacon of Winchester, they had as adversary a contentious egoist with a gift for expression and, one suspects, an incurable bent for martyrdom.

The affair over, Philpot was called to account for his outrageous behaviour by Gardiner, acting as his ordinary, and sent to the King's Bench Prison. But he was not to be silenced as easily as that. He at once wrote out his own story of what had been said and done in convocation and conveyed it into the hands of his sympathizers to be circulated at home and abroad. Within the twelvemonth it was on its way back to England in print, ostensibly from a press in Basle.[1] Yet still the authorities were not through with Philpot, nor he with them. Two years later, Bonner as Bishop of London got orders to try what could be done to bring him round. He was, after all, a man of standing, son of a Knight of the Bath,

[1] Philpot, *Trew Report* (1554); Foxe, VI, 395–411.

The Martyrs

a dignitary of the Church. He was consequently called up for examination a dozen times or more by a varied assortment of bishops, privy councillors and learned disputants brought up from one or other of the universities in the hope that he might be persuaded to conform. But his inquisitors soon found that they had caught a tartar. Philpot began by denying Bonner's jurisdiction, and refused to answer anything concerning the sacrament. For whatever he might have said on that subject in the recent convocation, he claimed that he was responsible only to his own ordinary, who had already examined and condemned him, and that he could not legally be charged a second time with the same offence. Besides, he had committed no offence. Whatever he had said in convocation he had had a right to say 'by the ancient and laudable custom of this realm'.

> I stand still upon my lawful plea ... that though it were as great a heresy as you suppose it, yet I ought not to be troubled therefore in respect of the privilege of the parliament house, whereof the convocation house is a member, where all men in matters propounded may frankly speak their minds.

He is being held, they say, under suspicion of heresy, but he demands what he calls the benefit of the subject – the right, that is, heretic or not, to be told wherewith in particular he is charged, why he is being held, and why, contrary to the common law of England, his living has been taken from him without public trial.

Finally, he yields sufficiently to argue with his inquisitors on the subject of the sacrament, and the argument revolves, as so often it did, in widening circles of semantic confusion. On any controverted matter, they ask, how shall one determine the truth? He answers, by the Word. But what if there is doubt concerning the meaning of the Word? The answer is, by the fathers and teachers of the primitive Church. And if they disagree? Then back to the Word. Thus, like all of his way of arguing, Philpot always comes back to the Word. If the Anabaptist Joan Boucher was to be burnt, as he holds that she deserved, it was because she stood against 'one of the manifest articles of our faith, contrary to the Scriptures'. When finally he himself went to the stake, it was in order to vindicate his notion of what the Scriptures require all men to accept for truth.

But he was to show the men who in a kind of desperation sent him there that to burn such as he might simply be to make their voices carry farther. In the intervals of his appearances before Bonner, Philpot was confined in what he calls the bishop's coal-house, but his friends still managed to supply him with food and other necessaries. On one occasion, Bonner complained, he was sent a pig with a knife in its belly, and on another a bag of powder to make ink. Writing materials he certainly received, for after each working over by the commission, he contrived to put down an account of questions asked and answers given, and to frame this dialogue in a vivid narrative of the accompanying action and stage-business, not omitting shrewd satirical thrusts at his in-quisitors, the cynical turncoat Lord Rich as well as the bumbling Bonner. Copies of these accounts were soon being passed about among his friends. They were published too late to be read in Mary's time, but not too late for the subjects of Elizabeth.[1]

Yet it was not the scattered publications of such personalities as Philpot which in the end brought disaster upon Mary's endeavour to re-establish the old religion in England, but the organized and sustained propaganda on behalf of the new religion which began with the three leading figures in the Tower. Such a campaign was set in motion by Ridley's directing hand and soon taken up by certain of his personal associates in exile on the Continent. Cran-mer, though the most eminent of the three, was a man given to long brooding over controverted issues before making up his mind, and he was likely to act impulsively and extravagantly. Latimer's genius was for the pulpit, and he was, besides, by sixteenth-century standards, an old man. It was Ridley, the youngest of the three and now in the full vigour of his age, who turned a disciplined intelligence and an executive temper to the work of party leadership. 'Wise he was of counsel, deep of wit,

---

[1] *Examination* (1559); Foxe, VII, 605–83.

and very politic in all his doings.'[1] It was, then, largely owing to his initiative that the case for the religion of the Word was so promptly put on record and into circulation for the confounding of Mary's plans and the edification of her and her successor's subjects.

That was one side of Ridley. But it was also said of him that though he had not been called until the eleventh hour, he had then become 'a faithful labourer terrible to the enemies for his excellent learning and therefore a meet man to rid out of the Lord's vineyard the sophistical thorns of wrangling disputants'.[2] This side of Ridley's mind and character came into play when, a prisoner in the Tower, he faced the certain prospect of having to reply to the test question concerning the nature and meaning of the sacrament of the altar. He knew that unless he subscribed to the doctrine now held for orthodox, the inquiry would quickly resolve itself into a discussion of subtle and abstruse conceptions of the meaning of the words, This is my body, and of the injunction, Take this and eat. Admitting, as Ridley did, that Christ was somehow present in the sacrament, what was the nature of that presence? Was Christ's body actually present under the appearance of bread and wine? Or did the bread and wine remain what they appeared to be while Christ, corporeally still in heaven, made His presence spiritually known to those who partook of the bread and wine in the spirit of the faith? Was the sacrifice offered by Christ on the Cross for the sins of man an act of propitiation which must be renewed over and over again on behalf of both living and dead? Or was that original act of propitiation sufficient once and for all to the end of time, a grace to be entered into by the faithful in the commemorative rite of communion?

To some minds the pressing of such questions as the crucial test both of spiritual faith and secular loyalty pointed to other questions of disturbing and far-reaching implications. Was any single answer on such a matter attainable by such procedures, or, indeed, by any rational procedure whatever? In any case, was it essential

[1] Foxe, VII, 407.
[2] Ridley, *Works* (Parker Society), 100.

31

for the ordinary man to be able at the peril of his soul, not to say his life, to answer such questions precisely as the men now in power in the Church would have him, especially in view of the fact that no one could tell how long that power would continue in their hands? Was his subscription to the required answer, whatever it might be, really essential to the security of the state and the preservation of civil order? Was there nothing more immediate and compelling in spiritual life than absolute certitude on such abstruse questions as these?

'Many things,' Ridley observed, 'confound a weak memory: a few places well weighed and perceived lighten the understanding. Truth is there to be searched for where it is certain to be had. Though God doth speak the truth by man, yet in man's word (which God has not revealed to be his) a man may doubt without mistrust in God.' That Ridley after three years at the Sorbonne mistrusted his own ability to answer the questions to be put to him by his opponents – men of the sort he had lived and disputed with most of his life – we can hardly suppose. Certainly when the time came he kept both his head and his courage. But he knew that the case was likely to be different with many others caught in the same danger with less knowledge and less self-assurance. To meet the need of such persons, he now prepared not such a treatise as Cranmer had published, but a brief statement in the form of questions and answers simply phrased and supplemented by texts from the New Testament and citations from the early fathers. After circulating for a time in written copies, this work was printed at Zürich in 1555 with the title *A brief declaration of the Lordes Supper*.

But, still in the Tower, Ridley's mind went on working at the problem of getting out something in written form to help confused minds and perhaps wavering souls when put to the ordeal of having to answer precisely as to the real presence in the sacrament. The result was another engaging tract, published on the Continent in 1556 after its author's death as *Certen godly, learned, and comfortable conferences betwene the two Reverende fathers and holye Martyrs of Christe, D. Nicolas Rydley late Byshoppe of London and M. Hughe*

The Martyrs

Latymer Sometyme Byshoppe of Worcester during the tyme of theyr emprisonmentes.[1]

We are told here that Ridley and Latimer were for a time kept apart in the Tower in retaliation for their refusal to hear Mass, but that Latimer's faithful attendant, Augustine Bernher, was nevertheless able to carry messages back and forth between them. In this situation Ridley is represented as taking the opportunity to draw up a statement in simple terms of the reasons for his refusal. These he sent to Latimer, who presently returned them with the comment that he had 'read over of late the New Testament three or four times' but had failed to find any support for those teachings and practices 'which be the very sinews and marrow-bones of the mass'. Yet, he confessed, 'I am sometimes so fearful that I would creep into a mouse-hole.' Ridley acknowledges the comfort he has received from the older man's words, but begs another draught of the same for his encouragement. 'For surely, except the Lord assist me with his gracious aid in the time of his service, I know I shall play but the part of a white-livered knight.'

Whether Latimer, having deliberately refused the offered opportunity to escape prosecution by running away, now seriously wished to hide in a mouse-hole, is much to be doubted. No less is it to be doubted that Ridley, fresh from directing the demolition of altars and images in London churches, not to mention defying the queen at Paul's Cross, really thought of himself as a 'white-livered knight' who must look to Latimer for courage or for arguments with which to face the ordeal he saw impending. One of his adversaries at Oxford probably came nearer to the truth when he said that on the matter of the sacrament 'Latimer leaneth to Cranmer, Cranmer to Ridley, and Ridley to the singularity of his own wit'.[2] Everything we know about the man suggests, indeed, a resolute character with a mind of his own. Face to face with their adversaries at Oxford, he was to prove the most resourceful, tough-minded disputant of the three.

But in the Tower he was thinking of less determined characters than himself, who might be fearful of giving way under the

[1] Foxe, VII, 410–23.   [2] Foxe, VIII, 538.

33   B

pressure soon to be put upon them to recant and conform. Two of his own chaplains and his own cousin were among the backsliders. His tract, therefore, is to be thought of not as a record of his own state of mind, but as a kind of dramatic dialogue in which, with the hope of steadying less confident spirits, he depicted himself applying to Latimer to confirm his judgment and fortify his resolution. Especially the latter, because Latimer was the patriarch of them all, the most famous preacher of the Word to all the people. And the prime argument against the Mass on which he expatiates in response to Ridley is the argument of a preacher, not a scholastic philosopher. Ridley had observed that the Mass 'is done in a strange tongue, which the people doth not understand'. Latimer elaborates, 'They speak into the air, the mind receiveth no profit; they are to one another as aliens.' 'They roll out their Latin language by heart, but in so doing they make the poor people of Christ altogether ignorant.'

Latimer's career had begun not with a change of mind concerning the doctrine of the sacrament but with an awakening to what he took to be the Holy Spirit revealed in the Scriptures and his discovery of the power of words in discourse. He had experienced the compulsion of the born evangelist to speak, to seek an audience and feel the ecstasy which the presence of an audience produces in such men. His rejection of the traditional conception of the sacrament had come as the effect of his long career in the pulpit, especially when he found the exponents of that conception more and more opposing his exercise of his gift. Thus the need to propitiate God by a ritual of sacrifice came to mean less to him than the need to bring what he took to be his knowledge of God's will home to men from the pulpit in language they could understand, and his conception of the one need was accommodated to his conviction concerning the other. This surely is what was meant by his followers calling him the Apostle to the English. 'The minister of the gospel,' he is represented as saying in the dialogue with Ridley, 'hath rather to do for Christ with the people, than for the people with God ... the office of reconciliation stands in preaching, not in offering.'

The Martyrs

So much by way of reassurance to wavering souls on the subject of the real presence. But something more was needed to stir imagination and steel resolution to endure what seemed certain to lie ahead. The office of the preacher, according to St Paul, was so to speak to every man as to make him believe that he was being called, as it were by name, to take upon himself a new character and a new mode of life. Doctrine, polemic, and moral exhortation might serve to this end up to a point, but every preacher depended in fact upon something more effective for evoking in his hearers the state of mind appropriate to the new life and for keeping it always keen and taut.

Here again Paul served for guide and model. What every elect soul had to look forward to in the present life was such a testing as now impended or, in a word, some measure great or small of martyrdom, and the prime image for inducing the mood required for that trial was the image of the warrior. The saint was to put on the armour of faith and fight the good fight under Christ's banner against Antichrist. And since there could be but one outcome to this battle and that certain and proximate, the image of spiritual war derived from St Paul merged inevitably into the image of Christ's second coming and final triumph in heaven and earth. This was a theme with many possibilities, and on this theme Ridley brought his artfully contrived narrative to a conclusion. 'Hitherto, ye see, good father,' he wrote, 'how I have in words only made, as it were, a flourish before the fight which I shortly look after.'

In Tynedale, where I was born, not far from the Scottish borders, I have known my countrymen watch day and night in their harness ... especially when they had any privy warning of the coming of the Scots. And so doing, although at every such bickering some of them spent their lives, yet by such means, like pretty men, they defended their country. And those that so died, I think that before God they died in a good quarrel, and their offspring and progeny, all the country loved them better for their fathers' sakes.

35

Should they not then also watch and go armed in Christ's quarrel with the enemy of mankind?

> I pray you, help me to buckle on this gear a little better; for ye know the deepness of Satan, being an old soldier ... But truly he will not be so willing, I think, to join with you, as with us younglings.

Ridley in the Tower could hardly take personal charge of the publication of his tract, but he could take a chance on Bernher's getting it into the hands of someone who would see that it reached those for whom it was intended. Unimportant perhaps in itself, it was a presage of what these men had in store for the Marian regime. The author and his two associates were held in the Tower while the queen and her government were occupied with the repression of rebellion in Kent and elsewhere, with arrangements for the queen's marriage, and with negotiations for the reconciliation of the realm with Rome.

These matters settled or on their way to being settled, the next thing was to dispose of resistance to these policies within the Church itself, and first of all with the intransigence of the three eminent figures being held in the Tower. Strictly speaking, until absolution came from Rome and reconciliation was actually effected, the technically still schismatic Church lacked authority to press the charge of heresy against these men to a decision. Nevertheless, it seemed imperative that they should be brought to submit in the most public fashion as an example to others. Consequently, in March 1554 the government ordered Cranmer, Ridley and Latimer to be brought to Oxford to be examined as to their beliefs concerning Christ's presence in the sacrament by a commission of doctors of both universities.

Most of what now can be known about this affair comes from the accused and the reports left by their friends and sympathizers, reports designed of course to justify the victims, not to do justice to their prosecutors.[1] According to these reports the government staged what purported to be a formal scholastic disputation on the

---

[1] Foxe, VI, 439–536.

question at issue, held in the university church and the divinity school before an audience of graduates, undergraduates, and townspeople. The accused were brought in one after the other and asked the usual questions, to which they made the usual and expected replies. There is no need to retrace the stages of this altercation between impassioned disputants arguing at cross purposes in the terms of an obsolete dialectic. Cranmer, Ridley and their opponents – Latimer was a law unto himself – matched texts with texts, syllogisms with syllogisms, citations with citations as though it were conceivable that the question could still be settled by such procedures. Cranmer was said to have answered 'very wittily, modestly and learnedly' and his inquisitors to have treated him with a measure of respect. At one point the prosecutor commended and thanked him for his 'wonderful gentle behaviour and modesty', and 'at this saying all the doctors gently put off their caps'.

Not so with Ridley, whom the members of the commission recognized as their most formidable antagonist. Their questions, Ridley said, sprang from a bitter and sour root, and his answers were reported to be 'sharp, witty and very learned'. At the close the prosecutor said of him, 'here you see the stubborn, the glorious, the crafty, the unconstant mind of this man.' As for Latimer, positive that nothing of the Mass was to be found in the New Testament, he posed as an ancient holy man who had forgotten his Latin, and he refused to argue.

The government's purpose in the affair, though they staged it as a formal disputation, was really to expose these leading exponents of the new faith to public condemnation. For something of more practical significance was involved than the metaphysical question of what happened to the elements in the sacrament of the altar. At stake was the authority of priesthood in the Church and of the Church in the national community, that is to say, the power to direct and control education, public opinion and the exchange of ideas in the age now at hand. Cranmer, Ridley and Latimer were condemned as heretics and remanded to prison, but in the struggle for this imponderable power over what people should think, the victory of their adversaries was but a hollow one. For the resort to force masked by scholastic debate gave the champions of the new faith the opportunity to reach after the imaginative sympathy of the oncoming vernacular public. Whether or not these men are to be venerated as saints and martyrs, they must be admitted to have been masters of the arts and devices of discourse, both those customary among members of the intellectual class of their time and those soon to become available to everybody for the general propagation of ideas and attitudes on all public questions.

Doubtless none of the three realized all the implications of the dispute in which they were engaged, but all were fully aware that the real issue was not one that could be settled then and there. They defended their position in respect to the sacrament as best they could, but they addressed themselves over the heads of their opponents to winning the attention and sympathy of people in general. Whatever they said they said for the record, and they or their friends saw to it that a record was kept and presently circulated where it would have most effect. Latimer's friend Bernher and Ridley's brother-in-law Shipside were in attendance and were probably present at the assemblages in St Mary's and the divinity school. They had in any case opportunity to collect reports from both witnesses and principals. Ridley himself, on the alert to forestall misrepresentation, prepared an account of his own examination directly after the event. In addition to the official scribes appointed by the commission to record the proceedings, Cranmer and Ridley were allowed to retain notaries to serve on their behalf, and Latimer was probably allowed to do the same.

One of the men chosen for the purpose was John Jewel, whose story illustrates the manner in which a rising young academic intellectual might be led to turn against the established regime and the old religion. He had arrived at Oxford in 1535 at the age of thirteen to become the favoured pupil of his tutor, John Parkhurst. At the age of twenty he was a Fellow of his college. In 1547, at the beginning of Edward's reign, he attached himself to Peter Martyr, whom Cranmer brought to Oxford at the same time that he brought the other great Strasbourg reformer, Martin Bucer, to

Cambridge. Martyr inspired his disciple with a passion for preaching to which he gave expression in a sermon at St Mary's on the occasion of his commencing B.D. in 1552.[1] 'This,' he declared, 'is our office, this we take upon us, and this we profess; and except we do this, we do nothing, we serve to no use.'

But the next year Mary came to the throne, and the preaching that Martyr's disciple was bent upon became at once suspect. Martyr went back to Strasbourg and Parkhurst went into exile, while their pupil, the moment before at the threshold of what promised to be a brilliant career in the university and the Church, remained behind to be harassed by the university authorities. He was required as public orator to compose a congratulatory address to the queen. He was turned out of his college fellowship. He was appointed to serve as notary to Cranmer and Ridley at the great disputation on the sacrament. Finally he was told that he must make formal subscription to orthodox doctrine on that subject, and word went about that he was to be called up to London to be examined by Bonner. He subscribed, but presently fled and rejoined Peter Martyr at Strasbourg, bearing report of what had happened at Oxford.

Cranmer, Ridley and Latimer were condemned as heretics and remanded to prison, but their execution was delayed for reunion with Rome to be completed and in the hope that they might still be induced to recant. In the interval, strangely enough, the authorities were unable or unprepared effectively to prevent them, condemned though they were for heresy, from committing their experiences, exhortations and appeals to writing and somehow conveying those writings to friends and sympathizers still at liberty at home or in exile abroad. Ridley, again taking the lead, made himself the centre of a spreading net of communication and propaganda. During the year and a half in which he was kept waiting for the expected end and in spite of the hardships of imprisonment, of which he often complained, he managed, as he had done before in the Tower, to address several tracts and epistles to his followers and associates, encouraging them to stand fast and

[1] Jewel, *Sermon made in Latin* (1586); *Works* (Parker Society), II, 950–64.

supplying them with reflections and arguments for use in case of need. These things usually found their way – just how there is no knowing – into the hands of Bernher or Shipside or possibly some other friend, to be transcribed and sent about. Some were intercepted and suppressed, but others were circulated in written copies at home and abroad and eventually found their way into print on the Continent and, after the fall of the regime, in London.

Meanwhile, Ridley's example was followed by two of the several men who had served under him as Bishop of London and were now awaiting their fate in London prisons. To be sure, Edmund West and Nicholas Grimald, having made their peace with the present regime, the one endeavoured to persuade him to do the same, and the other betrayed at least one of his writings to the government. But John Rogers, John Bradford and Edmund Grindal remained faithful. The first two were to be martyrs, and the other was to be the prime instrument for making the stories of their martyrdom known. Each of the three had been a Fellow of Pembroke while Ridley was Master, and had been brought by him up to London to preach the gospel. Rogers had spent some years on the Continent in Henry's time, assisting Tyndale with the Bible and preparing the so-called Matthews version for publication. Involved with Bradford after Mary's accession in a riotous scene at Paul's Cross, he was consigned to Newgate and there kept waiting until January 1555 to learn what was to be done with him. While there, however, he found means to pen an account of his experience in a little black book which he left hidden under the stairs in his prison. There his widow and his son found it when they came to gather up his effects after his death at Smithfield. That, at any rate, is the story which presently reached Grindal on the Continent.

Bradford, while reading law at the Inner Temple, had been spiritually bowled over by Latimer to such effect that he had gone to Cambridge, studied divinity under Martin Bucer and been picked by Ridley for a fellowship at Pembroke, a prebend at St Paul's and a royal chaplaincy under Edward. Arrested at the same time as Rogers, he was presently sent to the King's Bench prison. There, thanks to the slackness or indulgence of keepers, he preached to his fellow-prisoners, carried on an extensive correspondence with persons outside, and consorted with Laurence Saunders, a preacher like himself, awaiting his fate at the adjoining prison of the Marshalsea. Again, this is the story put into writing by the man himself and his friends and after his death conveyed to Grindal.

For Grindal providence held a different fate in store. Younger by some years than the other two, he had while a Fellow of Pembroke attracted Ridley's attention at the disputation on the sacrament at Cambridge in 1549 and been called up to London by him shortly afterwards. If things had gone as expected, the young man was marked out for a bishopric at the age of thirty-four, but things turning out as they did, he alone among Ridley's picked company of young men escaped to the Continent and thence presently resumed contact with his associates who had stayed behind in England.

Some time in the spring of 1555 the news reached Oxford of the burning of Rogers and the shortly to be expected burning of Bradford. Ridley at once wrote of the latter that he thanked God 'that ever I was acquainted with him, and that ever I had such a one in my house'. Of Rogers he said that he blessed God that he also was 'one of my calling to be a prebendary preacher of London'. Then his mind ran on to his own impending fate and to Grindal, now safe and away, who had been '*olim comprebendarius*' with the other two. 'And now because Grindal is gone ... I trust to God it shall please him to strengthen me to make up a trinity out of Paul's church to suffer for Christ.'

Not long afterward a letter came from Grindal written at Frankfurt on May 6th and bringing news of the exiles at that place, at Strasbourg and at Zürich. The writer lets Ridley know that they have received reports of his responses in the disputation at Oxford and of his writings in the Tower. They intend to have his treatise on the sacrament translated into Latin, but they will publish nothing for the present lest they provoke his persecutors to restrain him from writing further. Ridley replying sends news of himself, his two fellow-prisoners, and other friends in England. He wonders how his writings could have found their way into Grindal's hands, and he cautions him to credit no account of the disputation at Oxford except that which he himself has prepared. Grindal had made a sort of apology for having run away from the danger which had overtaken his fellows, but Ridley made the pregnant reply: 'seeing you say that there be in those parts with you of students and ministers so good a number, now therefore care you not for us, otherwise than to wish that God's glory may be set forth by us.' For Grindal and his fellow-exiles, when the time comes, will be enough to light and set up again the lantern of God's word in England.[1]

By the summer of 1555, when these words were written, the course of government action and of the reaction it evoked, of persecution countered by propaganda, was fixed. The leaders of the opposition to restoration of the Mass and reconciliation with Rome who had been held in prison in the hope that they might be induced to submit had not submitted, could not be silenced and were not prevented from communicating with their partisans. At the same time there was no falling off in the number of persons whom it seemed necessary to suspect and prosecute. Before long these unfortunates were also coming to think of themselves and to be thought of as martyrs for the truth and to have their stories passed from mouth to mouth and hand to hand.

The Marian martyrs' battle need not be fought over again in these pages, and the issues of that battle are not to be confused with those of later battles they could have known nothing about. Neither they nor the government which prosecuted them, let alone the host of people with no fixed opinions they were ready to kill or be killed for, supposed that liberty to believe or disbelieve as one chose was essential to the spiritual well-being of the nation. Practically everyone still assumed that society could exist only within the twofold framework of Church and state, that it was the sovereign's duty to maintain both and that the subject was bound on his allegiance to believe as the Church determined.

[1] Ridley, *Works* (Parker Society); Foxe, VII, 424–37.

The Martyrs

If anyone believed otherwise, he must expect to be called to account. If he denied the truth as determined by the Church, he was liable to be prosecuted in the tribunals of the Church for the crime of heresy, and upon conviction to suffer punishment at the hands of the civil magistrate. If he opposed the authority of the queen, he was liable to be prosecuted for treason and upon conviction to be punished accordingly. In either case formal indictment was usually tantamount to conviction, and torture might be employed to elicit testimony or confession. The punishment for treason in the case of persons of rank was beheading, and of all others, hanging and disembowelling. The punishment for heresy was burning, except that a convicted heretic might be let off if he confessed his error and did appropriate penance. But for a relapsed heretic there was usually no reprieve. The statute of Henry V, originally aimed at the Lollards, set up the procedure to be followed by the servants of the Crown in carrying out the judgments of the Church in particular cases. In practical effect the distinction between heresy and treason was nugatory, and the penalties, publicly administered for monitory effect, were equally horrible, but scarcely more revolting according to present standards than those meted out for numerous other capital offences under the law.

Heresy had traditionally been punished in such fashion on the Continent and continued to be so. It had been prosecuted after the same fashion by English monarchs at least since Henry V and by the queen's father both before and after his break with Rome. The statute *De heretico comburendo* had, to be sure, been repealed in the reign of Edward VI, but that had been done in the interest of the party then in power and was not taken as applying to Anabaptists and such, whom all parties put beyond the pale. Consistently enough therefore, parliament re-enacted the statute in December 1554 in order to regularize the present government's proceedings, and on February 4th the execution of persons still persisting in their rejection of the orthodox doctrine of the sacrament began with the burning of John Rogers at Smithfield. Ridley and Latimer suffered the same fate at Oxford in October, and Cranmer

43

in March of the following year. The burnings continued until November 10th, 1558, a week before Mary's death. During that period of not quite four years, it is estimated that something like two hundred and seventy-five persons were convicted of heresy by the tribunals of the Church and executed in the customary way by command of the queen's government. This does not include an undetermined number of persons who died in prison under similar charges before their cases were decided and sentence passed.

Of the total number of persons actually executed, besides Cranmer, Ridley and Latimer, four had been bishops, seventeen were clergy of lesser rank, fifty-five were women, and a few were described as gentlemen. The rest consisted of artisans, husbandmen, labourers, and other persons of humble status concerning whom little is told beyond their names and the fact and place of their execution. The notions for which many of these persons were executed were probably such as almost any government in that age would have prosecuted with more or less severity. Some just as guilty as the rest no doubt escaped because some bishops lacked the necessary zeal or were far enough from Westminster to avoid pressure from the government. The greatest concentration of cases occurred in and about London, because the impact of the new faith was greatest there, but also because that region was most directly under the eye of the privy council. Consequently Bonner as Bishop of London had to bear the heaviest responsibility for the burnings at the time, and, when Foxe's book had done its work, the greatest obloquy afterwards.

That any considerable number of people were deeply revolted by the burnings at the time of their occurrence, we have chiefly Foxe to witness. To most of the martyrs' immediate contemporaries, they were men who had been duly convicted of heresy; heresy was a capital crime for which the penalty was burning; and the punishment for heresy as for other capital crimes was to be administered as publicly as possible for its edifying effect. Many of Foxe's readers had no doubt witnessed such scenes, perhaps some of the very scenes described and depicted in his book. They would, before long, be relishing similarly revolting scenes in the

theatre. Several of the leading martyrs had themselves approved
the burning of convicted heretics under previous regimes, and
they resented nothing so much as having that particular accusation
directed against themselves. As for Foxe himself, he protested not
against the injustice of punishing heretics but against the inhumanity of punishing them in that manner.

Yet whatever may be said in extenuation of the burning of
Protestants by the Marian regime, it was a tactical blunder of the
greatest consequence for Gardiner, Bonner and their associates to
burn the men they did – eminent, able, resourceful men, leaders
of that body of articulate, university-bred intellectuals who would
have the pulpit and the press at their command, just so soon as the
present regime came to an end. True, no one in that age thought
of questioning the obligation of the civil magistrate to punish
persons convicted by the tribunals of the Church of religious error
wilfully persisted in. The magistrate was responsible for defending
the faith and the people in the faith, and Mary in her simple-
hearted devotion felt bound to put the sword entrusted to her
keeping at the Church's service. But the situation was not so
simple or clear-cut as all that, and this the men about her should
have known, no one better. The principle of two independent,
complementary, concurrent jurisdictions, secular and spiritual,
temporal and universal, had never been honoured in England
without reservations, and for twenty years it had been in more and
more nearly complete suspension. Henry VIII had, to be sure,
continued to profess adherence to traditional doctrine and practice
in other respects – he had even burned heretics – but the breach
he had made with the papacy had opened the way for other profoundly disturbing breaks with the past, not to mention many
deepening, ramifying differences of belief and practice within the
English Church itself.

The disintegration of the old order had been going steadily on
during the years in which Mary had been cut off from the main
currents of national life, leaving her with little understanding of
the difficulties she would encounter when she came to the throne.
A fundamental difficulty was that, coming to power in the face of

opposition with no idea but to undo what her father had done, she found no English subject at hand competent to advise her who had not come at least part of the way her father had marked out. This was as true of the men who now wished to stop short or turn back in that course as it was of those who sought to press on. Even Gardiner, the ablest and most experienced of them all, had supported Henry in divorcing her mother and bastardizing herself and had written a notable treatise, endorsed by Bonner, in defence of royal supremacy in the Church. There was hardly one of these men, now ready enough to turn back with her to the old order of things, who had not profited in some fashion or degree by its dissolution or who was prepared to relinquish whatever material advantage he had thus gained. Naturally she distrusted them all, and, in her tragic isolation, as the situation got more and more out of hand, turned more and more to foreign advisers who could not but fail her.

Meanwhile, the men to whom the administration of her government had perforce to be left were exposed to bitter attack upon their motives by others who refused to accommodate their consciences to her change of policy. Not all the bishops who kept their places under Mary took active part in persecuting people now adjudged to be heretics. That Gardiner and Bonner acted in good faith was evidenced by the fact that they had accepted deprivation under Edward. But they were all back in office, and Gardiner in particular was back in the privy council as the chief judicial officer of the Crown, charged with enforcing the laws. Inevitably the opponents of the Crown's policy in respect to the Church, finding themselves prosecuted as heretics, harped incessantly on the fact that their rivals' change of mind had not lacked reward. The Marian bishops would have been obtuse indeed if they had not felt themselves in some degree, justly or not, vulnerable to such criticism. While some of them consequently held back from taking extreme action against their critics, others were stung to justify themselves by greater severity. And once committed to that course, there was nothing to do but go on. For the queen and her government had got themselves into a position where any refusal

The Martyrs

to accede to their policy in respect to the Church had to be regarded as a threat to the security of the regime itself. Such opposition might of course have been prosecuted, as it was to be on occasion in the succeeding reign, as treason; but Mary saw it as heresy, and consequently it was as heretics that the Marian bishops were called upon to prosecute men who did not hesitate to assail them in return as betrayers of Christ and His Church.

Even so, this might not have mattered in the long run if the victims of persecution had consisted only of such persons of humble rank and little education as did in fact make up the majority of the Marian martyrs, and if the notions for which they suffered had been the usual Anabaptistical fantasies. But this was not the case. The Marian bishops found themselves pitted against a small but effective corps of men of their own kind, their own former associates and rivals in the universities and the Church, their peers, in some cases their superiors in rank, men whose course up to a point had been substantially little different from their own, men accustomed to speak with authority, men as ready to burn heretics as themselves. Resenting as they did the charge brought against them, they refused to acknowledge any difference between themselves and their adversaries except that the latter had betrayed what they themselves knew to be the truth.

This is not to say that this accusation was just or the reasoning behind it correct. Men in such a predicament may be mistaken and they may mislead. The important point, historically, is that they had the art, the learning and the address to give as good as they got in the war of ideas and to take their case to the public. Consequently, though in the whole number of Marian martyrs they were relatively few, their influence was out of all proportion to their numbers. For waiting in the wings, while Mary's tragedy worked itself out, were Elizabeth and the exiles, Elizabeth conning the first lesson of practical politics, which is to survive, the exiles getting ready to publicize the story and its lesson for the instruction of herself and her subjects.

CHAPTER II

The Exiles

~~~

WHATEVER else may be said about it, the burning of the chief spokesmen of the reform movement was a tactical mistake of the first order, and the mistake was compounded many times over by the letting of so many of the disciples and younger associates of these men escape to the Continent. The exodus began soon after the queen's accession and was made up of clergy and students preparing for the Church, gentry, a small number of men described as merchants, and a few printers and other artisans. They comprised in all about eight hundred persons, including wives, children and servants. The most numerous contingent, containing the largest proportion of clergy and others of academic education, settled in small groups keeping much to themselves in the cities of the Rhine valley and Switzerland, centres of the reformed religion, printing and the booktrade. Among these the most active spirits were men in their thirties and early forties who, if things had gone according to their expectations, would before long have succeeded to the places in the English Church held by the men who were now facing persecution at home in England. This leading group of exiles included such men as Richard Cox the displaced Vice-Chancellor of Oxford, Edmund Sandys the displaced Vice-Chancellor of Cambridge, John Ponet the displaced Bishop of Winchester, and Edmund Grindal who would soon have been promoted to a bishopric if the young king had lived.

These and others of the group of similar position and promise were men who had taken a leading part in affairs of the Church and were destined to do so again as soon as the present regime should come to an end. Most of them made their way first to

The Exiles

Strasbourg, whence Cranmer had called Martin Bucer and Peter Martyr, the one to Cambridge and the other to Oxford, and whither Martyr had now returned. In the disputes which presently arose concerning the government and form of worship to be followed by the English congregation at Frankfurt, this leading group of exiles, centred at Strasbourg, insisted on keeping as close as the circumstances allowed to the recently adopted Edwardian settlement, which they had had a hand in drafting. They were opposed, however, by another less numerous, less highly placed but not less able and determined group of exiles, headed by John Knox and William Whittingham, who were committed to the church order devised by Calvin at Geneva. Out-manœuvred and repulsed at Frankfurt, these men drew back to Geneva, and although they were never to attain high position in the Church under Elizabeth, they were nevertheless to have an important influence on the development of religious life among English-speaking peoples.[1]

The differences between the two groups of exiles at Frankfurt came in retrospect to seem of great significance, but at the time the thing that mattered most to all the exiles was the fact of exile itself against the stark background of persecution going on in England. It was that which broke up the normal course of their existence, set them thinking more intensely than ever about the convictions which had brought them to their present predicament, and gave them a common grievance and purpose. It left them with no hope of recovering their former position unless they could somehow stir up the English people to rise in support of their cause, and no way of getting at the people except through the arts of discourse and the devices of publicity. For whether either party realized it or not, neither would be able to make good its claim unless it could make good its hold upon the people, or upon enough of them, at any rate, to count with whatever government might be in power in the state. Either the one must evoke popular faith in the Word, or the other must win the people back to belief in the Mass, though this would also mean that each must labour to convince the people that their deliverance from sin depended upon

[1] William Whittingham, *Troubles at Frankfort* (1575).

their deliverance from the heresy of the one or the superstition of the other, as the case might be.

At the accession of Mary, after twenty years or more of violent change this way and that, many of the people were no doubt ready enough to welcome a return to old established ways; but the old established ways, especially in and about London, had been disrupted too long for many to be deeply attached to the faith of their fathers, or to understand very well what it meant or what it required of them. And the Marian regime never really got round to doing anything effective to allay the confusion, uncertainty and indifference of the popular mind. The government's efforts were directed to suppressing heresy, not to reviving religion, to making opponents and critics subscribe to the doctrine of the real presence, not to instructing the people in the meaning of that doctrine. Eventually the adherents of the old faith would launch a genuine effort to recapture the devotion of the people, but not until they had lost the initiative in this rivalry to the victims and survivors of the Marian persecution.

For persecution gave its victims the opportunity to dramatize their faith in the Word by embracing martyrdom, and its survivors the opportunity to exploit the testimony of the martyrs by the classic device of a martyrology. Persecution and exile gave the evangelists of the Word exactly the occasion they needed to make the idea that the Holy Spirit speaks directly to whom it will from the pages of the sacred book as appealing to the imagination as the great dramatic rite of propitiation in the Mass had ever been. And as it happened, their effort to this end fell in with the great advance of the popular language as the chief instrument of expression and of printing and the book-trade.

The problem of converting the English people to the religion of the Word was first of all a problem of language and style, and then one of the mechanics of communication, publication and distribution. In the beginning was the Word, but the Word had to be made English and put into print. The language of the Church, of academic education and intellectual intercourse, was still in large measure Latin, as it had always been. A man's native

Lord opē the king of Englands eies.

THE BURNING OF MASTER WILLIAM TYNDALL

speech was the speech of the region of his birth, of his neighbour-hood, his village, perhaps not English at all. Indispensable at home, it became less sufficient the farther he went from home and the more he found to think and talk about. But as the national state and along with it a national culture and a national economy developed and cohered about London, the language of the London region became familiar, useful and necessary to English-men everywhere. The history of their language from this time on is the history of the spreading of that London speech wherever in the world its users went, and of its progressive adaptation to their indefinitely multiplying occasions.

They were still having to learn how to express themselves in it with clarity and coherence, especially when they came to general ideas, but while helping themselves freely to what they wanted from other languages, they went ahead to bend their native tongue, redolent as it was of the household, the farmstead, the sheepfold, the market town and the sea, to the expression of any-thing they could think of about any subject whatever, however stirring or profound. This was the language into which Tyndale and Coverdale translated the Bible, in which Cranmer fashioned the prayer book, in which Latimer preached, in which the Marian martyrs told their stories, and in which preachers, writers of tracts, translators, chroniclers, playwrights and poets would presently be filling pulpits, book-stalls and theatres with such matter in such quantity as had never before been known in the vulgar tongue. Latin would continue to be the language of academic learning, but as Elizabeth's regime consolidated its hold upon the nation and as the nation grew more aware of itself, the queen's English would become more and more the language of all her subjects in all their concerns and for all their purposes. And with the advance of this vernacular speech and its extension throughout the British Isles and overseas, the religion of the Word was destined to keep pace.

Thus the endeavour initiated by the martyrs and exiles of Mary's reign to convert the English people to a religion based upon the reading of the Word in print became an inseparable part of the great folk movement of their age and nation. They and their successors might differ endlessly concerning the points of faith to be deduced from their reading of the Word, but their objective as spiritual leaders in the age of expansion about to begin would continue substantially the same for all of them. This was, regardless of differences, to awaken men to a more lively awareness of their present condition and predetermined fate as revealed to their understanding in the Scriptures. All must be made to realize their mortal condition, the brevity of life, the certainty of judgment. They must be made to understand that redemption must be expected to happen, if at all, as a transforming event in the consciousness of the individual, that it could happen as readily to one man as to another, but that it was not to be had for the asking, or at second hand, or for a price. God called a man, and the man knew himself called to a new life. The process of this regeneration, the Church was to set forth with all possible elaboration of detail drawn from the Scriptures and the experience of the elect in all ages.

For whether one believed that grace came as a purely unconditioned or as a partially induced event, the elect soul must nevertheless collaborate in the working of grace. The essential, imperative exercise of religious life, the one thing not to be omitted, was for everyone the reading of the Bible. This was what the reformers put in place of the Mass as the decisive high point of spiritual experience – instead of participation in the sacrament of the real presence on one's knees in church, they put encounter with the Holy Spirit in the familiar language of men on the printed page of the sacred text, in church services employing that text, and in preaching devoted to its explication and application.

The validity of that conception is not for us to consider here. The Bible has meant different things to different people at different times. The question here is, what did it come to mean to the English people at this particular time in their history when they were about to swarm out of their narrow island into the modern world? To reach a credible answer to that question we must somehow put ourselves into the frame of mind of people encountering that extraordinary book for the first time in their own language and in print while expecting the encounter to result in a visitation of divine grace. People were told that the book contained the rule of life by which all their acts and motives should be directed and would eventually be judged. But telling people to look for the rule of life in a book which mirrored life with such variety and intensity was like telling them to look in life itself.

The Bible was not chiefly a book of law, and in any case Moses was not Aristotle. There was no systematic statement of abstract general principles capable of universal application to be found in its pages. What the Bible offered was an imaginative representation of the life of a single people having a unique sense of their identity as a people set apart from all others by a peculiar destiny. It showed a people who thought of the present always as the manifestation of an antecedent design centred upon themselves and certain to be consummated in the proximate future. And this it did by means of poetic fables, epic sagas and dramatic legends accompanied by prophetic comment, lyric ejaculation and gnomic reflection, all bearing upon the relationships of family, Church and state, of parents and children, husbands and wives, prophets and kings, the nation itself and the nations round about, and of all these with the inscrutable power which determined the fate of all from the beginning.

The book-trade would presently be putting much other literature of great imaginative power before the English people, but no other literature like this. And the great writers who were to make the age of Elizabeth illustrious were, we must remember, for the most part not yet born. The popularization of this one book, not simply as a book like other books but also as revelation, was to have an incalculable effect, peculiar to itself and going far beyond the bounds of religion, on every aspect of public life. Thanks to the Bible, the vernacular public would henceforth have at its disposal a common code of familiar reference, of principles and judgments embodied in pregnant names, images, examples and legends, serving as a vocabulary for the formulation and expression of its thoughts on any subject with which it might deem itself concerned.

The disputes concerning Church government and discipline which arose among the exiles at Frankfurt, foreshadowing all the dissidence on those subjects among English-speaking peoples still to come, have received more than their due attention from historians and need not detain us here. The 'troubles at Frankfurt' did nothing to damp the ardour of either party for the purpose they held in common or to prevent the triumph of their cause in England, the triumph of the English nation in the impending struggle for world power with rivals of opposing faith, or the spreading of people of Protestant faith and English speech throughout the world. There would be plenty of time later for them to debate whether the Church should be patterned upon Canterbury or Geneva. The immediate and most pressing concern of the exiles both at Geneva and Strasbourg was to find means to induce their compatriots at home to embrace the faith to which their associates in England were at the moment testifying with their lives.

To this end they accomplished two things compared to which the 'troubles at Frankfurt' were of very little importance. These were a Book of Martyrs presenting the stories of the victims of the current persecution in England, and an English version of the Bible based upon Tyndale and Coverdale and suited to the needs and capacities of the vernacular-reading public. The first was the undertaking of Edmund Grindal at Strasbourg, brought to completion by John Foxe under his direction, but also under the influence of John Bale at Basle. The other was the work of exiles at Geneva under the direction of William Whittingham.

We have seen that the Marian regime either could not or did not prevent the leading figures among those it chose to prosecute for heresy from communicating with one another and with their friends and partisans at home and abroad. Thus Philpot's account of the dispute at convocation at the close of 1553 reached the exiles on the Continent in time to be printed soon afterwards; Ridley's tract on the sacrament reached them in time to be printed in 1555, and the story of his conference with Latimer in the Tower followed in the ensuing year. By that time, too, Peter Martyr and Grindal at Strasbourg had received Cranmer's rejoinder to Gardiner's reply to his earlier treatise on the sacrament, and were arranging for its translation and publication. Almost as soon as the burnings began in February 1555, reports of what was happening began reaching Grindal and his associates. By the spring of that year he was exchanging letters with Ridley at Oxford. By that time, too, reports had arrived through Jewel and others of the disputation at Oxford, followed by news of Bradford's fate and a little later of the execution of Latimer and Ridley. Word of Cranmer's end reached Peter Martyr within six weeks of the event, and as more stories of more burnings continued to come in, Grindal made plans for putting them into print.

He planned, he said, a 'book of martyrs' or history of the persecutions going on in England to be published in English and Latin, the Latin version to be prepared by John Foxe under his direction and patronage. The two versions were intended at first to be identical in content and to appear at the same time, but this plan was soon found to be impractical, because fresh material kept coming to hand and the necessity of depending on a number of people caused many delays. In June 1557 Grindal wrote to Foxe that the English book, which he had hoped would be ready for printing by that time, was still being held up. In December 1558, when news came of Mary's death, it was still not ready, and Grindal hurriedly wrote again advising Foxe to wait with the Latin version in the expectation that still more material would soon be available. In the end it was Foxe who produced both the Latin and the English versions of the book, the former at Basle in August 1559 and the latter in London four years later, still with the co-operation of Grindal and other returned exiles now back in the line of power and promotion.[1]

As for Foxe's own career, that may be said to have become the book itself. At the beginning of the period of exile he had been a hard-working, impecunious, unassuming, single-minded scholar and schoolmaster in his late thirties who, ten years before, had given up his fellowship at Magdalen, Oxford, probably under pressure, married and taken to teaching. In 1548 he joined the household of the widowed Duchess of Richmond as tutor to her

[1] Grindal, *Remains* (Parker Society); Strype, *Life and Acts of Edmund Grindal*; Foxe, VII, 424–37.

wards, children of the late Henry Howard, Earl of Surrey. There he met and made friends with John Bale, twenty-one years his elder, who was later to refer to him as for ten years his faithful Achates.[1] Bale, recently returned from exile, went off to take up an Irish bishopric, while Foxe continued as tutor to the Howard children until the spring of 1554. At that time he protested against the re-adoption of the repressive Act of Six Articles, and soon afterwards made his escape to the Continent. On his way to Strasbourg he turned aside to visit the birthplace of Erasmus at Rotterdam. He went from Strasbourg to Frankfurt not later than September 1555, where he encountered Grindal, possibly for the first time, and rejoined his friend Bale. These two presently settled at Basle, where Foxe found employment as a reader for the press in the printing establishment of Oporinus. At the same time Grindal enlisted his services and contributed to his support.

His principal task was the preparation of the Latin version of the Book of Martyrs from materials sent to him from time to time by Grindal at Strasbourg. A trait in Foxe's personal make-up may have had something to do with his undertaking such a work. He seems to have suffered a deep revulsion, quite unusual in his time, at the spectacle of physical pain deliberately inflicted. 'For such is my disposition,' he confessed almost apologetically, 'that I can scarce pass the shambles where beasts are slaughtered, but that my mind secretly recoils with a feeling of pain.' He admired God's mercy in decreeing that beasts to be sacrificed at the altar should be slain before being committed to the flames. He pleaded with John Rogers, who was himself to be burned, to intervene with Cranmer to save the Anabaptist Joan of Kent from the stake. Let her error be put down, but let her life be spared. She might infect a few, if allowed to live; by her death she would confirm many more in error. 'At least let another kind of death be chosen, answering better to the mildness of the gospel.'

The following year Foxe made the same plea for another condemned heretic, and later on he petitioned Elizabeth and the privy council to spare a group of such unfortunates. 'To burn up with a

[1] Bale, *Scriptorum illustrium ... Catalogus* (1557–9), 763.

fiery flame, blazing with pitch and sulphur, the living bodies of wretched men who err through blindness of judgment rather than deliberate will ... belongs [more] to the example of Rome than to the spirit of the gospel.' There are banishments, close confinements, chains, perpetual exiles, brandings, floggings and even gibbets to be used. But let not the fires of Smithfield be rekindled. 'The diseases I am now speaking of,' he declares, 'need spiritual medicine rather than bodily, for an erring faith can be compelled by no man; it can but be taught; and many men die orthodox that lived long as heretics.' He commends a Spanish friar who, preaching before King Philip, 'did earnestly inveigh against the bishops for burning of men, saying plainly that they learned it not in scripture to burn any for his conscience.'[1]

The Book of Martyrs in its final form was to include something more than the stories of the Marian martyrs transmitted to Foxe by Grindal, something more and something different from the collection of sensational tales of physical horror, padded out with many additions, to which the book was reduced in the popular versions issued to eighteenth- and nineteenth-century readers. Foxe set these stories of recent and remembered figures in what was for his own age a convincing, momentous, historical-scriptural perspective, made meaningful by the unfolding context of immediate events. Not the least important effect of his book was indeed to impress upon the contemporary mind a sense of the past and its meaning for the English nation in the present crisis. To the claim of the Catholic Church to an authority handed down from a divine founder through an apostolic priesthood, Protestant reformers in general had been opposing an argument which purported to be based on the facts of history as they were to be found in the Scriptures and other written records. How sound or exact their conception of historical process or their handling of historical evidence was, is here immaterial.

The importance of what they did lies in this: that just at this point in the historical development of European culture they put forth a defence of their cause conceived in historical terms and

[1] Foxe, VI, 704.

based on what purported to be documentary proof. The importance of what Foxe did, aside from his mere reporting of recent events, was that as he went on elaborating his book he incorporated the stories of the Marian martyrs into that historical argument, giving it a particular English bent and application. Grindal had called the book a book of martyrs, and the name stuck, but Foxe professed to write not merely of the sufferings of martyrs but of 'Acts and Monuments passed in the church and realm of England, wherein why should I be restrained from the free-walk of a [hi] story writer more than others that have gone before me'.[1] He would devote himself 'to the searching of times and antiquity and to the conservation of such acts and monuments as are behoovable for the church'. That is, he will relate the facts of history and produce the evidence.[2]

In all this he was following the line marked out for him by his friend John Bale, now settled near him at Basle, and previously marked out for Bale himself by John Leland.[3] Most historians who have given any attention at all to Bale have been so repelled by his extraordinary virtuosity in the art of verbal abuse that they have been unable or unwilling to assess his very real historical importance. In this respect, of course, his disciple Foxe has to a degree suffered from the same attitude. True, Bale's vocabulary reeks of the Suffolk earth from which he sprang, but what he said and what he signified we cannot on that account afford to ignore if we wish to understand the state of mind in which the Marian exiles and those of their way of thinking presently greeted the accession of Elizabeth. Bale came from a poor family in Suffolk and got his education in a Carmelite house in Norwich and at Jesus College, Cambridge. He began by writing a biographical history of his order, but by 1535 he had left the order, married and got himself into trouble for heresy.

However, he had made friends with John Leland, who had been commissioned by the king to search for books, manuscripts and what other evidences he could discover relating to the national

1 Foxe, III, 705.   2 Foxe, II, 14.
3 Bale, *Laboryouse Journey and serche of Johan Leyland* (1549).

past, and Leland interposed with Cromwell for his release. He then took to writing and perhaps performing in plays designed to win support for the policies his patron was putting through in the king's name. Bale was, of course, a child of the very system he was helping to bring to an end. His plays were written in the form of the medieval morality play, but they interwove with the conventional moral allegory legends from scripture and the English chronicles. In the most considerable of these performances, we still see Everyman beset by a series of temptations on his way to judgment, but the theme is treated as no medieval writer would have treated it. Bale's Everyman is King John, and the temptations which beset him are temptations to yield to the attacks by which the Pope and his agents and abettors are always seeking to undermine or overthrow the authority vested in royalty. Though the John of history actually shows but dimly through the veil of allegory, Bale was nevertheless making a start at turning national legends to the uses of propaganda in the national cause.[1]

The occasion for going on in that vein, though not in that form, was the reaction which presently led to Cromwell's fall and Gardiner's ascendancy and sent Bale packing into exile. Stephen Gardiner, Bishop of Winchester, was a great churchman of the type often drawn into the service of the Crown, an able and conscientious public servant, learned in the law, experienced in affairs, conservative in temper, and determined to maintain the established order. Not unreasonably he saw in any attack upon the position of the Church or upon its traditional doctrines the first motion towards such a disruption of society as the world was witnessing in Germany as the result of Luther's heresies. If Gardiner knew of Bale's fulminations, without doubt he viewed them in the same light. The effect of his ascendancy in Henry's government in the closing years of the reign was the Act of Six Articles, which made any person denying the accepted doctrine of the sacrament liable to prosecution for heresy. Gardiner's expectation, we must assume, was that the Act was in itself warning enough to head off serious

---

[1] W. T. Davies, *Bibliography of John Bale* (Oxford Bibliographical Society, 1940); H. McCusker, *John Bale, Dramatist and Antiquary* (1942).

violation of its provisions, but such a threat once made is always likely to provoke persons of fanatic temper or of a certain stubbornness of opinion and strength of character to challenge the determination of its makers and put them on the defensive in the eyes of the very people they are seeking to impress with the enormity of the supposed error.

Precisely such a person the authorities presently had to deal with in Anne Askew, a young woman of good family, well read in the Scriptures, opinionated, articulate and in her own way devout. Twice Edmund Bonner, Bishop of London, had her up for questioning concerning the notions she had expressed as to what happened to the bread and wine in the sacrament. Twice her inquisitors laboured with the greatest patience to set her right on the subject, and once they let her go. But each time she refused to budge from her view of the matter and, still worse, insisted upon arguing back. She also refused, though put to the rack, to incriminate anyone else. The authorities having gone that far, there was nothing more they could do with such a person but let the law take its course, in the hope that others would be deterred by her fate from falling into the same error.

There the affair might have ended, but that the victim herself, or someone writing in her name, put her story on paper and sent it to John Bale in Wesel. It is a singularly clear, unaffected, moving, dramatic narrative in which we see the accused as a true saint encountering the arguments of great worldly prelates with simple devotion to truth, and enduring torture with Christian fortitude.

Then the lieutenant caused me to be loosed from the rack. Incontinently I swooned, and then they recovered me again. After that I sat two long hours reasoning with my lord chancellor upon the bare floor, whereas he with many flattering words persuaded me to leave my opinion. But my Lord God (I thank His everlasting goodness) gave me grace to persevere, and will do (I hope) to the very end.[1]

[1] Bale, *First Examinacyon of Anne Askewe* (1548), *Lattre Examinacyon of Anne Askewe* (1547); *Select Works* (Parker Society); Foxe, V, 537–50.

The Exiles

Here was stuff much more compelling than old-fashioned allegory, and Bale promptly put it into print with characteristic comments of his own.

He was spending this his first period of exile in Switzerland and Germany, never very far from a printer, and continuing his attack upon the Roman Church in a number of works in which we see emerging what were to be the major themes of propaganda in the national cause for some time to come. In *A Brefe Chronicle concerning ... Sir John Oldcastle* Bale told the story of that fifteenth-century Lollard martyr. In *The Actes of the English Votaries* he exposed the iniquities of the celibate orders. In *The Image of Both Churches* he explicated Revelation as the key to the understanding of the past, present and future course of the Church. In *Illustrium maioris Britanniae Scriptorum Summarium* he undertook a conspectus of English history in the form of a biographical encyclopedia. In *The laboryouse Journey and serche of Johan Leyland*, published in England with his comments and additions directly after his return from exile, he followed Leland's lead in exploiting English antiquities for his purpose.

Bale tells us that as a child he saw a young man burned at Norwich for having the Lord's prayer in English and refusing to pray to the saints. That or some similar experience may explain the violence of language with which he assails the old regime in the Church. Yet the intensity of his resentment is also a reflection of the distress suffered by people of his station in East Anglia as the result of the break-up of the social and economic system of which the Church was so important a part. Nowhere had the presence of the Church been more pervasive. Nowhere were people riper for indoctrination in the new faith or, for that matter, in old heresies. On the Continent such conditions had more than once conduced to the rise of religious demagogues, promising the people the immediate overthrow of their oppressors, the imminent arrival of a redeemer, the dawn of the millennium, a new heaven and a new earth. It was indeed often such a renegade priest or friar as Bale who set himself up as such a messiah, with disastrous effect upon law and order. Such a thing, it was notorious, had only

61

recently occurred at Münster, and who could be sure that comparable conditions would not soon bring a comparable catastrophe in England?

Yet England was to prove no Münster and John Bale no John of Leyden. Things were bad enough in East Anglia, and Bale was full enough of apocalyptical urgings. In him, however, as a little later in the Marian exiles and among the English generally, apocalyptical urgings took a different turn. They led not to the pursuit of a millennium but to the aspiration after nationality, not to the expectation of a messiah out of the blue but to the idea of an hereditary monarch called by the grace of God to rule the realm and defend the faith, not to the desire to cast down the mighty but to the resolution to cast out the interloper. The reactionary policies of the closing years of Henry VIII caused no conflict of loyalties in Bale's mind. He could not but condemn the things being done in the king's name, but he put the blame not on Henry, not even, when the time came, on Mary, but on the evil counsellors who betrayed ruler and people to the adversary.

The adversary was of course the Pope, and the betrayers were high-ranking members of the hierarchy like Gardiner and Bonner. Bale therefore now took in bitter earnest to exploiting the antiquarian lore to which he had been prompted by Leland in order to demonstrate that it was always such evil counsellors as these who thrust themselves between the monarch and his vocation. 'I would wish some learned Englishman,' he wrote in his preface to the Oldcastle story, 'to set forth the English chronicles in their right shape ... all affections set apart. I cannot think a more necessary thing to be laboured to the honour of God, beauty of the realm, erudition of the people, and commodity of other lands next the sacred Scriptures ...' What he meant by this was that he wished the national legend as he found it in Polydore Vergil and the fifteenth-century chronicles upon which Polydore so largely drew might be purged of traditional assumptions and retold from his own stiffly nationalistic and secular point of view. Thus he himself retrieved the story of Oldcastle from the unfriendly pages of Polydore, Walsingham and *Fasciculi Zizaniorum*, and turned him into an authentic saint of the new faith, martyred at the hands not, of course, of the hero of Agincourt, but of Archbishop Arundel.[1]

Bale's most ambitious attempt to rewrite history nearer to his idea of the facts was a vast work purporting to record the lives and works of hundreds of writers he claims as countrymen from the very beginning of the British race down to his own time. This work in its first form, *Illustrium maioris Britanniae Scriptorum Summarium*, was a quarto of one hundred and forty-nine leaves, published at Wesel in 1548. The work in its final form, *Scriptorum Illustrium maioris Britanniae Catalogus*, the product of the author's second exile under Mary, was a folio of seven hundred and forty-two pages, published at Basle in 1557. It consisted of biographical sketches and lists of the writings, authentic or supposed, of some nine hundred mythical and historical persons, not only writers but all sorts of others, beginning with Japhet. The subjects were presented in roughly chronological order and arranged in nine divisions of a hundred each. A second part of two hundred and fifty pages, published two years later, added five hundred names and an index to the whole.

The main work goes on from the first mythical inhabitants of Britain to Brutus the mythical eponymous founder, Joseph of Arimathea, King Lucius, Helena and her son the Emperor Constantine, to Saxon and Norman kings, John, Henry II, Wyclif, Oldcastle and the Lollards, and so to Anne Askew and the Marian martyrs, Rogers, Bradford, Ridley, Latimer, Cranmer and the rest, whose stories Bale must have got from Foxe or Grindal, concluding with Foxe himself and Cardinal Pole. Interspersed at appropriate points were also included catalogues of Roman bishops and patriarchs, whom he characterized down to Gregory the Great as faithful pastors and preachers, and of popes from Boniface VIII on, presented as agents of Antichrist encroaching upon the authority of kings. To describe the work as a biographical dictionary of English literature is quite misleading. It is an encyclo-

[1] L. M. Oliver, 'Sir John Oldcastle: Legend or Literature,' *Library*, ser. 5, I, 1945-6.

pedia on the medieval pattern comprehending what the author understood as universal history but focused upon England and the immediate crisis in the relations of England to the Roman Church.

But for Bale, as for many another historian before and since, the function of history was to explain the present and reveal the future. The title-page of *Catalogus* tells us that along with everything else the book will make clear the meaning of St John's apocalyptic vision, a work which, the author tells us at another point, is 'the very complete sum and whole knitting up ... of the whole verities of the bible'. It explains the meaning of 'all the chronicles and most notable histories which hath been written since Christ's ascension, opening the true natures of their ages, times and seasons. He that hath store of them and shall diligently search them over, conferring the one with the other, time with time, and age with age, shall perceive most wonderful causes. For in the text [of Revelation] are they [the causes] only proposed in effect, and promised to follow in their seasons, and so ratified with other scriptures, but in the chronicles they are evidently seen by all ages fulfilled.'

And though Bale qualifies this statement by saying 'yet is the text a light to the chronicles and not the chronicles to the text', it is clear that he sees prophecy and history confirming one another and flowing together in one continuous revelation of the design of the Creator. While compiling his encyclopedia of national history, Bale was also composing a commentary on the Apocalypse with historical elucidations. This, *The Image of Both Churches*, is his most clearly conceived and carefully executed work, the one in which the gravity of the subject is most nearly matched by a style free from gross extravagance.

The intention of this work was to persuade the English people that the struggle between the believers in the Word and their persecutors was but one more engagement in the age-long contention of Christ and Antichrist described by St John in his vision. Bale was probably familiar with Luther's version of this idea, either directly from Luther's own writings or from the latter's follower and champion, Matthias Flacius Illyricus. At Basle in 1556 Flacius published *Catalogus Testium Veritatis*, a collection of testimonies by martyrs and others against the papacy, drawn from a wide variety of sources and going far back in time. Both Bale and Foxe were in Basle while this work was being printed by Oporinus, and both made use of it. Flacius also headed a group of Lutheran reformers at Magdeburg who were at this time compiling a history of the Church century by century from their point of view. The first volume of this truly formidable work of German scholarship, *Sexta Centuria Ecclesiasticae Historiae*, was published by Oporinus at Basle in 1562–3. At Geneva meanwhile Jean Crespin in 1554 published the first of several editions of a martyrology beginning with Wyclif and Huss which was conceived from a French Calvinist point of view. All these writers, however, including Bale and Foxe, were appropriating and adapting to their own purpose and occasion the conception of history and the legend of the Church which had been fixed by Eusebius and Augustine.

Eusebius's account of the first three hundred years of the Church initiated the legend that the apostles had established the Church in its primordial purity once for all, and that its history ever since had been the history of the unceasing endeavour of the elect people of God to maintain it in that condition from corruption within and attack from enemies without who were for ever seeking its downfall. The life of the elect, who were the true Church, was a life of struggle carried on at the risk of persecution and martyrdom, but sustained by confident expectation of the return of the Redeemer and universal Judge. They were the Church, their struggle was part of the Church's collective struggle against Antichrist, and the Church's temporal victory under Constantine over the forces of paganism was an earnest of its ultimate triumph over all its enemies.[1]

Eusebius, writing in the fourth century, was preoccupied with the events leading to that victory. Augustine, writing half a century later, was concerned with preserving the Church from barbarism. He extended Eusebius's view of history to cover the whole course of mankind's experience and the Church's part in it as set forth in the Scriptures and in other records so far as they

[1] Translated by Meredith Hanmer, *Ancient Ecclesiastical Histories* (1577).

could be accommodated to the record of Scripture. The course to be taken by man's life from the present to its proximate fore-ordained end was forecast in prophecy, of which the Apocalypse was the final summation. The history of mankind thus conceived fell into six periods of a thousand years each, taking a thousand to mean not a definite number of years but any grand division of time. The ages of the world extended from Adam to the flood, from Noah to Abraham, from Abraham to David, from David to the Babylonian captivity, from the captivity to Christ, from Christ to the present and so to the end. After the fall of Adam men lived under sentence of death according to the law, except for a mystical few elected to eternal life by divine grace. Christ's coming sealed the election of these few and caused Satan to be chained up for a thousand years.

This meant that, though he still roamed the world, the elect were for that time secure from persecution. He would be per-mitted to assail them again for a short period just before the end, but again without avail. The present and last age of the world would end with Christ's second coming, Satan's final overthrow, and the last judgment. Augustine rejected the idea that Christ at His second coming would establish an earthly kingdom over which He would rule with the saints for another thousand years while Satan lay bound in the bottomless pit. Christ's kingdom on earth was not a material state still to be expected, but a spiritual condition present since the beginning, the mystical realm in which dwelt those who had been singled out for redemption by divine grace. For Augustine the millennium was either the whole period of time since the election of these few or the whole period since the sealing of their election by Christ.

For the community of the elect, the City of God, was to be distinguished from all others, they being merely of this world. Any gathering of reasonable people bound together by agreement as to the objects of their love, Augustine declared to be a com-munity. The City of God is a community of people bound to one another by the love of God 'even to the contempt of self'. The city of this world is a community of people bound together by the love of self 'even to the contempt of God'. The Roman state is a community of the latter sort, which, united up to a point in the love of justice, has fallen short in the love of God and so has declined in virtue and power. The Church on the other hand is up to a point a godly community set apart from, when not actually opposed by, the civil republic.

Here, however, Augustine introduced another distinction. The corporate visible community known as the Church is not to be supposed identical in its totality with the City of God; nor can each of its members be counted on to love God more than himself. The true Church is the spiritual community composed of the elect of God, those and only those who truly love Him above everything else. This, the City of God, is a spiritual realm transcending every other, not excepting the visible church, and comprised of those who, their election having been sealed to them by Christ, are already of the kingdom of heaven.

Thus Eusebius and Augustine, confronted by the collapse of the pagan order, formulated a conception of the past to explain what was happening and what they desired to have happen in their own time. Eusebius conceived the history of the Church as the history of a band of faithful souls struggling to stand fast by an original unchanging revealed order constantly threatened by betrayal within and attack from without. Augustine conceived the whole history of mankind as occupied with the recurring opposition of two orders within every order, two cities within every city, two Churches within every Church, one of grace and election, the other of nature and reprobation, one ideal and transcendent, the other material and temporal. On these pregnant conceptions men in later ages had rung many changes, and sixteenth-century reformers, confronted by the collapse of the medieval order, seized upon them again to explain what was happening in their own time and what they would have happen in the time to come. To express these ideas afresh for the English public in its own vernacular, and incidentally for the inspiration of John Foxe, was Bale's most important accomplishment.

But since history was supposed to reveal the meaning of events

67

in the present, it was all the more necessary to confirm that revelation out of Revelation itself. In his *Image of Both Churches* Bale told his readers that that book was the sum and knitting up of all that preceded and all that was to follow in the chronicles of scripture. It was the whole story of the Church 'from Christ's ascension to the end of the world', set forth 'under pleasant figures and elegant tropes'. 'He that knoweth not this book knoweth not what the church is whereof he is a member ... He that delighteth not to behold the condition of his own city is thereunto no loving citizen. And after the true opinion of St Austin, either we are citizens in the New Jerusalem with Jesus Christ, or else in the old superstitious Babylon with antichrist the vicar of Satan.' What we are to learn from St John, however, is not that the New Jerusalem is about to descend upon us from the skies, but that it has been present on earth all along for us to love and defend – present, that is, in that communion of the elect which is the true Church.

As for the millennium, that was not a glorious time still to come, but the thousand years after Christ during which nothing that Satan had been able to accomplish by violence or deceit had sufficed to prevail against those who truly loved God. By the connivance of Pope Sylvester II, to be sure, the devil had broken loose again and made the Church of Rome his own, but Christ's true Church had not perished. Pious and learned men – he names among others Marsiglio, Petrarch, Wyclif, Huss, Luther, Bucer, Bullinger – renewed the war of the elect against Antichrist. That war was destined to continue until the end of time itself, which may come any tomorrow. This ever renewed contention of Christ and Antichrist, of the City of God and the city of this world, of the New Jerusalem and Babylon, is the focal theme of the whole history of mankind, while the history of the Church is merely a projection on a larger scale of the story of every martyr from those who appear in the pages of Eusebius down to Sir John Oldcastle and Anne Askew.

Since the world's beginning ... hath iniquity had his froward course, and shall have so still to the latter end thereof. In the very angels or spirits of heaven did God find an untoward stubbornness and an obstinate crookedness. What he hath had in the ungodly children of men since the days of Cain till this present age, it were much to write. Of that [which] was sometime the Church of Christ hath it made the synagogue of Satan ever since that adversary was set at large after the thousand years and somewhat afore, whose malignant members under the title of spirituality are always filthy whoremongers, murtherers, thieves, raverners, idolators, liars, dogs, swine, wolves, abominable workers, adversaries to God and devils incarnate.[1]

In all this Bale was following the same line of argument as propagandists for reform everywhere, but there was this difference between English martyrologists in general and their French and German counterparts: for Crespin, Flacius and the centuriators of Magdeburg it was enough for the martyr or other witness to be given a place in their pages if he had suffered under the Roman Antichrist whatever his nationality; while those to whom Bale gave place were preponderantly English as well. In his pages, as in those of English propagandists following him, the war between the two Churches within the Church, while still represented as filling all history, nevertheless settles down into an age-long contention of English rulers and people against the alien intruders for ever seeking to subvert the English state and corrupt the English Church by open violence or by false doctrine and evil example. Through all of Bale's writings ran the thread of a legend which, in a few years, loyal subjects of Elizabeth would seem to have known all their lives and which few would ever seriously question. The gospel of Christ, Bale told them, was brought to Britain by Joseph of Arimathea and disciples of the apostle Philip, and the Church was presently established throughout the realm by King Lucius. It was persecuted by heathen Saxon invaders, corrupted after Augustine by the agents of Rome, and again after the invasion of the Normans by monks and friars. Yet native kings

[1] Bale, *Yet a course at the Romyshe foxe* (1543).

combated tyranny and resisted corruption, while a long line of native teachers – Wyclif, Gower, Chaucer, Tyndal, Frith, Bilney and others since – kept the true faith alive.

'Now truly in this latter age and end of the world God, showing great mercy to his elected heritage, hath gathered them together from the perils of persecution by the voice of his holy gospel.' Bale was thinking of himself in this perspective when providence played the ironic jest of prompting King Edward to send him to preach the gospel to the Irish at Kilkenny. Put to flight before the year was up, he escaped with his life and little else, but comforted himself with the reflection that he was not alone in his experience of vocation, persecution and deliverance. Paul and Luke had been through the same experience, and in his thankfulness he lets his imagination take wing for a moment. 'For I fare like the bird which is delivered from the snare of the catcher. He flieth to a bough and rejoiceth in his deliverance, and even so do I. In the which rejoice[ing], I make not only myself merry but also all my loving friends.' This was written when, after various adventures and narrow escapes which he relates with great gusto, Bale had joined the other exiles on the Continent.[1]

He had first encountered John Foxe in 1548 when he returned from his first period of exile to be received into the household of the Duchess of Richmond. Foxe's interest in the English past and his conviction that the history of mankind had been occupied always with the contention of the two Churches dates from this time. So far he had published nothing but some translations from German reformers and a plea against the death penalty for adultery. When he arrived at Strasbourg in the late spring or early summer of 1554, he brought with him the manuscript of a work which he presently had printed at that place as an octavo of a hundred and twelve leaves, entitled *Commentarii rerum in ecclesia gestarum, maximarumque per totam Europam persecutionum a Wiclevi temporibus ad hanc usque aetatem descriptio. Liber primus*. This was designed to be the first part of a history of the movement for the reformation of the Church beginning with Wyclif and the Lol-

---

[1] *The vocacyon of Johan Bale* (1553).

lards and going on to Huss, Jerome of Prague and Savonarola. Meanwhile, either at Strasbourg or Frankfurt, Foxe rejoined Bale, and the two men presently settled down near one another at Basle, Bale to go on with his *Scriptorum Illustrium maioris Britanniae Catalogus*, and Foxe, while working for his living in Oporinus's printing house, to turn Grindal's martyr stories into Latin and make ready to incorporate them into the apocalyptical conception of history he had acquired from Bale.

The plan for the Book of Martyrs seems to have been that Foxe should bring his already published history of the Church down to the end of the reign of Henry VIII and continue the story from that point, making use of the materials supplied by Grindal. As we have seen, however, both English and Latin versions of the book were still hanging fire when the news came which made Grindal and his associates drop everything and hasten home. Foxe had no such occasion as they to hurry. Instead of suspending his part of their joint project as Grindal advised, he remained at Basle for the better part of a year and completed the work as best he could. It was published by Oporinus and Brylinger in August 1559 as a folio of seven hundred and thirty-two pages with the title, *Rerum in ecclesia gestarum, quae postremis et periculosis his temporibus evenerunt, maximarumque per Europam persecutionum, ad Sanctorum Dei martyrum, coeterumque rerum quae insignoris exemplisint, digesti per Regna et nationis Commentarii.*

The work opens with a statement of the familiar contention that history should be studied, especially by rulers, for the lessons it has to teach, and that more is to be learned from the examples of saints and martyrs than from the exploits of heroes and warriors. Foxe then reprints his *Commentarii* of 1554 and goes on to give an account, largely based on information published and unpublished supplied by Bale, of persecution under Henry VIII. Anne Askew's story appears in full, but without Bale's comments. At a later point Foxe introduces his own address to the nobility on behalf of his fellow-exiles, and the treatise of John Hooper on the sacrament. Most of the remaining five hundred pages are devoted to the stories of the Marian martyrs. They include a detailed account of

Lady Jane Grey, probably based on reports brought over by her former tutor John Aylmer; John Philpot's account, already in print, of the convocation of 1553, followed later in the volume by the story of his examination and burning; a report, substantial but not as full as that in later editions, of the disputation at Oxford in April 1554 and the subsequent examination and execution of Ridley, Latimer and Cranmer; and finally the stories of the notable martyrs of 1555–6, Rogers, Hooper, Saunders, Taylor, Bradford and the rest. The book closes by enumerating some eighty persons who were sent to the stake between the time of Cranmer's death and the end of the reign in November 1558.

Some years later Foxe was to say of his book that it was begun 'in the far parts of Germany, where few friends, no conference, and small information could be had'.[1] Though there may be some exaggeration in this statement, nevertheless the work gives evidence of having been put together under some pressure. It does not for one thing do all that the title promises. It leaves the history of persecution on the Continent to a second part, to be completed as things turned out by another hand and published separately at a later date. Foxe's part is still therefore mainly Grindal's Book of Martyrs put into Latin. Yet though *Rerum in ecclesia gestarum* reflects less of that apocalyptical conception of history which the author had acquired from Bale than appears in the later English version of the book, it still announces the great themes of propaganda which were now to be heard on behalf of the religion of the Word in pulpit, press and parliament. Once in print, even in Latin, the story of what had been done under the late regime to such well known figures in the Henrician and Edwardian Church as Cranmer, Ridley and Latimer was bound to become common talk and lead in the circumstances of the reign which followed to translation and further elaboration in English.

More than ever the purpose would now be to identify the religion of the Word, as opposed to the religion of the Mass, with the cause of the national state, and the effect would be to give depth and range to the people's sense of being a people with an identity

---

[1] Foxe, III, 384.

of their own distinct from any other. The religion for which the martyrs in Foxe's book died was the religion of the Word in English. From the beginning the movement for reform in England, so far as it directly affected the way people thought and felt about religion rather than the way rulers attempted to reconstitute the relations of the ecclesiastical and civil states, had centred on getting the Bible translated, printed and circulated in the vulgar tongue. Henry VIII had gone so far as to authorize the Bible derived from Tyndale and Coverdale for reading in churches. Edward's government had authorized an English liturgy based upon that Bible. Popular interest in the Bible encouraged preaching and the publication of other printed books as well. The Bible, the prayer-book, the pulpit and the book-trade, working together, were to produce a change in the mental lives of the people basic to the whole process of change about to come. Yet the fact was that so far the only English Bibles actually accessible to people in general were still bulky, expensive, black-letter folios suitable only for use in churches. The technical and editorial problem of turning out a book of such volume and complexity for private use, equipped with the necessary apparatus for the instruction of unaccustomed readers, had still to be worked out.

Its working out was the accomplishment of the group of exiles at Geneva under the direction of William Whittingham, lately Fellow of All Souls, now pastor of the English congregation at Geneva, a disciple of Calvin and his kinsman by marriage, an able, learned, widely travelled man in his early thirties. His wish, he said, was to bring the Scriptures 'to the simple lambs, which partly are already in the fold of Christ ... and partly wandering astray by ignorance'. At Geneva he had access to original texts and to translations in other languages, to the advice of Calvin, Beza and other men learned in the Scriptures, and to printers and other artisans. By 1557 he and his associates were ready with their version of the New Testament and in 1560 with the complete text.

The result was the English Bible of the Elizabethan public, of the Scottish Reformation, of the English voyagers and the first English settlers in North America. In form the book was typically a manageable quarto, having the text divided for the first time into numbered chapters and verses with a topical heading for each page, an introductory summary for each chapter, and a preliminary 'argument' for each book. There was also a running commentary in the margin designed to help the reader to understand what he read from page to page and to form a connected idea of the whole. The 'arguments' were designed not only, it was said, for those 'already advanced in the knowledge of the scriptures, but also for the simple and unlearned'. The marginal glosses were designed for persons who could not afford learned commentaries or who lacked opportunity and leisure to read them 'because of their prolixity'. There were in addition maps, woodcut illustrations, tables of names, topics and the ages of the world.

What the Geneva Bible did was to set before the reader in comprehensible terms keyed to the Scriptures a statement in the common tongue of the conception of man's inner life derived from Paul by way of Augustine and Calvin. It enabled the reader to discover for himself from the text before him that the life of man is governed from the beginning to the end of time by the design of his Creator, and that this design is revealed in the record of events. Man begins in innocent harmony with this law of his being, and this is the way of life. He contravenes the law on his own volition, and this is the way of death. From death there would be no escape, did not the Lord of life call men from time to time in their fallen condition once more to believe in Him, obey His will, and live again. Such were the elect, called out of the generality of men to strive against the spirit of disobedience, first in themselves, but then also in others.

Here were the essentials of the great doctrine of salvation by the election of divine grace alone, and on these points there was and continued to be substantial agreement among all English exiles and reformers, whether they held by the English or the Genevan settlement of church worship and government. When doctrinal deviation or dispute occurred, as it usually did wherever Calvin's systematic formulation of these ideas penetrated, it was over the question, who and how many were called, and on what terms. On this matter the English, while they were all Calvinists up to a point, were seldom Calvinists in a strict Genevan sense. Many of them had imbibed the doctrine of grace not directly from Calvin, but in modified form from Bucer at Cambridge and Peter Martyr at Oxford. They had followed the latter back to Strasbourg, and some of them had gone on to listen to Zwingli's disciple Bullinger at Zürich, with whom they were to keep in frequent communication after their return to England.

Under these influences they learned to hedge in some degree on the rigorous form of predestinated election worked out by Calvin in a situation very different from their own. The situation which awaited them on their return from exile would be one in which they would have to preach and go on preaching for, so to speak, their very lives. Under these conditions, while not faltering as to the all-sufficiency of grace, they would naturally preach it as though there were something the people they were trying to convert could do to participate in the process of their own redemption. Vocation was still essential, and still God's doing. But the elect were called to co-operate with the Lord as though they were indeed His chosen agents, confident that His purposes could not fail and that He would never let them down unless they let him down first. Far from suggesting to the subjects of Elizabeth that they might safely sit back and leave everything to the Lord's determination, the effect was to encourage them to suppose that, whatever they might choose to undertake, the Lord's hand would be in it.

What with the Geneva Bible and the legends of the recent martyrs for whose faith the Bible was the prime vehicle, the effect of the propaganda initiated by the Marian exiles would be felt in all phases of public life in the reign of Elizabeth. Government would more and more have to be carried on to the accompaniment of discussion by men with the confidence in their own opinions bred by such a faith, an increasingly passionate interest in the affairs of the realm, and a familiar apparatus of images and ideas for speculation, expression and communication. Nothing like this on any such scale had ever happened in England before. The beast of many heads was becoming a public with many voices. Consequently all parties concerned with the theory of state as well as with the practice of government presently found themselves impaled upon the horns of a dilemma. Men who disagreed about almost everything else were at one in doing at least lip-service to the idea that all men were obliged by the law revealed in nature, scripture and history to obey the rulers God set over them, and that God held rulers responsible for the manner in which they exercised the authority entrusted to them. If either failed in his duty – the ruler to God only, the people to God in him – God would punish the offence in His own way in His own time.

This was all very well as a way of rationalizing the consolidation of the national state under the Crown and the liberation of the Crown from subjection to the papacy or other outside authority. It was all very well, that is, so long as no one had seriously to face the question what to think or do when God seemed plainly to command one thing and his vice-gerent the opposite. In that case the problem was not so simple, and it was further complicated by the course which events took in England. Theory and tradition held that such questions were for the Church to determine, since it was the exponent of the universal laws of God as distinct from the temporal laws of states and kings. In fact, of course, the authority of rulers had been limited by their actual power to impose their will upon vassals whose ability to resist was sometimes greater than that of their overlords to compel. But by the middle of the sixteenth century English monarchs had made firm their hold upon the state, and Henry VIII had extended his hold over the Church. Thus he became, in fact if not in principle, the arbiter in any case to which the universal law binding both kings and subjects applied. The effect was to make dissent from the religion of the monarch tantamount to treason and to require the subject in that case to choose between disobeying the civil ruler and betraying his faith.

More and Fisher had chosen to keep to the faith at the cost of disobeying the king, but the generality of Henry's subjects, lay and cleric alike, had bowed to his supremacy, and Cranmer and

Gardiner both had defended it in print. Hence the accession of a monarch determined to restore the Church to its former authority and herself and her people to their former obedience confronted conscientious adherents to the new faith with the same tragic necessity to choose which had confronted the adherents of the old under her father, and would again under her sister. Subjects who had repudiated the Pope were bound to obey the king as head under God of both Church and state. But what should they do when the heir to the authority they were pledged to obey in both realms revoked her claim to their obedience in the spiritual realm, while as their civil ruler she called on them to yield obedience to a spiritual authority which her predecessor had ordered them on their allegiance to reject as contrary to the laws of God? Were they to obey God's vice-gerent at the risk of disobeying God? Or were they to obey God at the cost of disobeying God's anointed? Rebellion offered one way out of the difficulty, martyrdom another, and martyrdom was a kind of rebellion or could be made to serve as such, while both martyrdom and rebellion could be argued to be not disobedience at all, but obedience to a higher authority than that of any earthly ruler.

Such considerations became increasingly apposite and pressing in the circumstances of the sixteenth century. Government might continue to be regarded as the personal affair of the hereditary monarch, and defenders of royal supremacy might argue to their hearts' content that kings were responsible only to God. Yet the fact to which rulers would have to accommodate themselves as best they could was the emergence of increasingly precise and exacting notions concerning the responsibilities of rulers under God which subjects would deduce from the Bible, the teachings of the pulpit, the Book of Martyrs, the English chronicles, and the overflowing products of the book-trade. The prince by divine right would be expected to be a godly prince, a David, a Solomon, a Josiah; but godliness would call for definition and discussion, subject to all the winds of doctrine which coursed through the heads of a more and more articulate public. Under these conditions the subject's duty of civil obedience, while in principle as absolute as ever, would in fact become more and more conditional. No ruler could ever be certain that his people would submit quietly to the denial of what they might regard as their interests or convictions, let alone to martyrdom, simply on theoretical or dogmatic grounds. They would at any rate not submit without speaking up and arguing back.

The Marian exiles, having eschewed martyrdom, far from keeping silence, sent a steady stream of subversive and abusive publications back to England, directed for the most part not against the queen herself but against the authorities and doctrines of her Church and government. In particular John Ponet, John Knox, and Christopher Goodman demonstrated how scripture could be used to support an attack not on the principle of kingship, but on the title of a given individual to exercise its powers. Ponet's *A Short Treatise of politike power, and of the true Obedience which subjects owe to kynges and other civile Governours* was published at Strasbourg in 1556. Knox's *The First Blast of the Trumpet against the monstruous regiment of Women* was published at Geneva in 1558, and in the same place and year appeared Goodman's *How Superior Powers ought to be obeyed of their subjects*, with a commendatory address by William Whittingham. All four of these writers proceeded from the premiss that the function of the state is to preserve the people in their obedience to the law of God as revealed in His Word. By that, they held, every act and decree of rulers was bound to be judged. Their attitude in this, though expressed with an exaggeration which approached absurdity, was one which governments would have more and more to deal with from this time on. All four men accepted without question the principle of complete independent autonomy in the national state under monarchical rule, but seeing that the state in England and in Scotland was now being governed contrary to their idea of what the law of God required, they repudiated the claim of the present rulers to the unconditional obedience of the people.

Knox and Goodman were as certain as any pope had ever been that earthly rulers were subject to God's universal law, of which the Church was the appointed exponent, but they were just as certain that the voice of the Church was to be heard not in the decrees of the hierarchy centred at Rome but in the utterances of the preaching ministry. In Knox's words, 'we in our miserable age are bound to admonish the world and the tyrants thereof'. They must make the truth known, 'unless that to our own condemnation we list to wrap up and hide the talent committed to our charge'. They must speak as did Isaiah, Jeremiah, Ezekiel and Daniel when Israel took to worshipping idols. They must say with Paul, 'Woe be to me if I preach not the Evangile,' or as Peter and John said to the high priests and the Sadducees, 'Judge whether it be just before God to obey you rather than God.'

This was in effect an argument for the right of preachers – though a right it soon proved impossible to limit to the pulpit – to hold rulers accountable under whatever might be taken to be the law revealed in scripture. Knox and Goodman – by 1558 Ponet was dead – employed the liberty they assumed to be theirs to observe that the persons then presuming to rule over England and Scotland were both women, and to point out with unmistakable emphasis that for women to rule over men was clearly forbidden by God in the Scriptures. The conclusion to this reasoning was obvious, but the moment for putting it forward was most untimely, since the next thing that happened was that the English crown fell to another woman, one who proved to be any man's match in the art of governing and whom it behoved exiles returning from Geneva as well as Strasbourg and elsewhere to obey without demur. There would be nothing for any of them to gain under her regiment by pressing the argument that God might in some circumstances absolve men from having to obey her. There would on the contrary be everything to gain by turning the argument that God requires men to obey His vice-gerent in the state against those who were prepared to deny her authority to rule the Church.

But the returning exiles would have to do more than that to counter the endeavour soon to be put forth by their adversaries to accomplish that revival of the old faith they had failed to accomplish under Mary. The evangels of the new religion would have more than ever to put forth the experience of the Word over against participation in the Mass as the indispensable element in every man's religious life. They must advance their conception of the Church as the whole body of the elect against the conception of the Church as an apostolic hierarchy charged with transmitting God's message to the people. And the next step would be to associate the idea of the communion of true believers with the Church of England, the Church with the nation, and the nation with the indispensable though enigmatic young woman now coming to the throne. There was no telling in advance how much stock she would take in their notions and pretensions, but that could not be allowed to matter. Providence must have called her to her present station for a purpose, and the returning exiles could afford to have no doubt as to what that purpose was. England was to lead the world to its redemption in the final reformation of the Church, and Elizabeth was to be the ruler and representative of England in that work.

In dedicating their Bible to her, the Geneva translators said:

> For the eyes of all that fear God in all places behold your country as an example to all that believe, and the prayers of all the godly at all times are directed to God for the preservation of your majesty. For considering God's wonderful mercies toward you at all seasons, who hath pulled you out of the mouth of the lions, and how that from your youth you have been brought up in the holy scriptures, the hope of all men is so increased that they cannot but look that God should bring to pass some wonderful work by your grace to the universal comfort of his church.

Let her therefore be bold and strong in God's quarrel with Satan, the old dragon.

> For albeit other kingdoms and monarchies, as the Babylonians, Persians, Grecians and Romans, have fallen and taken end, yet the Church of Christ even under the Cross hath from the beginning of the world been victorious, and shall be

everlasting. Truth it is, that sometime it seemeth to be shadowed with a cloud, or driven with a stormy persecution, yet suddenly the beams of Christ, the sun of justice, shine and bring it to light and liberty. If for a time it lie covered with ashes, yet it is quickly kindled again by the wind of God's spirit; though it seemed drowned in the sea, or parched and pined in the wilderness, yet God giveth ever good success, for He punisheth the enemies, and delivereth His, nourisheth them and still preserveth them under His wings.

CHAPTER III

A Godly Queen

ᏨᏯᎷᏯᎦ

ON November 17th, 1558, Queen Mary died, Elizabeth at once succeeded, and within six months most of the exiles were back in England. Thirteen of them were presently appointed to episcopal sees; Grindal to London, Cox to Ely, Jewel to Salisbury, Parkhurst to Norwich. Others were assigned to posts of only somewhat less influence and elevated later. Most were of the group which had followed Peter Martyr to Strasbourg. That they should have been called to take so large a part in the Church under the new regime was not surprising. They were the natural successors to the men who had been the leaders of the Church under Edward and had been made to suffer for it under Mary. During the period of exile they had kept as closely as they could to the Edwardian settlement. Their devotion to the principle of royal supremacy was beyond question. Not surprisingly, too, the Geneva men, fewer in number and differing in their views of Church government and discipline, were accorded less favourable positions. Whittingham was made Dean of Durham, but Knox was obliged to go back to his native Scotland, taking Goodman with him.

The man picked by Cecil and Bacon for the queen to appoint Archbishop of Canterbury was their fellow-Cantabrigian, Matthew Parker. He had managed to avoid going into exile, but there could be no doubt where his sympathies lay. He had arrived in Cambridge from Norfolk in the fifteen twenties in time to come under the influence of Bilney and Latimer. In 1531 he had ridden over to Norwich to be present at Bilney's martyrdom, and years later he gave Foxe an account of what he had witnessed on that occasion.[1]

[1] Foxe, IV, 652.

Cranmer licensed him to preach. Anne Boleyn gave him her patronage during her brief ascendancy and pledged him to be always faithful to her daughter. Notwithstanding her fall and his having to repel an accusation of heresy, he rose steadily from post to post in the university and the Church. Under Edward, vicechancellor a second time, he made friends with Martin Bucer and preached at his funeral. When Northumberland reached Cambridge in his vain attempt to overtake Mary, Parker was among those present to receive him, and when Mary succeeded in establishing herself, he was obliged to take refuge among friends and kinsfolk in Norfolk. He continued in touch with the exiles, however, and from someone among them received a copy of John Ponet's book in defence of the marriage of priests, published at Zürich in 1555. Parker, himself married, took up the argument in Ponet's support.

In the preface to this work,[1] not published until 1567, he gave expression to the humiliation and apprehension to which he had been subjected under Mary. 'If any indifferent learned man,' he wrote, should undertake to write the history of those unhappy times, 'it would rise to a huge volume ... what cruelty was seen executed by firing old men and women, young men and maids ... what proscriptions and banishments of learned men ... and such as tarried within the realm, how they were driven to corners, spoiled and impoverished ... Which heavy infelicities English children yet unborn shall weep and wail to consider the same'.

His resentment was still to be heard in his account of himself and his two predecessors in his *De Antiquitate Britannicae Ecclesiae*. There he told again the by-that-time familiar story of the examination, degradation and burning of Cranmer and his two associates at Oxford. Parker was grateful to the Lord that, while inflicting Pole upon England as punishment for her sins, he still showed his loving care of her by preserving Elizabeth. In writing of himself he dwelt on the many learned men who had been driven by papal tyranny in those days to flee abroad or hide at home, and he

[1] Parker, *Defence of priests marriages* (1567).

83

described their exultancy when at Elizabeth's accession the burnings stopped and the exiles returned.

They returned, however, to a situation full of uncertainties, not
the least of which was Elizabeth herself. It was perplexing enough
to have a woman for ruler, but Elizabeth was besides a perplexing
character, self-assured, intelligent, well educated after the manner
of the time, adept in the language of godliness, determined to have
her way, but in a very feminine way unpredictable and unscru-
pulous. None of the anxieties which beset those who looked to her
security for their own safety and success could be dispelled so long
as she remained unmarried, and they could not be expected to
cease altogether if she married a subject, still less a foreigner, least
of all – or so it seemed – if she chose not to marry at all. Her
supporters would never be able to put aside the question, who
would succeed, bringing what changes, when she was gone. The
returned exiles in particular would never be free from apprehension lest what they had had to endure under the one Mary they
would have to endure again if the other came to the throne. It was
that apprehension which made them now look to Elizabeth as the
avatar of their religious faith and of the faith of the nation in itself.

Although as exiles they had escaped martyrdom, martyrdom
had left its mark upon them none the less. While they had been
fleeing to safety, their fellows had been enduring the fate which
might as easily have been their own, and sending reports of the
experience after them. To suffer martyrdom at second hand was
to suffer its effects with special poignancy another way. The
essence of the martyrs' experience as reported by the martyrs
themselves lay in the assurance that came to each of them that he
was being singled out to give witness to the truth by the author of
truth himself. Persecution confirmed its victims in their sense of
election, making them capable of enduring what otherwise would
be beyond endurance. As for those who escaped into exile, if their
having fled the fire left them at all doubtful of their own election,
banishment went a long way towards easing compunction by
assuring them that they had been reserved for a purpose which
could not fail to be presently achieved and in which they were

bound to participate. If they kept much to themselves in their banishment, it was because they felt themselves to be dedicated men, sojourners in spirit as well as in fact, waiting to be called back to England to resume the building of the New Jerusalem.

Hence the legends and prophecies of the Old Testament – of the escape of the chosen people out of Egypt to the promised land, of the fall of Babylon and the recovery of Zion, of a fifth and last monarchy to succeed and put an end to all that had gone before – these and the New Testament promise of the return of the Redeemer, and St John's vision of the casting out of Antichrist and the overthrow of the spiritual Babylon, all took on a special meaning and relevance. Other reformers, remembering Münster and John of Leyden, might be chary of attaching too much practical importance to such fantasies. Too often they had been used by mystagogues of one sort or another to stir up distressed peasants and proletarians to disrupt the civil order. But the English exiles were not dreamers deluding themselves or the vulgar with notions of new heaven and new earth, but high-ranking members of a displaced hierarchy and intellectual class cherishing a real prospect of returning by legitimate means to legitimate power.

Ordinary eschatalogical dreamers might find in Revelation excuse for turning their backs on reality and history. The same texts set fire in these English exiles to not impossible hopes of recovering their position in the realm of England itself. The outcome might have been different if they had been kept wandering in the wilderness for forty years, but with the death of Mary in not much more than four years the apocalypse they had been looking for seemed actually to have arrived. The promptitude with which providence thus brought about their anticipated deliverance confirmed their sense of their election, and they at once made ready to participate in the fulfilment of its design. For there is nothing like a thumping obsession with the idea that something is going to happen, whether or no, to make some men spend their lives seeing that it does happen.

And yet that providence should be left to shape its ends as it would, or the new queen her policies, was the last thing to occur to the returning exiles and their partisans. Believing that they had everything to lose if she should fail them, they undertook at once to impose upon her, her government and the public their conception of the role which the Lord expected her to play. They announced at once that a great new age was about to begin for the Church and the nation, and that Elizabeth was the appointed agent for bringing it about. Thus the notion of a great climactic Elizabethan age, though not as yet so designated, may be said to have sprung full blown from the apocalyptical imaginings with which the Marian exiles kept up their courage during the years of their discontent.

Whether they had any real idea of what manner of woman Elizabeth was is doubtful, but by the time they reached home she had displayed, if not her readiness to pursue the policy they prescribed, her gift for acting the part which they were about to devise for her and which her public was prepared to appreciate. At her coronation on January 15th, the citizens of London staged five pageants to greet her on her way from the Tower to the Abbey. One scene displayed York and Lancaster united in her person. Another invoked the beatitudes upon her with the assurance that God, having brought her safely through all her recent perils, would give her strength to fulfil His purposes for herself and for England. Another showed her Time leading forth his daughter Truth with the Word of Truth in her hand. 'And Time,' Elizabeth exclaimed, 'hath brought me hither.' They presented her with a Bible, and she clasped it to her bosom, kissed it, held it up for all to see, and promised to read it. In the last scene of all they showed her Deborah 'with her estates, consulting for the good government of Israel'.[1]

The whole affair from beginning to end showed above everything else that she knew when it was her cue to speak, what to say, and how to say it so as not simply to exact the obedience to which she was entitled, but to command the attention and the devotion so necessary to her security. This gift was never to fail her even under the most trying circumstances. A few weeks later

[1] *The Passage of our most dread Sovereign Lady* (1558).

the holdover bishops from her sister's regime urged her to acknowledge the subjection of her Church and realm to the Pope. She replied in the words of Joshua, 'I and my house will serve the Lord,' adding that as Josiah assembled the elders to make covenant with the Lord, so she had assembled her parliament and clergy to covenant with God, not with the Bishop of Rome.[1]

The role the exiles proposed for Elizabeth to play, announced in high prophetic strain by the Geneva translators in their dedication, was stated even more explicitly in the rejoinder which John Aylmer made to John Knox's ill-timed argument against women rulers. Formerly tutor to Lady Jane Grey, Aylmer was a friend of Elizabeth's former tutor Roger Ascham. On the eve of his return to England he composed a tract called *An Harborowe for faithfull and true subjectes*, published by John Day in London with a Strasbourg imprint and the date April 26th, 1559. Having first regularly demolished Knox's offensive syllogism, Aylmer pictured Elizabeth under her sister's rule as the faithful godly princess saved from martyrdom only in the nick of time for England's sake by divine intervention. This story, based probably on information supplied by Ascham, anticipated the classic version of the same legend to be set in circulation by John Foxe.

Having thus sketched the portrait of the godly princess now happily elevated to the throne, Aylmer went on to exhort all Englishmen to stand ready to spend their lives and their money in her defence. They should thank God for letting them be born Englishmen rather than Italians, Frenchmen or Germans. For England abounds in all good things – beef, mutton, cheese, beer, ale, tin, lead, wool, leather – and God and His angels fight on her side against all her enemies. 'God is English,' the writer exclaims in the margin. 'For you fight not only in the quarrel of your country but also and chiefly in defence of His true religion and of His dear son Christ.' England says to her children,

God hath brought forth in me the greatest and excellentest treasure that He hath for your comfort and all the worlds.

[1] Strype, *Annals*, vol. I, pt. i, 206–8.

He would that out of my womb should come that servant of Christ John Wyclif, who begat Huss, who begat Luther, who begat the truth. What greater honour could you or I have than that it pleased Christ as it were in a second birth to be born again of me among you?

This was indeed to give the apocalyptical dream of Christ's reappearance upon earth an English turn, and Aylmer went on to make clear what role England and Elizabeth were called to play in the new age now at hand. 'You cannot be my children,' England says, 'if you be not her subjects. I will none of you, if you will none of her.' Therefore 'let us requite her with thankfulness, which studyeth to keep us in quietness. Let us daily call to God with lifted up hearts and hands for her preservation and long life, that she may many years carry the sword of our defence, and therewith cut off the head of that Hydra, the Antichrist of Rome, in such sort as it may never grow again in this realm of England.'

The fact that in all this Aylmer may have been speaking for no considerable number of his countrymen is neither here nor there. He spoke for a highly articulate group of intellectuals with a common grievance, a common purpose, a common body of ideas, a common vocabulary for making their ideas known, and a vital stake in the security of Elizabeth's person and the success of her regime. From her point of view, whether she liked it or not, they were the men she could most surely depend on to acknowledge her supremacy and to whom she was therefore obliged at the outset of her reign to entrust the administration of the Church. Their attitude towards her, moreover, as well as towards matters of religion was shared in considerable measure by the men she could most surely depend on for the administration of civil government and by many of those who would presently sit in the parliaments she was obliged to call to Westminster.

The question of the Church was of course crucial, and up to a point her supporters were at one in pressing for reform. If they differed among themselves, it was only as to the form and direction reformation should take and the extent to which it should

Henricus the emperor, with his wife and child, barefoot and barelegd

waiting on pope Hildebrand, three daies and three nights, at the gates of Canusium, before he could be suffered to come in.

King John offering his Crowne to Pandulphus, Legate.

go, not at all as to the necessity of opposing the religion of the Word to the religion of the Mass or of defending the Church of England against the Church of Rome. Their judgments on these matters might not tally exactly with Elizabeth's own. Their zeal might soon outrun discretion, good manners, and her own notion of what was due to her position or best for the nation. Yet the only quarrel that any of them from the soberest councillor to the hottest gospeller ever had with her was due at bottom to nothing more than her apparent disinclination to proceed farther and faster in the direction to which she was already perforce in some measure committed.

Yet the problem of reform was by no means simple or clear-cut. There were two objectives to be served in reorganizing the relations of Church and state on a national basis; first, to provide for the promotion of Christian faith among the people based upon the experience of the Word, and, at the same time, to reconstitute the Church as a national institution under the Crown. The one purpose was the primary concern of the survivors, especially among the clergy, of the recent persecution. The other was the necessary concern of the queen and her government. The one called for evangelical effort by a ministry dedicated to preaching. The other called for agreement on a common body of doctrine and a liturgy under an episcopate answerable to the Crown. The two objectives were not necessarily incompatible, but to accomplish both at the same time required a degree of accommodation which the queen's government was bound to insist upon in the interest of civil order but which was never wholly satisfactory to everybody concerned.

But again we must remember that the first question to be decided at the accession of Elizabeth was not whether English-speaking peoples were to be Anglicans or Puritans, conformists or Nonconformists, Episcopalians or Presbyterians or whatever one will. The late martyrs had died and the exiles had endured banishment not for the sake of wearing or not wearing vestments, following or not following the prayer book, but for what they took to be the truth revealed to them in the Scriptures. This belief which they held in common was more significant in its effect upon English-speaking civilization than any of the many disagreements which sprang up among them in consequence. The great question which at this stage concerned them all was whether they were to be free to develop a religious life of their own based upon the experience of the book, which is to say, whether the English Church and the English state were to be free to develop their own potentialities in their own English way with whatever inner strains might be involved. This would not be possible unless Elizabeth could hold her place, and this she might easily fail to do unless she and her people could be held to what everyone understood to be the essential feature of the reformed faith. Hence the common objective of all parties, no matter what differences might presently spring up among them, continued to be to make the Word known to the people in their own language in the services of the Church, in the pulpit, and, as things turned out, more and more through the printed page.

Aylmer, settling down as Archdeacon of Lincoln, later Bishop of London, found nothing more to say in print for the purpose of investing the figure of Elizabeth with the aura of apocalypse. The idea of a national Church dedicated to the religion of the Word under the providentially appointed rule of a godly prince was given its fullest and finest expression in the early years of the reign by John Jewel, who was back in England by March 1559. Since July 1556 he had been living at Zürich and had undoubtedly heard the hundred sermons which Bullinger preached on the Apocalypse and shortly afterwards published with a dedication to the refugees gathered there – Italian, French and German, as well as English. John Day was soon to issue the book in London in both Latin and English.

Jewel arrived in England just as the reform leaders were seeking to reopen the fatal debate on the sacrament which had ended four years before in the burning of Cranmer, Ridley and Latimer. Eight defenders of the Word, of whom seven, including Grindal and Jewel, were returned exiles, were to be pitted against eight defenders of the Mass headed by Henry Cole, Dean of St Paul's, a contemporary of Jewel's at Oxford who had conformed under Henry and Edward but under Mary had taken a leading part in the affair at Oxford and had preached at Cranmer's recantation and burning. Nothing came of this attempt to turn the tables on the spokesmen for the old faith, because they refused to discuss a question which they now held to be closed. The Lord Keeper, Sir Nicholas Bacon, who presided, concluded the proceedings by telling them, 'for that ye would not that we should hear you, you may shortly hear of us'. Intended or not there was something grimly ominous in this remark. The men who now came swarming back from exile or out of hiding would have been something less or more than human if none of them had any notion of paying back their late oppressors in their own coin, persecution for persecution, always, of course, from the highest motives and in the name of religious unity.

But the experience of the late reign showed that persecution could easily defeat its own purpose, and the current experience of continental governments showed that religious zeal, if allowed to go unchecked, ended in religious war and civil disorder. Elizabeth, having learned the lesson of her sister's mistakes, was prepared to take no such risk if she could possibly avoid it. So far as she was concerned people might believe as they liked, but they must obey her commands and keep the peace. Churchmen who refused to acknowledge her supremacy were removed from their posts and imprisoned or allowed to go into exile, but the advocates of the new religion were obliged to limit their efforts at retaliation to preaching and other forms of publicity, and not too much of those.

For more than any of her predecessors Elizabeth was under the necessity of carrying on her government and maintaining the theoretically absolute authority of the Crown in the face of unsought and often unwelcome advice, instruction and admonition from self-appointed counsellors who, with the infallible Word at their command, arrogated to themselves an authority assumed to be no less absolute in its way than hers. Elizabeth had seen what had happened when Mary let churchmen of one persuasion get out of hand. She was determined not to let those of any other upset the apple-cart. Hence she began as Mary had done by forbidding all preaching, a prohibition she never attempted to enforce completely, and she never ceased to keep a tight rein on the pulpit and a wary eye on churchmen.

The fact was, of course, that she could no more do without the preachers than they could do without her. While she stood between them and a return of persecution, they stood between her and popular disaffection in the mounting crises of her reign. So, though there would be no end to the government's need for keeping preachers of the Word and their partisans in parliament from taking over the whole direction of the Church on the pretext of making reformation more perfect and the regime more secure, there would also be the best of political reasons for never reducing them to complete silence. They had in fact to be made use of, and Elizabeth had not been many days on the throne when the astute, indefatigable Cecil was drawing up lists of preachers having the strongest personal reasons for loyalty to the new regime, many of them returned exiles, to be called to address the people at Paul's Cross.

Jewel was called to preach at that place in June 1559, shortly after which he was sent on a commission of visitation to the western counties. On his return he was named Bishop of Salisbury, and thereafter frequently called to preach both at Paul's Cross and at court. Not forgetting the danger and humiliation to which he had been subjected at Oxford four years before, he took these occasions to reiterate a sweeping challenge to his old antagonists. If any of them, or if any learned man whatever, would produce proof from the Scriptures or from the ancient teachers, fathers, councils or historians of the Church of the doctrine of the sacrament to which he and others had been made to subscribe under threat of prosecution or for praying in a strange language or for forbidding the people to read the Word of God in their own tongue, he would give over and again subscribe.[1]

The challenge was taken up first by Henry Cole, his former

[1] Jewel, *The Copie of a Sermon* (1560); *Copies of the Letters* (1560); *Works* (Parker Society), I.

contemporary at Oxford and one of his adversaries in the late abortive disputation at Westminster. This was all that was needed to provoke Jewel to come forward with what was immediately accepted as the authoritative statement of the English position, now annealed and fixed by persecution and exile. The book was published in Latin in 1562 as *Apologia Ecclesiae Anglicanae*. Archbishop Parker at once saw to its publication also in English. Lady Bacon, wife of the Lord Keeper, presently translated it a second time, and Parker again arranged to have it published, this time with a laudatory epistle from himself. The argument in rebuttal was then taken up by Thomas Harding, another contemporary of Jewel's at Oxford, one who, like him, had conformed under Edward and again subscribed under Mary, but unlike him was now standing fast by his reconversion. Jewel had found him installed in a prebend at Salisbury, but he was now taking his turn at exile. He published his *Answer to Master Jewelles Apology* at Louvain in 1564.

Jewel argued that the prime source of revealed truth was the Scriptures, that the prime function of the Church was to preach the Word, and that the sacraments were but seals of the faith which sprang from the experience of the Word. These truths were the same which had been revealed to the apostles, the same for which the faithful in all ages had been persecuted, the same for which the late martyrs had died. To this Harding made the rejoinder that, because both heretics and true believers had on occasion been made to suffer, it did not follow that heresy was anything but heresy. The truth was not whatever this man or that might suppose had been revealed to him in the Scriptures. It was that which had been revealed to the apostles and continuously conveyed to mankind by the Church as the living embodiment and vehicle of truth on earth.

But any dialectical advantage to which Harding could fairly lay claim availed him little. Jewel's command of the techniques of formal controversy was equal to his own, and he commanded in addition an art and a freedom of public discourse not now available to his opponent. In *A Defence of the Apology*, running to hundreds of folio pages, he entered a counter-rebuttal to Harding's rebuttal. More important, in sermons at Paul's Cross, at court and at Salisbury and in printed discourses of the same character, he saw to it that the queen, her government, parliament and the people should not be allowed to forget that the rulers of the Church in the late regime, backed by an alien power, had made martyrs of Englishmen for reading, hearing, preaching, believing the Word, the Word in their own language. What these enemies of the Word had done before, they would do again if the occasion offered. Starting from this point, Jewel projected the main features of the case for the national Church and the supporting legend its champions drew from scripture and history.

The faith now preached in England had been brought to its shores directly from the apostles, embraced and fostered through the ages by native kings, beset time and again by alien, mis-believing tyrants and intruders, but never totally rooted out. Now it was once more being revived and sustained by a godly prince. Privately in a letter to Peter Martyr, Jewel might express regret that 'this woman, excellent as she is and earnest as she is in the cause of true religion', could not be induced to proceed more rapidly and thoroughly with reforming the Church in accordance with the ideas he had brought back from Zürich. There was still that little silver cross on view in the royal chapel, besides a deplorable paucity of men competent to preach the gospel.[1] But publicly, in the face of any pressure brought to bear against Elizabeth, all Jewel's doubts vanished in a blaze of devotion. 'When it pleased God to send a blessing upon us, He gave us His servant Elizabeth to be our queen, and to be an instrument of His glory in the sight of the world.'[2] Before her coming there had been nothing but darkness and affliction, as there still was in all neighbouring kingdoms, but now England was entering upon a new day.

Let us consider how mercifully God hath dealt with us. He

---

[1] *Works*, IV.
[2] *View of a seditious Bul* (1582); *Works*, IV, 1145.

hath restored unto us the light of His gospel, and hath taught us the secrets of His heavenly will. We hear Him talk with us familiarly in the scriptures, as a father talketh with His child. Thereby He kindleth our faith, and strengtheneth our hope; thereby our hearts receive joy and comfort. We have the holy ministration of the sacraments: we know the covenant and mystery of the Lord's supper. We fall down together and confess our life before God; we pray together, and we understand what we pray. This was the order of the primitive church. This was the order of the apostles of Christ. If we compare this with the former, we shall soon see the difference between light and darkness. The kingdom of God now suffereth violence. The sound of the gospel hath gone over all the world, and the whole world is awakened therewith and draweth to it. The sun is risen: the day is open: God hath made His kingdom wonderful among us. It is now time, now is it time, that we should arise from sleep; for now is our salvation near.[1]

The new day was to bring many changes, but behind all the changes to come in the structure of Church and state, there was also to occur a fundamental change in the way people thought about themselves, their institutions, the meaning of existence, the past of mankind in general, and the history and destiny of their own nation in particular. Whether we call this change a religious or an ideological revolution, it underlay every other phase of change and traversed every difference of creed, sect, party and class. For there was one common operative factor in the situation which no one could get away from, the popularization of the vernacular Bible through the combined agency of pulpit and press. When Elizabeth came to the throne the earlier printed versions had had twenty-five years in which to accumulate in public places where people could get at the book if they wished, and now came the Geneva Bible. The printing of that version, so carefully calculated to meet popular need, continued to be carried

[1] *Works*, II.

A Godly Queen

on at Geneva, but the importation of the book was authorized and John Bodley was granted the privilege of printing it in England. He refrained from exercising the privilege, possibly because of some demurring at some of the translations and the tenor of the commentary, but in 1575 publication was finally transferred to London and continued there year after year well into the seventeenth century.[1]

Meanwhile, in 1572 Parker saw to the publication of still another translation by a commission of bishops, to be used chiefly in churches. And all this time preachers were promoting demand for the book by explicating its meaning as they understood it in application to every conceivable situation in life, while the booktrade battened on the results of their activities. 'Public and continual preaching of God's word,' Grindal told the queen, not very much to her liking, 'is the ordinary mean and instrument of the salvation of mankind'. By preaching God's glory was enlarged, faith nourished, charity increased, the ignorant instructed, the negligent incited, the stubborn rebuked, the weak comforted, and the wicked warned of the wrath of God. 'By preaching also due obedience to Christian princes is planted in the hearts: for obedience proceedeth of conscience, conscience is grounded upon the word of God, the word of God worketh its effect by preaching.' And 'no prince ever had more lively experience hereof than your Majesty hath had in your time, and may have daily,' let her come to her city of London never so often.[2]

The intellectual procedures by which preachers essayed to deduce general principles of belief and conduct from the antique fabric of legend, poetry and precept they knew as the Bible may seem to the modern mind incomprehensible and in a sense absurd. The preacher framed his discourse on the assumption that his audience had a degree of familiarity with the sacred text and a respect for it which is quite beyond us. The present-day reader of his sermon feels no such concern for every point in his exposition

[1] W. W. Greg, 'Books and Bookmen in the Correspondence of Archbishop Parker', *Library*, ser. 4, vol. XVI, 1935.
[2] Grindal, *Remains* (Parker Society).

as held his original audience listening, it might be, by the hour. But it held them, and we must ask in all seriousness how and why and to what end.

The preacher, in an age when long-established certitudes were being undermined and swept away, taught people to see themselves, their own predicaments, the predicaments of their time, mirrored in the scriptural saga of spiritual striving. He demonstrated by what they could not but take for incontrovertible proof the way of escape from frustration, doubt and confusion, and he described the inner process by which such relief would make its coming known, the way of life that must inevitably follow, and the ineffable reward. The preacher set forth an enthralling drama of self-examination leading to the resolution of uncertainties and inhibitions and so to a life of positive endeavour and a sense of achievement. Whether anyone could by his own effort do anything to bring on such an experience in himself might be a matter of debate, but practically that hardly mattered. There could be no question but that salvation was written plain in the Bible for all to read about and hope for, and what men hope for ardently enough, they do not as a rule expect to be denied. Whatever position a preacher might presently take concerning vestments, liturgy, discipline and Church government, such was still the burden and effect of his teaching in the pulpit.

Needless to say, many more sermons were preached than ever were printed, and not every published sermon was printed exactly as it was delivered. Preaching directed to the spiritual needs of ordinary people did not generally begin to find its way into print until later in the reign, in the publications of such physicians of the soul as Greenham and Rogers. The sermons most likely to be published in the early years of Elizabeth's reign were those preached before special audiences on special occasions by men specially chosen for the purpose. This is not to say that preachers called to hold forth on such occasions neglected to edify their hearers in the doctrine of salvation by the Word, but they took pains to extend the application of that doctrine from personal to national experience.

The most notable master, down to his death in 1572, of this art of bringing biblical legend to bear upon the spiritual exigencies of national life was the indefatigable author of the *Apology for the Church of England*, and we see him at his most eloquent in the sermon which he preached either at court or Paul's Cross on November 17th, 1569, the anniversary of Elizabeth's accession.[1] The moment was an anxious one. The Queen of Scots had now fallen out with her subjects, and Elizabeth had had her on her hands for more than a year, during which time Mary had been intriguing with the northern earls for Elizabeth's overthrow and her own marriage with the Duke of Norfolk. The sixth chapter of Joshua provided Jewel with a text with many scriptural parallels for assuring the elect that with the Lord on their side they had nothing to fear from the powers of this world – Jericho, Babylon, Rome, Spain, the Queen of Scots.

Nothing could have been more appropriate to the occasion. Elizabeth's supporters were painfully conscious of being few in numbers and weak in military strength compared with their adversaries. They were, moreover, standing alone, with a woman for ruler, unmarried at that. But the fall of Jericho was a story hard to spoil in the telling, and Jewel made the most of it. The people within that wall might laugh the Lord's elect to scorn, but they, God's people, marching about with the ark of the Lord, 'lifted up their voices, and shouted with a great shout . . . the trumpets blew in every corner; the whole heaven and earth was full of their noise; and the wall fell down flat'. And from that point the preacher went on weaving together scriptural and historical instances to show that 'the Lord which was mighty to save Daniel in the midst of the lions, and Jonas in the whale's belly, and His three servants in the flaming fire, and Israel in the Red Sea ... was also able to make His own cause good, to give courage to His servants and trembling and anguish of mind to their enemies.' There were some – Jewel was no doubt thinking of the northern earls and the Duke of Norfolk – who, growing sick of the manna of the Lord and yearning after the gourds and onions of Egypt, were trying to build Jericho up again. But God was with His elect,

---

[1] Jewel, *Certaine Sermons* (1583); *Works* (Parker Society), II.

and neither the Queen of Scots, the Pope, nor the King of Spain could stand against them. 'Upon this day' – Elizabeth had been on the throne eleven years – 'even upon this day, God sent His handmaid and delivered us ... then was our mouth filled with laughter and our tongue with joy ... The Lord hath done great things for us, whereof we rejoice.'

By Good Friday, which came four months later on March 24th, the rebellion in the north had been quashed, Mary's intrigues thwarted, and Norfolk sent to the Tower. But the Pope had excommunicated Elizabeth, absolving her subjects from any sin of disobedience, and the situation still seemed full of danger for the faithful. In these circumstances Grindal, now Bishop of London, called upon his old associate John Foxe to preach the Good Friday sermon at Paul's Cross, knowing no doubt that the latter had just completed what amounted to the final version of their jointly projected Book of Martyrs. Foxe's sermon[1] on 'Christ Crucified', in two parts for morning and afternoon, showed the preacher still preoccupied with the central theme of that book – the fall of man, the election of the saints, their reconciliation with God, their contention through all the ages of the world with the spirit of disobedience within themselves and in mankind at large, the war of the two Churches which fills all time.

As in the book Foxe had tried to show the sufferings of the martyrs in the late reign in the perspective of history thus conceived, so now he depicted in the same framework the dangers through which the queen and her faithful subjects had just passed and by which they were still threatened. They were to keep in mind that Christ had accomplished the reconciliation of the elect with God once for all, and that His sacrifice of Himself on their behalf had but to be embraced by faith and need not be again and again renewed. The preacher would have his countrymen therefore to be reconciled with one another, and he proposed that those too stiff and wayward to get on peaceably with their fellows, 'stoical stomachs and unsociable natures', be sent *ad rem publicam*

---

[1] Foxe, *A Sermon of Christ crucified* (1570; other editions 1575, 1577, 1585, 1609, 1759 with preface by George Whitfield).

Platonis or *Mr. More's Utopia,* either to live with themselves or else where as none may live to offend them'. They were to be banished, that is, not for their errors but for their unregenerate, uncharitable tempers.

Preachers, on the other hand, were to be 'physicians of souls' and declare to the people 'the promise of grace, the word of life, the glorious treasures and abundant riches, not of this present world here, but laid up for us hereafter in Christ to come'.

> They that be true Christians and have regard to their souls must learn by their preachers and understand by the scriptures that besides this life, besides this world, this kingdom, these things here present, there be other things and much greater things, another world to be looked for.

And it will follow that the people, having learned to contemn both the glories and the hardships of this world, 'neither being dejected by adversity nor yet puffed up with prosperity', will be ready with Moses to climb the hill Nebo for a view of that 'spiritual country and glorious kingdom whereof I preach unto you'.

> There shall you see your factor and agent ... Christ Jesus taking possession for you in heaven ... There shall you see our noble and triumphant captain Joshua, our saviour Jesus, with His priests and Levites and His people following Him, seven times going about the great city Jericho with trumpets of jubilee in their hands. And I doubt not but He hath gone six times about already. And when the seventh blast shall come, then beware, great Jericho.

Beware, the rich and mighty of this world, the great Turk, and the great caliph of Damascus. Beware, also, the great caliph of old Rome and 'all other cruel tyrants and potentates of this world which have abused their sword to the destruction of Christ's saints'.

On this familiar note Foxe concluded the first or morning half of his sermon. Actually his hopes for the immediate fall of Jericho may have been less sanguine then they had been ten years before. At any rate, his afternoon sermon was designed to allay the fears and perplexities evoked by recent events. The ultimate

and certain triumph of the elect depended, he said, not on the will
or the fate of this person or that, but upon the will of God alone.
The elect were to have faith, and the answer of faith to whatever
the adversary might say or do was that devotion which enables
those who love God to endure anything done to them for His
sake. The type and exemplar of such devotion was Christ, and of
all persecutors, Satan. Into the mouth of Christ on the Cross Foxe
put such a reply to Satan as the martyrs in his book had been
directing at Gardiner and Bonner. The occasion for this was the
news that the Bishop of Rome had lately sent proctors and
messengers to reconcile the English people to him. Foxe replied,
'Our message is that ye will be reconciled unto the living God.'

> His friendship if ye desire, ye need not seek it far; it is here
> offered unto you for taking. But then ye must take it while
> it is offered. Behold now the acceptable year; yet is the good
> time; yet is the day of salvation; yet to-day lasteth and the gate
> is yet open wherein the wise virgins may enter ... Take there-
> fore while it is offered. Refuse not, lest ye be refused ... Be
> bold and fear not. For what should let you to be bold, having
> such a patron to make your way for you?

This sounds as though Foxe meant that grace was offered to all
men to accept or not as they chose, an error or ambiguity which
preachers easily slipped into when carried away in the pulpit by
their own eloquence and their zeal for saving souls. But the
preacher would undoubtedly have repudiated the idea. He was
not at this point reflecting on the condition of mankind in general.
He was addressing his fellow-subjects in the loyal city of London
on the morrow of the defeat of the queen's enemies. What more
natural on such an occasion than to speak as though they were
indeed the Lord's elect? 'Dearly beloved brethren and countrymen, how dearly he hath loved you, ye see ... Yesterday ye were
sick and weak; this day with his blood he hath recovered you ...
Yesterday ye were sinners; this day he hath purged you and made
you righteous.' So the preacher goes on, multiplying the familiar
instances of the Lord's intervention on behalf of His chosen.

Sound enough doctrine at any time, but especially apposite on Good Friday, 1570.

For at that particular juncture of events there was no forgetting the danger which threatened England and the English Church, or the grace that God had vouchsafed to the faithful everywhere by putting Elizabeth on the throne and keeping her there. The Turk has been driving the Church back and back into a 'little angle of the west', while the Bishop of Rome has been everywhere 'stirring up his bishops to burn us, his confederates to conspire our destruction, setting kings against their subjects, and subjects disloyally to rebel against their princes', Christians against Christians, Papists against Protestants, Protestants against one another.

But upon England, 'after storms of persecution and cruel murder of so many martyrs', God has bestowed halcyon days, which Foxe prays may continue no matter how the friends of the Bishop of Rome may grudge and mutter, conspire and take on. God has given His people a queen 'so calm, so patient, so merciful, more like a natural mother than a princess ... such as neither they nor their ancestors ever read of in the stories of this land before'. 'As thou hast given her unto us and hast from so manifold dangers preserved her before she was queen,' so now the preacher begs that 'she may continually be preserved, not only from the hands but from all the malignant devices wrought, attempted, or conceived of enemies both ghostly and bodily against her.' Yet he does not forget to add the petition, 'in this her government be her governor'.

Thus Foxe on Good Friday, 1570. Meanwhile, Jewel had also denounced the Pope's bull in a sermon at Salisbury,[1] assuring the people, as they were to be assured again and again from many a pulpit, that 'when it pleased God to send a blessing upon us, He gave us his servant Elizabeth to be our queen and to be the instrument of His glory in the sight of the world ... By her He restored the truth; by her He sent us the light of His word; by her He hath relieved the hearts of the people.' Jewel quotes the words which, he says, he heard the queen speak to her council and judges, 'Have

[1] Jewel, *View of a seditious Bul* (1582); *Works* (Parker society), IV.

a care over my people ... See unto them; for they are my charge. I charge you, even as God hath charged me.'

We do not know who preached at court or at Paul's Cross when Accession Day came round in 1570, for surely someone must have been called up for the occasion; but from this time forth there was never any lack of sermons on that day to ring the changes on the themes that Jewel and Foxe had set going. And beginning in 1570 courtiers tilted in honour of the day before the queen, church bells were rung at Oxford and before long all over the realm, and by 1575 special services were being held in churches.

But at all times there was preaching and still more preaching on the themes and after the fashion represented here by Jewel and Foxe – at court, at Paul's Cross, before parliament, at the Inns of Court, on market days and at assizes, in cathedrals and country churches, in London pulpits. We hear much from preachers themselves and their partisans about the lack of preaching, of the paucity of men fit to preach, and of the scarcity of provision for their support, but we need not take such complaints at face value. The truth was that the collapse of Mary's misconceived endeavour to force a return to the old obedience upon her subjects opened wide the door to that close-knit corps of university-bred professional intellectuals, reformers, preachers, talkers, and writers who had been so bitterly antagonized by being driven into hiding at home or exile abroad while their leaders were being prosecuted for heresy.

Out of this body of men there developed in the opening years of the new reign what became in effect a veritable if unrecognized and unacknowledged evangelical order bent upon exploiting the vernacular Bible for setting forth their conception of spiritual redemption. Returned exiles clothed with episcopal authority made haste to ordain and license as many recruits as they could find capable of preaching, and if a man lacked academic learning, it could be enough if he knew his Bible and had the gift of expounding it. Study groups known as 'prophesyings' were presently formed in various places for the discussion of scripture texts and the training of such persons in the art of the pulpit.

The result of such activities on the part of the brotherhood was that before long the number of men eager and after a fashion qualified to preach outran the resources at the disposal of the hierarchy available for their support. But neither the zeal nor the demand for preaching was to be thwarted by such shortage. College fellowships and university chairs, chaplaincies and tutorships in great households, lectureships salaried by voluntary contributions, and private patronage in one form and another were all forthcoming and went a long way to make up for the lack of beneficed posts. Besides, the book-trade now offered a resource of great possibilities for men whose first call might be to the pulpit but some of whom soon began turning to authorship in addition or even instead.

Eventually the pulpit would have to yield at least equal place to the printing-press, but in the meantime the masters of the special art of applying apposite concepts and images drawn from the infallible Word to present exigencies of every kind were best able to sway the minds of the vernacular public. It was soon apparent, however, that their influence did not uniformly conduce to the smooth functioning of a system of government which still in theory revolved about an ecclesiastical and a civil authority, each absolute in its sphere, but a system which in fact depended for its stability upon the skilful manipulation of often conflicting human passions by a woman ruler with a passion and a genius for political survival. The preachers, never questioning her supremacy, urged the people as one man to expect that under her rule the long-awaited reformation of the Church would at last be consummated. But how fast it was necessary to proceed to that end and precisely how the reformed Church should be constituted, they were never able to agree with one another, let alone with the queen and her government.

In 1570, with Catholic discontent coming to a head in the north, the demand of the more impatient reformers for instant action also came to a head in the proposal elaborated by the Lady Margaret professor of divinity at Cambridge, Thomas Cartwright, that the government and discipline of the national Church should be at once made over according to the pattern which, it was held, had been plainly set forth in the Scriptures. Pressed to its logical conclusion, this proposal would have entailed the replacing of the existing episcopate, responsible to the Crown, by a system of elective representative assemblies or presbyteries patterned upon Geneva and Scotland. The practical effect would have been to put the actual control of the Church into the hands of the preaching order. Many of that order, Foxe among them, remained loyal to the principle of royal supremacy and took no part in the agitation for presbyterian church government. Nevertheless, Cartwright spoke for an increasingly active and aggressive faction of the brotherhood of the pulpit, largely drawn, like himself, from the second generation of reformers and preachers which had sprung up since the return from exile. Moreover, these Puritans, as they now came to be called, drew formidable support from the class which, having a large material stake in the security of the queen and her regime, was reaching after more power for itself in the state and turning up in increasing numbers in parliament.

Our concern here, however, is not with the question of Church government, on which English Protestants were never to agree, but with the idea as to which they were all substantially at one, namely that the Church was essentially a communion of elect souls possessed by faith in the Word. That idea with its implicit sanctions was now to be extended to the nation as a community set apart by God from all others for purposes of His own. In the elaboration of that conception Matthew Parker, in spite of or perhaps because of the difficulties of his position, was to play just at this stage a particularly significant role. It fell to his lot to have to initiate the episcopate of the Elizabethan settlement under the conditions of Elizabeth's early years, made trying enough by the Catholics and still more trying by the Puritans and by the queen's objections to their repeated efforts to force her hand. He was not, however, simply the prototype of Anglican parsons still to come, harassed by nonconformity and turning for relief to scholarly and antiquarian pursuits. He shared the apocalyptical expectations with which the returned exiles greeted Elizabeth's accession. As archbishop he endorsed twice over Jewel's championship of the new religion. He became John Foxe's most important patron. He looked forward from the start to using the influence of his position to spread the light of the Word among the people.

At the same time, however, Parker was inclined by temperament and inured by experience in university administration to the need for working with the men and means actually at hand, which meant first of all working with the unaccountable young woman now on the throne. He felt a personal devotion to her as the daughter of his former patroness, and he did not doubt that she was God's instrument for making good the hopes inspired by her coming to power. Yet he also did not doubt that, if he was to accomplish anything for the cause he had at heart, it would have to be under the conditions imposed by that unpredictable political genius. She met all the specifications for a godly prince. She had perfect command of the language of godliness and could speak it with what seemed perfect conviction. She kept up a suitable piety in her personal devotions, featuring sermons and the Bible as well as prayer book and vestments. But she let him know that she would not allow religion to be made the pretext or preaching the occasion for putting any limitation on her prerogative as the Church's supreme governor. The truth was that she distrusted all preachers and most churchmen. For her experience with parliament soon convinced her that the fuller her subjects' heads became of pulpit notions and scripture instances, the more inclined they were to suppose that they knew better than she how the Lord expected her to conduct the nation's, the Church's and her own affairs.

Here from her point of view was reason enough to keep a curb on preaching, but there was a practical reason as well. Preaching required men of ability and education, which cost money, and she needed to put her hands on money wherever it was to be had. The Church, even after the depredations it had already undergone, still offered a stock of capital wealth to which she and the men who served her in government and at court could help themselves. Men who had long battened on the Church were not inclined to desist now, let alone disgorge what they had already got. Mary had alienated them by proposing to restore the Church's propery

A Godly Queen

to the Church's use. Elizabeth found it more practical to bind them to her at the Church's expense. But from Parker's point of view, how were the people to be awakened to a more lively apprehension of God's Word unless the ministry of the Church could be replenished with men able to preach the Word? And how were such men to be got if every time a church living were to be filled the income were diverted to some secular pocket or use?

But that was not all. Keeping the Church poor did not keep preaching down. It merely made preachers turn for support to other sources difficult for the episcopacy to control, in many cases to patrons of the very class which had been enriched out of the emoluments of the Church. In short, as Parker saw it, the queen's policy merely played into the hands of that faction which, in its haste to escape from Rome, was seeking to drive the nation headlong towards Geneva. He would have countered this Puritan attack on the establishment, coming as it did at the same time as Catholic conspiracy on behalf of Mary Stuart, by devoting far more of the resources of the establishment to the pastoral and evangelical functions of the Church. But his letters to Cecil, the queen's principal secretary and his own personal friend, are full of bitter complaints that Elizabeth, while holding him responsible for what happened in the ecclesiastical realm, begrudged him the means to do the Church's necessary work. 'The comfort these puritans have and their continuance is marvellous, and therefore if her Highness with her council ... step not to it, I see the likelihood of a pitiful commonwealth to follow. *Deus misereatur nostri.* Where Almighty God is so much English as He is, should we not requite his mercy with some earnesty to prefer His honour and true religion?'[1]

What Parker meant by saying that God was so much English as He was was something more precise than what Aylmer had expressed, but not essentially different. His thinking was still premised by the concept of two realms, spiritual and civil, revolving about each other in orbits complementary but independent, and each somehow involved also in a presumed universal

[1] Parker, *Correspondence* (Parker Society), 418–19.

107

civil and spiritual order. The problem was to dissociate that idea from the notion of a unique, comprehensive jurisdiction vested in the Roman hierarchy, and to attach it or its equivalent to the national Church and monarchy. England must be shown to be an empire and its Church a true apostolic Church each in its own right. To this purpose he dedicated himself in the hope of justifying the demands he was making on the queen as well as the resistance he was offering to Puritan excesses and Catholic pretensions. 'Because neither my health nor my quiet,' he told Cecil, 'would suffer me to be a common preacher, yet I thought it not unfit for me to be occupied in some points of religion.'[1] What he did to occupy himself was to see to the collecting and publishing of documentary historical proof of the independent origin and authority of the English Church and monarchy.

The fruit of his labours was a new translation of the Bible for use in churches, with an editorial apparatus suited to the purpose, and a history of the original establishment of the Church in Britain followed by a history of the see of Canterbury. In all this Parker was resuming the work begun by Leland and Bale of recovering what could be retrieved of the historical materials dispersed at the dissolution of the monasteries. To this end he enlisted the co-operation of bishops and other Church officials in the work of translation and in the search for books and manuscripts. He procured a letter from the privy council requiring all persons to allow him and his agents access to ancient records in their possession. He encouraged antiquarians and chroniclers such as Foxe, Stowe and Lambard. He set his chaplains to collecting books, compiling historical information, editing and translating Anglo-Saxon texts. Authorized by the queen to keep forty men in livery besides the customary number of household servants, he gathered about him a staff skilled in various arts relating to the production and preservation of books – copyists, draughtsmen, painters, illuminators, engravers, book-binders. He had one man in his employ who commanded the perhaps questionable ability 'to make old books complete ... that the character might seem to be the same through-

[1] *Correspondence*, 424–6.

out'.[1] He enlisted the services of London printers. When he died he bequeathed his collection to Corpus Christi College, Cambridge, with strict injunctions for its preservation.

As Archbishop of Canterbury, Parker was kept by the queen in a constant state of frustration and suspense. Reserving all decision to herself, she habitually deferred action until compelled by circumstance, and then shifted any onus of blame upon her servants. Meanwhile, she disarmed complaint by dazzling performance in the role which the reformers had pressed upon her of godly prince. Parker chafed – 'I was well chidden at my prince's hands, but with one ear I heard her harsh words and with the other and in my conscience and heart I heard God' – but he submitted.[2]

There was, indeed, nothing else that he could do. But he was not the only one she kept in such a condition. Sir John Neale has described in fascinating detail how she kept successive parliaments similarly suspended between impatience with her evasive ways and devotion to her person. Other historians have described the ins and outs of the dissension which followed the Puritan attempt to force her hand in the matter of Church government and discipline. Here our concern is not with the differences in regard to the Church which kept Elizabeth and her subjects at odds, but with the attitudes of mind which kept them in respect of the national interest nevertheless at one. Devotees of the Word might debate and disagree endlessly on one point or another, but on certain essential matters their thoughts moved together in the same common direction. All found it natural to assume that the true Church was a mystical communion of believers elected once for all by grace to salvation, that the Church thus conceived had been assailed through all the ages of the world by the spirit of disobedience and rebellion, but that the last age of the world and the final triumph of the elect were at hand, and that in that final engagement England was called to lead mankind and Elizabeth to lead England to ultimate redemption.

[1] Strype, *Parker*, Bk. IV.   [2] Parker, *Correspondence*, 309–16.

CHAPTER IV

The Book of Martyrs

ᑢᗯᓝ

THE invention of printing, according to John Foxe, was a miracle performed by the Lord for the express purpose of bringing the reformation of His Church to its final consummation. 'The Lord began to work for His Church not with sword and target to subdue His exalted adversary, but with printing, writing and reading ... How many printing presses there be in the world, so many block-houses there be against the high castle of St Angelo, so that either the pope must abolish knowledge and printing or printing at length will root him out.'[1] However that may be, certainly one of the most formidable 'block-houses' against the return of the old religion to England was the press and bookseller's shop of John Day, over Aldersgate, from which presently issued the successive editions of the Book of Martyrs in English.

Foxe, having seen the Latin version of the book through the press at Basle, was back in London by October 1559, and at once joined forces with Day in what was to be a lifelong association. In November the two men gave notice of their intention to publish the stories of the late martyrs by issuing in a neat octavo Ridley's *Friendly Farewel*, written shortly before the author's burning at Oxford. In a prefatory address to the reader Foxe announced that this was but one of many such histories they had in hand and intended to print 'of such as of late days have been persecuted, murdered and martyred for the true gospel of Christ'. The reader was asked to accept the little volume as earnest of others, 'which we are about, touching the full history, process, and examination of all our blessed brethren, lately persecuted for righteousness

[1] Foxe, III, 718–22.

sake'. The martyrs having done their part, the writer and the printer propose to do theirs. 'Thus double ways are we bound to the Lord, who not only by the Word and death of the saints confirmeth the testimony of his truth but also besides their death leaveth such monuments behind them which no less confound the adversary as confirm the godly.'

The resurgence of Protestantism in England and of Catholic persecution on the Continent at the accession of Elizabeth came at an opportune moment for the English book-trade. London artisans of various sorts engaged in the production of books had been a recognized craft of long standing, but had enjoyed no authorized monopoly. With the advance in the market for printed matter, they grew concerned for their proprietary rights, while the Crown at the same time grew insistent upon its claim to control the trade and share in its profits. The result was that Philip and Mary in 1557 issued a charter to ninety-seven named persons engaged in the business, known henceforth as the Company of Stationers, granting them certain privileges and imposing certain regulations. Two years later Elizabeth confirmed the charter and issued injunctions also confirming the regulations for licensing books which had been instituted by her father and continued under Edward and Mary.

Meanwhile the Marian exiles had returned better prepared by their sojourn in the centres of book-production in Germany and Switzerland to make use of the press, and in their train came an influx of foreign refugees skilled in various crafts associated with printing. English Catholics, on the other hand, now taking their turn at exile, took their turn also at plying their countrymen with books printed on the Continent or clandestinely at home. The result was that book-production in England soon became not only a flourishing trade but in its effects a major factor and a major problem in public life.

Several of the leading members of the Stationers' Company had sided with the reform party under Henry and, having served the Protestant cause openly under Edward, were excluded from business under Mary. Some were given a taste of persecution and exile, and engaged in clandestine printing at home and abroad. Of these John Day, now in his middle thirties, was and continued to be until his death in 1584 one of the most active and prosperous figures in the trade. Under Henry he and his partner William Seres had printed or reprinted Bale's *Image of bothe Churches*, and in the opening years of Mary's reign he probably had a hand in printing Bale's surreptitious translation of Gardiner's *De vera Obedientia*, including Bonner's preface. But his most notable publications before Elizabeth's accession were the sermons of Hugh Latimer and the tracts of Thomas Becon. Each of these made a wide, continuing appeal to the Elizabethan public, no doubt much to the profit of the publisher.

Latimer's sermons Day apparently procured for publication from someone attached to the household of the Duchess of Suffolk, the widow of Henry VIII's favourite Charles Brandon, an ardent and enthusiastic Protestant, and Latimer's patroness and protectress. The first of these discourses to appear in print was the sermon preached at St Paul's on January 15th, 1548, and commonly known as 'the sermon on the plough'. Next came the seven sermons preached the following year at court before the young king. These appear to have been taken down at the time of their delivery by Thomas Some and immediately conveyed to the printer. The sermons preached by Latimer before the king in 1550 and those preached later in the same year at Stamford were also promptly put into print. We get some inkling, perhaps, of what Day had in mind from the epistle to the reader prefixed to the second of the seven sermons to the king. 'Then must we as well live the word as talk the word, or else, if good life do not ensue and follow upon our reading to the example of other[s], we might as well spend that time in reading of profane histories, of canterbury tales, or a fit of Robin Hood.'

For such vain matter Day offered his public a suitable substitute in the tracts of Thomas Becon, a writer whose career supplies an excellent illustration of the ease with which preachers turned to something like professional authorship.[1] His career had begun at

[1] D. S. Bailey, *Thomas Becon and the Reformation of the Church of England* (1952).

Cambridge twenty years earlier, when, he said, Latimer was proving 'that the holy scriptures ought to be read in the English tongue of all Christian peoples'.[1] After Cambridge, Becon went to a living in Norfolk where he presently brought upon himself a charge of heresy, which he recanted. He then withdrew to Kent, and there produced a number of tracts under the name of Theodorus Basil which were published by John Mayler.

But these works were soon proscribed, and the author was again charged with heresy and again induced to recant. When Edward came to the throne, he resumed writing, and Day took over the printing of his tracts. When Mary came in, Becon was again apprehended but, according to Foxe, escaped from the Tower through Gardiner's mistaking his name.[2] He fled to the Continent and probably had a hand in writing subversive tracts to be printed by Day or one of his confederates and circulated illicitly in England. As a writer Becon made it his business to transpose traditional moral teachings and pious practices into fluent, unexacting English, with Protestant unction laid on with appropriate biblical illustrations. He told his readers how to conduct their lives according to the familiar pattern of godly behaviour brought up to date, how to repent their sins, how to pray, how to marry, how to die. With all this, he did not neglect also to exhort them to thank God for bestowing the light of His Word and a godly prince upon England.

Day was also arrested at Mary's accession and sent to prison for printing offensive books. There he encountered John Rogers waiting for martyrdom, and was told by him, 'Thou shalt live to see the alteration of this religion and the gospel freely to be preached again.'[3] On his release from prison, Day took part with others either at home or abroad in printing the fugitive pamphlets with which the exiles continued to pester the Marian regime. At its close he was apparently responsible for printing Aylmer's *Harborowe*, and soon after Mary's death he was back in his shop in Aldersgate with a new and superior set of type-faces imported

[1] Becon, *Jewel of Joy* (1553); *Works* (Parker Society), III, 413–76.
[2] Foxe, V, 696.   [3] Foxe, VI, 610.

from the Continent, with foreign refugees working for him, and before long with John Foxe as his editor and reader for the press and Archbishop Parker as his patron.

Within a year after Elizabeth's accession he had begun publishing more books than he had ever done before or than any other printer at the time, more books in the Protestant interest, books better printed than any produced in England since Caxton. One of the earliest of his publications after the queen's accession was, for example, William Cuningham's *The Cosmographicall Glasse*, a handsome folio of over two hundred pages, dated by the author '18 July 1559', entered in the Stationers' Register on November 6th, and published later in the same year with a dedication to the queen's favourite, Sir Robert Dudley. The book had also an elaborately engraved title-page border, a portrait of the author, decorative initials, charts, diagrams, tables, a map of the city of Norwich, and accompanying the printer's colophon a carefully designed and executed engraving showing two figures against a background of sea and wooded mountainside contemplating a skeleton on an elaborately carved bier out of whose breast sprang a tree bearing the legend *Etsi mors indies accelerat, post funera virtus vivet tamen.*

Where the means came from which enabled Day to resume his activities so promptly and on such a scale is easily enough explained. He was on close terms with returned exiles now in positions of influence and with important persons associated with the new government, such as Cecil and Dudley. Such persons were doubtless ready to encourage a printer of resource and tested devotion to the cause. These facts would account for the number of publications of significant interest to the supporters of the new regime which appeared with Day's imprint in the early years of the reign: Ridley's *Friendly Farewel*, which has already been mentioned; Jewel's challenge sermon of 1560, and his ensuing interchange of letters with Cole; the metrical version of the psalms prepared by Parker during his Marian eclipse, also published in 1560; the Latin original and the English translation of Bullinger's hundred sermons on the Apocalypse in 1561; the letters of the late martyrs with an epistle by Miles Coverdale in 1564; and, of course, the English version of the Book of Martyrs. Besides all this Day was presently granted the exclusive privilege of printing ABC books, the English service book, the Sternhold and Hopkins psalmody with notation for singing, and the English catechism.

Archbishop Parker called on Day whenever he had something to be printed which required special skill or unusual facilities. Thus when the archbishop came upon a sermon by Ælfric which seemed to set forth the Protestant conception of the sacrament, it was Day who printed the work in Anglo-Saxon type cut and cast for the occasion (1567).[1] Using the same type he also served his patron by printing the Anglo-Saxon translation of the gospel (1571),[2] to which he had Foxe contribute an introductory epistle, and a little later, oddly enough, Asser's Latin chronicle of King Alfred (1574). Again it was Day whom Parker called in to print his sumptuous *De Antiquitate Britannicae Ecclesiae* for presentation to the queen and the members of her court and council (1572).

An episode occurring about the same time suggests that the archbishop's favoured printer did not go unrewarded for his services. Nicholas Sanders had recently published an attack on the queen, and Burghley turned to Parker to see to the preparation and publication of a suitable reply. Parker brought a scholar up from Cambridge to do the writing and called on Day for the printing. But the work being in Latin, Day had to provide a new set of type at a cost of £26 and seized the occasion to beg a *quid pro quo*. Since Aldersgate where his shop was located was an out-of-the-way spot, he had obtained the lease of a plot of ground in St Paul's churchyard on which he proposed to erect at the cost of forty or fifty pounds a small building for the sale of books. The structure was to be strong enough and low enough for men to stand upon in any triumph or show. His competitors, however, were seeking to persuade the city authorities to forbid the project. So he applied to Parker, and Parker applied to Burghley to enlist

[1] *A Testimonie of Antiquitie* (1567); Foxe, V, 275–89.
[2] *The Gospels of the fower Evangelistes translated in the olde Saxon tyme* (1571).

the queen's favour on the printer's behalf, with what success unfortunately we are not told.[1]

But not least important for the prosperity of Day's business was
the fact that he promptly resumed the publication of Latimer's
sermons and Becon's tracts. He was in close touch with Augustine
Bernher, who had attended Latimer right up to the closing scene
at Oxford and who was still attached to Latimer's friend and
patroness the Duchess of Suffolk, now returned from exile and
restored to her estates and her former activities. In 1562 Day
brought all of Latimer's extant sermons together in two volumes.
The first, 27 *Sermons Preached by … Maister Hugh Latimer*, included
the seven sermons preached before Edward VI which Day had
previously printed from copies supplied by Thomas Some and
now reprinted with a dedication by Some to the duchess. The
other volume, *Certayn Godly Sermons*, contained chiefly sermons
delivered before that lady in Lincolnshire, printed now with a
dedication to her signed by Bernher. The latter gives some
account of Latimer's sufferings under persecution, but breaks off
with the statement, 'because these things be at large described in
the book of martyrs,' perhaps then going through the press, 'by
that most godly learned and excellent instrument of God, Master
John Foxe, I will not spend the time now to rehearse the same'.
Day reissued Latimer's sermons several times in a volume called
Fruitfull Sermons.

Some time in the twelvemonth beginning July 1558, Day
entered for publication in the Stationers' Register a work by
Thomas Becon called *The Sycke Mans Salve*, one of the most often
reprinted books of the century. It was a Protestant adaptation of a
long line of pious manuals going back to the medieval *Ars
Moriendi* instructing good Christians in the business of winding
up all their affairs both worldly and spiritual when they found
themselves about to die. The earliest extant copy of Becon's book
bears the date 1561 and includes a portrait of the author, a list of
twenty-five of his previously published works, and at the end the
same tomb device which Day had used in Cuningham's *Cosmo-*

[1] Parker, *Correspondence* (Parker Society), 411.

graphicall Glasse. By 1577 the publisher had reissued *The Sycke Mans Salve* at least six times. Meanwhile, in 1560, he published a 600-page folio of Becon's writings including *The Sycke Mans Salve* along with all of that author's tracts which he himself had printed before 1553. Three years later Day published a folio volume of 800 pages containing all of Becon's acknowledged writings composed during his exile and since his return. Finally came a folio of over a thousand pages containing all of Becon's writings which had previously been issued from the press of John Mayler.

Thus John Day after his re-emergence at the accession of Elizabeth appears to have been the most accomplished and productive printer in London, devoted to the cause of the national Church and favoured by important persons in the new regime making use of his abilities. Of all his publications, however, the most important was that English book of martyrs which had originally been projected by Grindal and his associates at Strasbourg and was now left to Foxe to see through to completion. As for Foxe, he was not the kind of person to seek or to invite important preferment in the Church. Convinced that the greatest danger now to be guarded against was the return of Catholics to power, he chose to keep clear of obligations that would take him away from London and the forefront of that conflict.

But he was not left entirely unprovided for. He was, for one thing, welcomed home by his old pupil Thomas Howard, now Duke of Norfolk, and was for several years domiciled in his patron's household in London. He was also given a pension which was continued even after Norfolk got himself fatally entangled with the Queen of Scots. Meanwhile, in January 1560, Grindal ordained Foxe and licensed him to preach, and shortly afterwards he went with his family to visit Parkhurst, now Bishop of Norwich. By midsummer he was back in London working with John Day at the Book of Martyrs. Upon the publication of the book in 1563 he was presented through Cecil's influence to a prebend at Salisbury, which with permission he let out on lease, and later to another at Durham which, since it required residence, he resigned. He was to spend the rest of his life in London in the employ of

John Day. His ashes rest with John Milton's in what remains after the last war of the church of St Giles.

Foxe left the work of translating *Rerum in Ecclesia Gestarum*, so much of it as he decided to retain, to assistants, while he himself searched for more material in episcopal registers and other sources, and corrected and amplified that already in hand. The book appeared in March 1563, a folio consisting of twenty pages of preliminary matter followed by eighteen hundred pages of text. It was entitled *Actes and Monuments of these latter and perillous dayes, touching matters of the Church, wherein ar comprehended and described the great persecutions & horrible troubles, that have bene wrought and practised by the Romishe Prelates, speciallye in this Realme of England and Scotlande, from the yeare of our Lorde a thousande, unto the tyme nowe present. Gathered and collected according to the true copies & wrytinges certificatorie as wel of the parties them selves that suffered, as also out of the Bishops Registers, which wer the doers thereof, by John Foxe.*

This title was enclosed in an engraved border similar in execution to that in Cuningham's *Cosmographicall Glasse* and possibly by the same engraver. It depicted the last judgment according to the conception of the two Churches which Foxe had taken over from Bale, showing the Lord sitting on high with trumpeting angels about Him and the world at His feet. The risen saints kneel on His right with trumpets at their lips and palms in their hands. Below them the martyrs are blowing trumpets while burning at the stake, and below the martyrs the people sit listening to the Word with Bibles in their laps. On the Lord's left the priests of the other Church are being cast by demons out of heaven, while below them others kneel at the elevation of the host, and below them a procession marches towards the crucifix and people sit listening to a becapped and vested priest while telling their beads.

The twenty pages of preliminary matter were designed to attract and impress various classes of possible readers. They included: 1. a 'Kalendar' listing month by month certain traditional holy days along with days commemorating English and a few Continental Protestant reformers and martyrs, some of them set out in red; 2. 'a little short table declaring the increasing and decreasing of the dayes by the approaching and declination of the Sunne', and concluding with rules for finding the date of Easter; 3. a Latin dedication of the book as a thank-offering to Christ; 4. an English dedication to the queen, opening with an ornamental capital depicting Elizabeth enthroned with counsellors at her right hand and likening her to Constantine and the author to Eusebius; 5. a Latin address 'ad doctum lectorum', contrasting the work with the *Legenda aurea*; 6. an address 'To the Persecutors of Gods truth, commonly called Papists', exulting over the oppressors of the victims of the late regime; 7. 'A declaration concerning the utilitie and profite of thys history', translated from the Latin *Proemium* of 1559. After these preliminaries came the eighteen hundred pages of text in black letter, with no less than fifty-six woodcut illustrations interspersed throughout the volume, and an index of names and topics. The work concluded with Day's tomb device as tail-piece, and over the page his portrait at the age of forty, dated 1562, and his colophon, 'Imprinted at London by John Day, dwelling over Aldersgate beneth saynt Martins, Anno 1563 [n.s.], the 20 of March.'

The book expressed the exultancy of the returned exiles at the intervention of providence in their behalf, but also their increasing concern lest divine justice be given occasion to withdraw the favour divine grace had bestowed. There was reason for their concern. The queen appeared to be committed to their cause by the circumstances of her birth and position and to be dependent on them in some degree for support against her rivals. But they could not be certain that her dependence upon them was as absolute as theirs upon her. For them she was indispensable and irreplaceable, so that, although they naturally could not trust her woman's judgment as they did their own, or her devotion to the cause they had at heart, they dared not allow their devotion to her to flag.

Yet it was a devotion more and more mixed with anxiety lest she should fail to live up to their idea of her or hold to the course they had charted for her, and lest her failure should provoke the

Lord to strike at her and them with sudden death or with rebellion and invasion. Protestants of all shades of opinion in respect to the Church were at one, therefore, in urging her to make certain of a Protestant succession by marrying and producing an heir, or, failing that, by naming a suitable successor. But after four years all they had got from her was promises, and their anxiety grew all the greater when the Queen of Scots returned to Scotland free to marry again and likely to do so, still more when, in October 1562, Elizabeth nearly died of smallpox.

It was while these things were going on that Foxe prepared the English version of the Book of Martyrs for the press. At the close of 1562, compelled by her need for money, Elizabeth summoned parliament, and the book was no doubt going through the press while the members were assembling at Westminster. In March, when it went on sale at John Day's shop at Aldersgate, they were still pestering the queen to marry or name a successor. Thus circumstances gave the book an extraordinary timeliness, a timeliness which grew still more acute as the situation grew still more uncertain for Elizabeth and the cause she represented or was supposed to represent, and as men grew more and more convinced that her survival was bound up with the survival of Protestantism, and the survival of Protestantism with the survival of England.

At this moment Foxe put into men's hands what appeared to be authentic copies of the reports which the victims of Catholic persecution in the preceding reign had dispatched to their friends then in exile but now on hand ready to testify to what had happened at that time and might easily happen again. These were not legends of martyrs long ago but reports of known and identifiable persons, some of them chief actors in events everyone had heard of, some of them ordinary folk in whom anyone might see himself, but all of them engaged in the same conflict with the same still active adversary. The stories were set, moreover, in a circumstantial report of the events which had led to the situation now pressing upon the nation, and this account was linked to the history of the reform movement at home and abroad and the struggle of

The burning of Tharchbishop of Cant. D. Tho. Cranmer in the town dich at
Oxford, with his hand first thrust into the tyre, wherwith he subscribed before.

past English rulers to defend themselves and their people against alien intruders. The stories of recent English martyrs were, finally, declared to be all one with the experience of Christian martyrs of all ages.

> Now then if martyrs are to be compared with martyrs, I see no reason why the martyrs of our time deserve not as great commendation as the others in the primitive church, which assuredly are inferior unto them in no point of praise, whether we look upon the number of them that suffered or the greatness of their torments or their constancy in dying ... All these things duly of our parts considered and marked, seeing that we have found so famous martyrs in this our age, let us not fail them in publishing and setting forth their doings.[1]

In 1559 the book had opened with the story of Wyclif. Now Foxe introduced his account of Wyclif with an account running to a little less than a hundred pages of the war of the two Churches within the Church since the beginning, of the first establishment of the faith in Britain, of the betrayal of the true spiritual calling of the Church by Hildebrand and his successors at Rome, of the increasing encroachments of popes upon the authority vested in civil rulers, and of the struggles of Henry II and John in England against the agents and allies of Rome. From that point Foxe went on for something a little short of eight hundred pages to tell of Wyclif and the reform movement instituted by him and carried on ever since by his disciples and successors in England and on the Continent, of the persecution of the faithful in England by popish bishops, and of the final liberation of Church and state from papal tyranny by Henry VIII. The treatment of Henry's own part in all this is necessarily guarded. Foxe would have his readers understand that the persons chiefly responsible for the afflictions of the saints in that king's time were his evil counsellors, especially the popish bishops, most especially Gardiner. The chief actor in the liberation of Church and state was represented to have been Cromwell, who 'alone, through the dexterity of his wit and counsel, brought to

---

[1] Foxe, I, 522.

pass that which even unto this day no prince or king throughout all Europe dare or can bring to pass'.[1] Then, from qualified commendation of Henry – he unhorsed the Pope but left him with 'trappings and stirrups whereby the prelates went about to set him on his horse again'[2] – Foxe goes on to the interval of Edward's brief reign, foreshadowing the true dawn to come with Elizabeth. All this part of the book was to be still more greatly expanded when Foxe came to reissue the work in 1570.

From this point he goes on in 1563 for eight hundred pages, nearly half the whole, to relate what happened in 'the horrible and bloody time of Queen Mary'. Of the material previously published he now omits Hooper's tract on transubstantiation, but retells most of the stories of persecution, where possible in fuller, more realistic detail, and he adds numerous stories of other martyrs reported to him since his return. Thanks to the assistance of Parker and Grindal, he was able to give a more detailed account of Cranmer, Ridley and Latimer in the Tower and at Oxford. He prints letters of Ridley and Bradford written in prison, letters and sermons of Latimer, and reports of such incidents as the exhumation and burning of the remains of Bucer and Fagius at Cambridge. Most of these stories he gives in what purports to be the very words of the persons concerned or of witnesses close to the time and event. He accompanies all this material with supporting documents of various kinds – official proclamations and communications, verbatim reports of disputations and examinations, treatises, sermons, letters, personal narratives, all, in the words of the title-page, 'gathered and collected according to the true copies and writings certificatory, as well of the parties themselves that suffered, as also out of the bishops' registers which were the doers thereof'. This assemblage of stories and documents, that is to say of 'acts and monuments', was accompanied by a running account of the events of Mary's unhappy reign which militant Protestants were anxious that people should not forget.

The reportorial effectiveness of this outpouring of circumstantial detail was further heightened by the fifty-odd woodcuts

[1] Foxe, V, 362–402. [2] Foxe, V, 697.

distributed throughout the text, the work probably of Flemish or German engravers working in England. Of these a third were conventionalized single-column representations of martyrs wreathed in flames, though none show the degree of sensationalism, the straining to exploit interest in physical suffering for its own sake, which characterizes the illustrations added to the book in the nineteenth century. Most of the half or full-page cuts, two-thirds of the total number in the original editions, were designed to serve one or both of two purposes: to illustrate a memorable scene, often of course the final scene, in the story of the given martyr or martyrs, and to score a point off the adversary in the manner of a satirical cartoon. The climax of the given story, especially one dealing with a well-known figure, was likely to be marked by a vividly executed illustration depicting priests, monks, friars, even bishops in their familiar habiliments, intermingled with civil officers, soldiers and bystanders mounted or on foot and bearing swords, halberds, lances and lighted faggots, all in action and all action centred on the figure at the stake.

The picture of Tyndale, for example, showed the full figure vigorously drawn, undraped, masculine, erect, his persecutors weaponed or gowned thronging about him, the executioner chaining him to the stake, and 'Lord open the king of England's eyes' springing in a ribbon from his lips. The burning of Huss, Oldcastle, Anne Askew, Bilney, Bradford, Rogers, Ridley, Latimer, Cranmer and a dozen others was pictured in the same dramatic fashion, the illustrations varying in detail according to circumstances but coming always pat to the climax and point of the story. The subject was by no means always a burning. Readers were also shown the emperor kept waiting barefoot in the snow with his wife and child outside the Pope's gate at Canossa, King John surrendering his crown to the legate and later poisoned by a monk at Swinstead, Wyclif's bones being dug up and poured into the stream at Lutterworth, Bilney being dragged from his pulpit by the friars at Ipswich, the bones and the books of Bucer and Fagius being burned in the market place at Cambridge, Cranmer recanting his recantation amid the fury of his adversaries in

St Mary's at Oxford, Bonner flogging one of the faithful in his orchard at Fulham.

Actes and Monuments in 1563 was the most elaborate expression of the apocalyptical expectancy with which the returned exiles and their party greeted Elizabeth at her accession. Naturally, therefore, the book was dedicated to her, and hers was the crowning story in its pages. The dedication likened her to Constantine bringing healing peace to the Church after an era of hatred and persecution, and the author to Eusebius begging only for the privilege of writing the history of the sufferings of the saints which she had brought to an end. A little later in the same year, having received a copy of Elizabeth's recent speech to the scholars at Cambridge, Foxe addressed a letter to her asking leave to transmit her words to posterity along with 'other monuments of historical matters'. It was a grief to him that 'when I am preparing a full account of you ... many things are wanting which are yet unknown to me and cannot be known but by your majesty'. And, he continued, if he were permitted to make them known, they could not 'be described better by any than by your own commentary, which I wish might be obtained by your most excellent wit in this time and space of your life'.[1] This was nothing less than an invitation to Elizabeth to add her own story to those of the other victims of persecution in the late reign. Fuller tells us that she called him Father Foxe,[2] but we are left only to imagine what a story she might have told if she had risen to the lure of her indefatigable collector of monuments of historical matters.

But he could not on that account leave her out of his book. He never wrote the promised history of her reign, but from information which probably came to him from Roger Ascham, Mistress Ashley and other members of her household, he rounded out his Book of Martyrs with an account of the person he regarded as the most illustrious victim of them all.[3] In the elaborately conceited style in which Elizabeth's subjects and Elizabeth herself

---

[1] Strype, *Annals*, vol. I, pt. ii, 108–12.
[2] Fuller, *Church-History of Britain* (1655), Bk. IX, 76.
[3] Foxe, VIII, 600–28

liked to wrap up their thoughts on formal occasions, Foxe opens his account of her experiences before she came to the throne by playing again on the theme of the godly prince, the part that Edward had not lived to act out and that the Lady Jane had not been permitted to bring off.

For what man reputing with himself the singular ornaments and noble graces given of God to this so princely a Lady and puissant princess, the mildness of her nature, the clemency of her royal estate and majesty, the peaceableness of her reign, who a virgin so mildly ruleth men, governeth her subjects, keepeth all things in order, quieteth foreign nations, recovereth towns, enlargeth her kingdom, nourisheth and [re]concileth amity, uniteth hearts and love with foreign enemies, helpeth neighbours, reformeth religion, quencheth persecution, redresseth dross, frameth the things out of joint, so feared with such love, and so loved with such fear.

This was, of course, a way of instructing his royal mistress in the way she should conduct her affairs by praising her for already having done so. But fortunately the writer soon lays aside the style of courtship. Lest it should happen to her as it had happened to her brother to be extolled while living but soon forgotten when dead – she had just nearly died after reigning fewer years than he had done – Foxe undertakes to write her history up to the present. It is a story which the responsible biographer should be chary of crediting in every detail, but a well-told story for all that.

It is the kind of tale which people at all times love to be told about royalty, though no such tale about a reigning monarch as Foxe now told about Elizabeth had ever before been told in English print. He begins by glancing back at the account he had given earlier in the book of her birth and baptism with Cranmer for godfather. He pictures her modest, studious girlhood as Ascham was to picture it again in *The Scholemaster*. He goes on to tell of the trials she had had to endure under her hard-hearted sister's rule – how she was rudely summoned to Westminster and accused of complicity in Wyatt's rebellion, sent to the Tower, nearly drowned at the shooting of the bridge, landed at the Traitors' Gate and held under false suspicion of treason, then dispatched to Woodstock under a boorish jailer, next brought back to Hampton Court to be examined by Gardiner and the privy council in the hope of getting her to incriminate herself, summoned in the night to a last audience with the queen in the royal bedchamber, Mary grim, suspicious and withdrawn, her husband listening 'behind a cloth and not seen'. Finally, of course, we have Elizabeth coming to the throne at Mary's death amid the rejoicing of the people.

All this is told with seeming artlessness, but with great skill in the handling of action and dialogue and the depiction of character, and with effective touches of sentiment and humour. A little boy in the Tower garden brings the princess flowers at the risk of a whipping. Villagers on the road to Woodstock ring the bells at her passing and are put in the stocks for their devotion. A merry conceited fellow, in order to amuse her and annoy her keeper, picks up the goat pastured in the enclosure where she takes her recreation and brings the creature to Bedingfield her keeper, saying 'what talk they have had I cannot tell. For I understand him not, but he should seem to me some stranger, and I think verily a Welshman.'

There is above all Elizabeth herself, princely and gracious with her friends and the people, steadfast and self-possessed in the presence of her enemies. 'This that I have said,' Foxe reports her to have told Gardiner, 'I will stand to. For I will never belie myself.' (Her portraits bore the legend *Semper eadem*.) 'Well,' we are told that Queen Mary said in that last interview at Hampton Court, 'you stiffly still persevere in your truth. Belike you will not confess but that you have been wrongfully punished?' and Elizabeth replies, 'I must not say so, if it please your majesty, to you.' 'Why then,' says the queen, 'belike you will to other[s],' and the princess, guarding every utterance, 'No, if it please your majesty ... I have borne the burden and must bear it.' Probably by 1563 there were others who had analysed Elizabeth's qualities as shrewdly as Foxe, but had anyone else depicted so convincingly the character which legend was to fix upon her? Or had any monarch ever been so served by a writer with such a sense of what people would delight to hear concerning their ruler?

The conclusion Foxe intended his readers to draw from the story was unmistakable. If Elizabeth was not herself actually one of the martyrs, it was only because providence in its care for the English nation had intervened to save her.

Such was then the wickedness and rage of that time, wherein what dangers and troubles were among the inferior subjects of this realm of England may be easily gathered when such a princess ... could not escape without her cross. And therefore as we have hitherto discoursed the afflictions and persecutions of the other poor members of Christ comprehended in this history before, so likewise I see no cause why the communion of her grace's afflictions also ... ought to be suppressed in silence ... And though I should through ingratitude or silence pass over the same, yet the thing itself is so manifest, that what Englishman is he which knoweth not the afflictions of her grace to have been far above the condition of a king's daughter. For there was [nothing lacking] to make a very Iphigenia of her but her offering up upon the altar of the scaffold.

Such was the story which John Foxe and John Day between them brought out in March 1563 while members of parliament were pressing the queen to relieve their anxieties by taking a husband or naming a successor, but when on April 3rd she sent them away again, they still had nothing more definite than a promise. Some of them may have carried *Actes and Monuments* home with them, and surely not a few had at least heard of the book when, again needing money, the queen called them back to Westminster in September 1566. Their anxieties had not abated in the interval. Elizabeth seemed as far from marrying as ever and no more inclined to name a successor. Meanwhile, the Queen of Scots had remarried, contrary to Elizabeth's wishes, and produced a son. Parliament consequently redoubled its importunity, but only to be finessed in a brilliant display of royal histrionics and sent home again with more promises.

Shortly afterwards the whole situation grew suddenly even more difficult and alarming. The Catholic party in France, egged on by Mary's relatives, reopened its war on the Huguenots. Under orders from Philip of Spain, Alva set out to exterminate the Protestants of the Netherlands. There was no telling when one or the other of these powers would turn about and come to the aid of the disaffected Catholics in England. Then in May 1568 Mary, fleeing from the troubles she had brought upon herself in Scotland, took refuge on the English side of the border, and made herself the centre of Catholic intrigue against Elizabeth. The outcome was open revolt, followed by a papal bull, which as it happened came too late, excommunicating Elizabeth and absolving her rebellious subjects from the sin of disobedience. The affair was brought sharply home to Foxe by the fact that in spite of his admonitions the Duke of Norfolk, under whose roof he and his family were living, let himself be induced by the hope of marrying Mary into countenancing the challenge to the authority of Elizabeth. Two years later he was to expiate his folly on the scaffold, with his former tutor beside him to give what spiritual comfort he could.

While the Catholic rebellion was coming to a head in the north, author and publisher of *Actes and Monuments* were making ready to issue a new and greatly enlarged edition of their book. Their labours were drawing to a conclusion as the uprising was being suppressed, and the book appeared towards the close of 1570 as the queen was being constrained by the public outcry against the Queen of Scots and the rebellious earls to summon another parliament.

The edition of 1570 fixed the Book of Martyrs in the form which was to remain substantially unchanged through six subsequent editions down to the eighteenth century. Of the two large folio volumes the first was entitled *The First Volume of the Ecclesiasticall history contaynyng the Actes and Monumentes of thynges passed in every kynges tyme in this Realme ... from the primitive tyme till the reigne of K. Henry VIII.* The second volume was described as going on *from the tyme of K. Henry VIII to Queene Elizabeth our gratious Lady now reignyng.*

The two volumes taken together showed how much author and publisher had learned about suiting a work of such a character, scope and size to the needs of their public. The book was printed as before in black letter, as was still the custom with books in the vernacular. But it was now much better printed on a larger page, with a much fuller apparatus of titles, sub-titles, running heads, dates, names of reigning kings, and marginal notes supplying both information and comment. There were additional woodcut illustrations. There was again an elaborate index of names and topics but also at the beginning of Volume I a list of 'The names of the authors alleged in this book', followed by another of 'The names of the Martyrs in this booke conteined'. The remaining prefatory matter was also revised with the ordinary reader in mind. The representation of the two Churches at the last judgment appeared on the title-page of each volume. Also retained was the address to the Christian reader on 'what utilitie is to be taken by readyng of these Historyes', but the Kalendar and the Latin prefaces of 1563 gave place to two new addresses in English, one 'to the true and faithfull congregation of Christes universall Church', the other 'to all the professed frendes and folowers of the Popes procedynges', and finally there was an entirely new dedication addressed to the queen.

In the text of the work Foxe now made some revisions, corrections and additions in his accounts of the Marian martyrs, rearranged the order of presentation here and there, translated or summarized Latin documents, but otherwise left this part of the work substantially the same as before. Where, however, he had formerly taken at most a hundred pages to relate the history of the Church and the nation before Wyclif, he now took five hundred, and where he had formerly taken something less than eight hundred pages to get from Wyclif to Mary, he now took over a thousand, the type-pages being at least a third larger. That is, he now led up to his account of Mary's reign and the stories of the Marian martyrs with a much extended account of the whole

course of the history of Church and nation from the very beginning to the crisis in which the queen and her people now found
themselves. Most important, he thus set before the Elizabethan
public the current Protestant version of the traditional Christian
conception of the meaning of history, its application to England,
and the lessons to be deduced from it for the instruction of the
queen no less than her subjects.

No one, of course, would now think of turning to Foxe for
information concerning the history of the Christian Church or the
English nation before his own time. Every part of his book is
deeply coloured by the passions and prejudices of the man and his
age. But all writing of history is a rewriting of history nearer to
the historian's own notion of what must have happened, and
the question here is not, did Foxe tell the truth as we would
have it told, but what did he take the truth to be and induce so
many of his countrymen in so critical a moment to accept as such.

In dedicating his first English edition to the queen he had likened
Elizabeth to Constantine and himself to Eusebius. The comparison
was appropriate, since it was no new thing in the history of Christianity for an upsurge of the religious spirit to find expression in a
rewriting of history. History was what Christianity was about.
What Christian teachers had to tell mankind that was different
from the teachings of rival cults was a story of mankind's past and
what it portended for the future. The telling and retelling of that
story had been the occupation of Christians in every age of active
faith.

For the essence of that faith was the conviction, the certain
knowledge as they supposed, that at a particular moment in time
a particular event had occurred which was both the consummation
of everything that had occurred before and the revelation of
everything that it behoved men to know of what was still to
come in so much of time as still remained. To seek escape from
history like the millenarians, or to think of it like the pagans as an
endless succession of revolving circumstance, was to reject Christianity. To hold faithfully to the idea of history thus conceived
was to be of that true Church which had come down in the

process of time from the prime witnesses of the unique event which gives history its meaning and reveals its purpose. Meaning and purpose were always the same. History had always the same story to tell of men condemned for disobedience to God's command and of men saved from time to time by God's grace from the consequences of their fall, of grace manifested in the faithfulness of the elect under temptation and affliction. This story, of which the Scriptures were the prime authentic record, it was the historian's business to relate to the conditions of men in his own time.

But as the history of mankind was the subject of Christian faith, so the history of the Church was the subject which preoccupied Christian historians, and the effect of the Reformation was merely to give the subject a new turn and a fresh relevance. Catholics, regarding the visible Church as the appointed vehicle for the transmission of truth revealed in scripture and history, demanded of Protestant reformers, where was your Church before Luther? Protestant reformers, denying the identification of a fallible priesthood with the Church, turned to the supposedly infallible record of the Scriptures. The whole history of the Church must be reviewed and rewritten according to the Word as set down in the book, the one book of unique authority, though in the event that turned out to mean not only that book but a multitude of others now being put into men's hands by the printing-press and the book-trade.

The uniqueness claimed for scriptural authority lay in this, that in the Scriptures the record of accomplished fact and the revelation of universal truth authenticated one another. The future which the prophets foretold had either become the past which the chroniclers had recorded, or was on its way to becoming so. Nothing that had ever happened had in truth been unforeseen; nothing that was still to happen had been unforetold. History and prophecy were in effect one continuing revelation of divine providence working upon the life of mankind. Thus in the Scriptures historians were provided with a key to the authentication and interpretation of all other records of the past and all tradition of whatever origin. Not the least important effect of the Reformation, aside from its effect upon religious life as such, was to make the art and science of historiography of momentous concern.

From this point of view the ancient classical notion that time and the universe run on for ever, and that the course of events is determined by chance for ever repeating itself, was untenable. Granted a creator, creation must have a beginning and an end, a principle and a purpose revealed in the record of things past and foretold, which it is for the historian to elucidate and demonstrate. For though the life of mankind does not go round and round with fortune's wheel, it does move in successive waves to break finally upon a predestined shore. It moves from age to age and so on to a concluding age, always more or less imminent. As to the exact chronological limits of these ages of the world's history, there might be some variation of opinion, but there could be no doubt as to the fact of their procession one after the other in a definite order through time towards an inevitable conclusion.

The history of mankind in general followed the same order as the history of man in particular. In every age of the world some man or men, however obscure or few, love God and obey him in innocence of heart. In every age as it proceeds men fall into disobedience and corruption from which there would be no escape did not God from time to time again interpose His grace in the lives of men chosen by Him to that end. In every age of the world, out of the generality of fallen men, some are called to believe, obey, and be saved and to show the way of salvation to others – some one man it might be, some one family, some one people, Noah, Abraham, the children of Israel, the tribe of Judah, the house of David, the apostles and Church of Christ. Thus mankind was believed to have been moving from the beginning through alternating lapses and recoveries, from crisis to crisis, always towards one greater crisis still to come, in which the whole process of history was to reach its final consummation in accordance with the foreordained scheme of things revealed in prophecy and the record of things past.

The Book of Martyrs

The Christian historian did not think of this process as one of development or progress from one stage to another, from lower to higher, primitive to advanced, simple to complex. He did not concern himself with the evolution and effect of laws and institutions. These things were works of creation, not products of growth. They became corrupt as men became corrupt through disobedience, and they were renewed as men were renewed by the grace of God, but they did not evolve or progress. Through grace men regain their lost knowledge of truth and their power to obey it, but such knowledge and power come as new and original acts of creation or revelation, the will of God making itself felt as a spontaneous, authentic experience in the consciousness of one man at a time, not as the cumulative result of the experience of one man following and building upon another. The prime factor in historical causation was not human determination or conditioning circumstance. There was no such thing as accident, only providence, no learning by trial and error, only the creative will of God working in this man or that, this people or that.

The historian must centre his attention, therefore, first and last on the experience of individual souls, beginning with his own, on their reawakening one by one to knowledge of truth and their adhering to truth through the compulsion of what they know. The significant facts of history, report of which he was bound to credit and transmit, were the facts of spiritual experience presented as nearly as possible in the testimony of the individuals concerned or as reported by those nearest to them. And since the essence of spiritual experience in this life is a kind or measure of martyrdom, the history of the elect, which is to say of the Church, is a story of martyrdom.

Here was the basic conception of history which Foxe found in Christian historians from Eusebius and Augustine to Bale and Flacius. Adapting it in his own way to his own purposes in the circumstances of his own time, he transmitted it to the generations who pored over his famous book or had it retailed to them through one channel or another. To object to his lack of originality or to his misrepresentation of facts is beside the point. The primary

133

enterprise of writers and publishers of books in his age was to get the literature and accumulated knowledge of past ages transposed into English and put into print. His accomplishment was to transpose the traditional Christian conception of history into terms that would be comprehensible to his own people in his own time. This meant to rewrite the history of the Church from an English Protestant point of view fitted to present circumstances. His people must be made to understand the whole pattern of events from the beginning to the present in order that they should realize their own place as a nation in that process, their immediate responsibility, the destiny to which they were called. Only thus could they rightly grasp the meaning of the current struggle with alien powers threatening their destruction and the necessity of supporting the queen and her government.

That the grounds for such a view of England's place in history were to be looked for first in scripture was, of course, beyond dispute. The will of God had made itself known directly to the people of Israel as to no people before or since. It followed that the record of Israel's experience was the most authentic and authoritative record of God's will that ever was, and that the history of every other people, notably now the English people, was to be understood only by the light of the record of that chosen nation as brought to fulfilment in Christ and His church.

This meant that the whole body of prophecy and chronicle in scripture was relevant to the whole course of events to the end of time, and the summation of the whole, foreshadowing the whole history of Christ's people clear through to their ultimate triumph with Christ over Antichrist, was the Apocalypse of St John. Bale had advanced this idea in his *Image of Both Churches*. Bullinger had expounded it at length to the English and other exiles at Zürich. Day had published Bullinger's exposition shortly after resuming business at Elizabeth's accession, and the translator had assured his readers that the book of Revelation thus expounded was 'as it were an ecclesiastical history of the troubles and persecutions of the church, especially from the apostles' time until the last day, wherein Christ ... shall come a righteous judge to condemn Anti-

christ and all antichristian hypocrites and bloody persecutors, but
to receive his elect people and to crown them with glory.'[1]

Thus in his new and extended version of the Book of Martyrs
Foxe endeavoured to place the stories of the recent victims of
Catholic persecution in England in the perspective of history as
conceived by Christian historians all the way back to Eusebius and
Augustine. It is a conception which sees history, as he explains at
the very start, occupied throughout by conflict between the world
and the kingdom of Christ, the world consisting of 'all such as be
without or against Christ', the kingdom of Christ consisting of
'all them which belong to the faith of Christ, and here take his
part in this world against the world'. Two sorts of people made
up the Church as we know it in this world, 'such as be of outward
profession only' and 'such as by election inwardly are joined to
Christ'. The first are of the visible Church only, partaking of the
sacraments but not of Christ's inward blessing. The others are of
'the invisible church ... partaking not only of the sacraments, but
also the heavenly blessings and grace of Christ'. And 'as between
the world and the kingdom of Christ there is a continual repugnance, so between the two parts of this visible church aforesaid
groweth great variance and mortal persecution, insomuch that
sometimes the true church of Christ hath no greater enemies than
those of their own profession and company.'[2]

So it was in the time of Christ Himself and His apostles; so it
has been ever since; so it is in these latter days. The history of the
Church, like the history of mankind in general and of man in
particular, has always to do with the contention of Christ and
Antichrist for possession of man's soul. Hence the pattern to be
looked for in the record of events is always one of lapse and
recovery, of falling away due to the weakness and wickedness of
men and of recovery due to renewal of divine grace, of Antichrist
breaking out again and again and of Christ intervening to redeem
His own and cast the devil out. History was the process by which

[1] Bullinger, *A Hundred Sermons upon the Apocalips*, translated by John Daus
(1561).

[2] Foxe, I, 87–8.

God sifted out the souls of His elect through trial and conflict, made endurable for them by the inner assurance that, God's purpose fulfilled, they would see a new heaven and a new earth. But God's purpose within the limits of time was not to bring forth a state of things that had never existed before – Foxe was no John of Münster – but to recover and keep what had been lost and might be lost again.

His intention, he tells his readers, is to show that the Church as now established in England was 'not the beginning of any new church of our own' but 'the renewing of the old ancient church of Christ'.[1] The reformed Church had not swerved from Rome; Rome had swerved from itself. Following the pattern revealed in scripture, the Church in its history had passed first through a time of trial and martyrdom, next a time of flourishing and growth, next a time of backsliding and declining, next a time of oppression and persecution renewed, and finally a time of reformation continuing to the present and pointing forward to a day of perfect restoration and triumph, after which time would be no more.

The chronology of this progression from period to period was made clear in Revelation. The Church's pristine era of trial had lasted, as John foretold, forty-two months, which, counting each month as a week of years, meant the two hundred and ninety-four years from the death of Christ in the thirtieth year of His age to the victory of Constantine over Maxentius. Six years more to the overthrow of Licinius made three hundred years to the end of persecution, in which period Satan had driven the Church into the wilderness (Rev. XIII) and the beast had afflicted the saints (Rev. XIV). Then the Lord sent Constantine 'to bridle and snaffle the power of the old serpent and give rest unto his church for the term of a thousand years', that is, according to Foxe's calculation, until the year of the Lord 1324, which was thirty years from Christ's nativity plus two hundred and ninety-four years from His crucifixion plus a thousand years from Constantine. During that millennium the Church had been free to preach the gospel; the

[1] Foxe, I, 9.

elect had been free from persecution; Satan had been confined (Rev. xx).

Yet before that time was up, the Church, while still free from oppression from without, had begun to fall away through weakness within itself. This falling away came not from the beginning nor all at once, 'but with long working and continuance of time by little and little' through the succession of bishops at Rome – Silvester who took upon himself the title of pope, Gregory VII or Hildebrand who arrogated to himself authority over kings and emperors, Innocent III who let loose the rabble of monks and friars. In 1294, thirty years short of the thousand years after Constantine's ending of the persecution of the primitive Church, came Boniface VIII who 'made the sixth book of the decretals, confirmed the orders of friars, and privileged them with great freedoms'. Thirty years later, 1324 years after the Lord's nativity, Satan broke loose again and made war on God's people unopposed until about the year 1371, when the Lord called up Wyclif and after him others here and there to reaffirm the truth revealed in scripture and betrayed by the bishops of Rome. 'The durance of which time hath continued hitherto about the space of two hundred and four score years; and how long it shall continue more, the Lord and Governor of all times, he only knoweth.'[1]

Having thus set the time-scheme of the age-long contention of Christ and Antichrist, of the Church and the world, and of the two Churches within the Church, Foxe went on in Book I to 'the three hundred years next after Christ', the first of the five periods of Church history. The one hundred and thirty-five pages which follow, based largely on Eusebius, are chiefly devoted to the ten legendary persecutions of the primitive Church by the pagan rulers of the empire. But the author announces at the start that he will also treat of 'the first conversion of Christian realms to the faith of Christ, namely of this realm of England and Scotland'. He concludes this portion of his story with a brief account of the conversion of Britain, to be covered more fully in Book II, leading to the conquest and conversion of the empire by Con-

[1] Foxe, I, 4–5, 87, 288–92, 724–7; IV, 104–9.

stantine, 'the great and worthy emperor, [who was] not only a Briton born by his mother Helena (being king Coilus' daughter) but [who] also by the help of the British army ... obtained ... peace and tranquillity to the whole universal church of Christ.' For the British part of this legend Foxe probably depended on the compilations of Bale and Flacius and the chronicle of Fabyan, who drew upon Gildas, Bede and Geoffrey. Neither he nor his public was of course at all interested in the discovery of facts never known before. His intention was to apprise his readers of what had long been known and attested by the best and most ancient authorities. His accomplishment was to retell the legend of the early Christian martyrs with an English Protestant turn and application and to cap this classic body of Christian fables with the epic tale of Constantine.

He does not omit the lessons which this history has to teach the English people and their ruler at the moment of writing. 'Thus have we,' he says, 'the unquiet and miserable state of the emperors of Rome until the time of the Christian Constantine, with the examples ... of God's severe justice upon them.' And in like manner, he continues, 'to come more near home ... I could infer [the same lessons] of this our country of England.' Gildas had preached repentance to the ancient Britons and they had laughed him to scorn. 'What followed? God sent in their enemies on every side and destroyed them and gave the land to other nations.' Wyclif had exhorted the people to amend their lives and forsake idolatry and papistry, and they had despised him and after his death burned his bones and his books. 'What followed? They slew their right king and set up three wrong kings on a row, under whom all the noble blood was slain up and half the commons thereto.'

Foxe next looks ahead to the treatment which had been accorded to Tyndale, Bilney, Frith, and Barnes when they too preached repentance to their countrymen, but this was indeed coming close to home, and he breaks off simply with an exhortation to the godly wise to judge for themselves whether or not the nation has since had to suffer for its offences. 'Neither is it here any need to speak of these our lower and latter days.' Enough to say 'that God yet once again is come on visitation to this church of England, yea and that more lovingly and beneficially than ever he did afore. For in this his visitation he hath redressed many abuses and cleansed his church of much ungodliness and super-stition and made it a glorious church, if it be compared to the old form and state'.[1]

'If it be compared to the old form and state.' Foxe was not losing sight of what was for him the main issue. He was all for determined action in support of the national faith, and he hoped for a still more perfect reformation. But he perceived that the probable effect of the proposals put forth by Cartwright in this critical year of 1570 would be to jeopardize everything that had been gained so far in the war of the two Churches by stirring up unnecessary internal strife and weakening the power of the queen. For in his judgment the accomplishment of the more perfect reformation in the face of Catholic opposition depended every-where on the security and success of the regime then established under Elizabeth in England. Consequently he would take no part in the Puritan attempt to force Elizabeth's hand at this time, and he designed his book in its extended form to set forth the lessons which history, especially English history, had to teach both queen and people concerning their mutual obligations under the law of God.

---

[1] Foxe, I, 93-4.

CHAPTER V

The Lessons of History

IN the new dedication of his book in 1570 Foxe assured the queen that, since the work was written in the popular tongue, it was not intended for her particular reading, but this statement is not to be taken at face value. What he really had in mind in addressing her comes out in the statement which immediately follows. Knowing the care she is taking for furnishing her realm with 'the voice of Christ's gospel and faithful preaching of His word', the writer intends 'to adjoin unto this [her] godly proceedings and to the office of the ministry the knowledge also of ecclesiastical history ... that like as by the one the people may learn the rules and precepts of doctrine so by the other they may have examples of God's mighty working in His church.' Thus they may learn about the acts of martyrs, but also – and here surely he is speaking as much to Elizabeth herself as to her subjects – about God's mercies and judgments 'in overthrowing tyrants, in confounding pride, in altering states and kingdoms, in conserving religion against errors and dissensions, in relieving the godly, in bridling the wicked, in loosing and tying up again of Satan the disturber of commonweals.'

Foxe would have the people obey whatever ruler God set over them, but he would counterbalance the absolute authority vested in the ruler by the requirement of godliness and the absolute subjection required of the people by the assumption that he and such as he were vested with authority to instruct the ruler in the obligations godliness required princes to fulfil. To be sure, if the ruler proved a godly prince indeed, that was due to the grace which God bestows from time to time upon His elect, not to the people's deserving. If the prince fell short in his duties under the law of God, that was a judgment on the people for transgressions of their own, not justification for disobedience and rebellion. If however they rebelled, that, while still an offence, was at the same time a judgment on the prince for his own derelictions. Nothing therefore behoved both prince and people more than that they should have brought before them the examples of God's judgments on their predecessors in past ages.

Foxe had now come in his narrative to the millennium after Constantine during which Satan had been under restraint, persecution suspended, the gospel preached, and the Church left free to flourish. Within this period also, however, the Church – that is to say the visible Church – had begun to fall away from the faith and example of the apostles through the progressive betrayal by the bishops of Rome of their true spiritual function. In the pages which follow, therefore, Foxe supplies his readers with what was in substance the standard Protestant account of the growing corruption of the papacy and the countervailing movement for reform. This account he drew largely from Bale, Flacius and the centuriators of Magdeburg, but he did not allow it to stand by itself alone. Since his plan called for an account of England's part in history, his account of the Church at large is from this point on interwoven with 'such domestical histories as more nearly concern this our country ... here at home'.[1]

The next three hundred and fifty pages take the reader through the history of persons and events in England under British, Roman, Saxon, Danish and Norman rulers, proceeding by stages of three hundred years each from Constantine to Egbert in Book II, from Egbert to William the Conqueror in Book III, from William to Edward III and so to Wyclif in Book IV.

The significance of this expansion of Foxe's original narrative is more easily mistaken than exaggerated. What he now did was to incorporate the legends concerning the national past which sixteenth-century chroniclers were currently putting into print with his Protestant version of the history of the Church and the reformation in general, bringing the whole down to date with his

[1] Foxe, I, 305.

account of the Marian persecution and the accession of Elizabeth.

The result was something much more than a hodge-podge of fabulous tales topped off with a martyrology and redeemed only by the inclusion of certain unique documents. It was for its own time and for several succeeding generations a comprehensive history of England based upon a conception of human nature and of the meaning and course of history which few of its readers were in any state of mind to do anything but accept as universally true. Though it was studded here and there with documents or 'monuments' of one sort or another, it was not a mere omnium gatherum of the raw materials of historical scholarship. Though it made use of material drawn from the chronicles, it was not presented in the disconnected form still practised by contemporary annalists. Documents and legends were framed in a coherent narrative from a single sustained point of view, a point of view shared by increasing numbers of the author's countrymen. Except for Polydore Vergil, who wrote from a very different point of view, no previous writer had attempted a work of such character and scope. No one had issued such a work in English print.

In all this Foxe was turning to his own use the more or less legendary material which contemporary chroniclers were at the same time putting into print. With the accession of Elizabeth the compilation and publication of annals of the nation's past started up again on an unprecedented scale. For the legendary beginnings and the early centuries of national existence, the compilers, while drawing freely upon one another, went back to fifteenth-century monastic chroniclers, to the *Brut* and the *Polychronicon*, and so to Geoffrey, Bede and Gildas, all of whom were now becoming more and more available, thanks to the antiquarian activities of Leland, Bale, Parker and others.

But Elizabethan chroniclers, by no means excepting Foxe, also owed much to Polydore Vergil, more than they cared to acknowledge but more in substance than in spirit and method. The debt and the difference were both significant. Polydore was an Italian humanist who came to England in the reign of Henry VII as deputy collector of Peter's Pence. He stayed on to serve the Church and the court in various capacities and to write a history of England in the interest of the newly established dynasty. The first part of his *Anglica Historia*, covering the subject to 1509, was published at Basle in 1535, the second, continuing to the reign of Mary, in 1556, after which the author retired to his native Urbino. A second edition appeared at Basle in 1570. An early English translation of the first part of the work is extant in manuscript.[1]

Anglica Historia is a well-ordered, continuous narrative patterned on classical models but making use of materials drawn from both classical and medieval sources. It begins with the mythical founding of Britain by the Trojan Brutus and carries the account through the reigns of legendary and authentic kings to the dynastic conflict of the preceding century and the establishment of the Tudor monarchy. Thus Polydore fixed the lines of the national legend which Elizabethan chroniclers, poets and playwrights were to tell and retell with variations in one form and another.

There was much in the story which could be made to serve the ideas and purposes of Protestant propaganda, as well as much that did not. In the story of Joseph of Arimathea and King Lucius Polydore laid claim to the early introduction of the faith and establishment of the Church in Britain, and he went on to assert their renewal at the coming of St Augustine from Rome, their persistence in the face of many dangers, and their present flourishing state. He capped the tale of British kings with the story of Constantine, born of a British mother and made emperor on British soil, with the result, he says, 'that even at this present the kings of England according to the usage of their ancestors do wear the imperial diadem as a gift exhibited of Constantinus to his successors.' Polydore's account of the contentions of York and Lancaster, following the same line of Tudor propaganda as More, is aimed at exemplifying the consequences which follow violation of the law of legitimate succession.

[1] *The Anglica Historia of Polydore Vergil A. D. 1485–1537*, edited with a translation by Denys Hay (1950); *Polydore Vergil's English History from an early translation*, edited by Sir Henry Ellis (Camden Society, 1848).

The Lessons of History

On all these matters the Elizabethans were in full accord with Polydore, but there were other points on which they could not but disagree. His sceptical, not to say contemptuous, attitude towards Geoffrey's saga of Uther and Arthur was bound to give offence. His Catholic view of Henry VIII's defection from Rome was, of course, strongly condemned. Most important, what Polydore saw in history, true to his classical background, was mutability, the endless cycle of chance and change in all things. 'And thus,' he says at the conclusion of his account of the Norman Conquest, 'do all human affairs ebb and flow, so that nothing is so certain as uncertainty itself and continual change into better or into worse.'

But Elizabethan chroniclers were much closer in spirit and method to their medieval forerunners. The 'principal commodity' of such writing, Grafton says in dedicating his work to Dudley, the queen's favourite, 'is the setting forth of God's doings.' 'You have not,' he continues, 'in reading of histories uncertainly yielded your judgment to fortune or nature but Christianly acknowledged the merciful providence of God,' and he means to direct the whole course of his own labours to the same end. For the Elizabethan as for the monastic chronicler the true significance of events lay in the fact that everything that happens happens not casually, but according to the design of the Creator. The chronicler set out, therefore, as though to record the whole course of events as they occurred one after the other from the first day of creation to the present moment and place, always with a view to discovering the divine intention behind each event, and always in anticipation of the winding up and conclusion of the whole process.

Yet these men were not cloistered monks, but sixteenth-century Englishmen living at the focus of national life, keenly aware of the dangers crowding in upon the present regime and on the faith with which its security and their own appeared to be bound up. Hence, while keeping to the annalistic pattern of their medieval models, they made the chronicle serve a very unmedieval purpose. Grafton says, as he goes on in his dedication, that he was moved 'by the singular goodness of God toward my native country in this, that he hath relieved the ruinous state of England with the most wise and godly government of our most gracious sovereign lady, whom he hath through infinite dangers preserved to defend us from imminent perils and present destruction.' Thomas Norton reiterates the point in his commendatory epistle to Grafton's work. 'Each man may have a glass to see things past, whereby to judge justly of things present and wisely of things to come ... and finally all men in seeing the course of God's doings may learn to dread his judgments and love his providence ... And above all things forget not to give God thanks for the queen's majesty's most gracious reign, so far in comparison exceeding the times that here thou readest of.'[1]

These productions of the book-trade, kept up to date from time to time in successive editions of various shapes and sizes from duo-decimo to folio, were all designed to keep the Elizabethan public supplied with what appeared to be precise information consisting of names, dates and factual details which would enable readers to perceive the continuity of the present moment in their own and the nation's existence with the whole sequence of providentially directed events since the first day of creation. Usually chroniclers included a table of the ages of the world variously reckoned but invariably placing the present moment in the last or next to the last age of all, and they frequently added another table listing all the rulers of England down to Elizabeth. Thus any reader could work out for himself how the English people came down from Adam and Noah by way of Japhet, how English kings came down from the heroes of Troy by way of Brut and Arthur, how the English Church came down from the apostles by way of Joseph of Arimathea. He could read, too, how alien powers of alien faith had ever and again intruded upon English affairs, fomenting dis-obedience and disruption, and how sooner or later they had all been driven out or else subdued to the common English order by faithful princes and the grace of God.

Thus through all the seemingly disconnected annals put to-

[1] Richard Grafton, *An Abridgement of the Chronicles of England* (1563); later expanded as *A Chronicle at large* (1568).

gether by Elizabethan chroniclers, there ran the thread of a story of national origins and national destiny in which the subjects of Elizabeth could see their present predicament foreshadowed, Elizabeth could be apprised of the role she was expected to play, and both could be assured of the predestined outcome. As for her, she already knew the story when she came to the throne and was quite prepared to make use of it for her purposes. When the displaced bishops shortly after her accession assured her that history justified the claims of the Roman Church to her obedience, she told them that 'the records and chronicles of our realm testify to the contrary', that Gildas 'testifieth Joseph of Arimathea to be the first preacher of the word of God within our realm', and that already 'when Austin came from Rome, this our realm had bishops and priests therein'.[1]

The printing of chronicles in the vulgar tongue embodying the national legend for the indoctrination of the people had been started by Caxton and carried on by Pynson early in the development of the book-trade, but an important advance in the production of such things came at the end of Henry VIII's reign and under Edward VI. In 1542 Thomas Berthelet published Edward Halle's *Union of the Two Noble and Illustre Families of Lancastre and York*, presenting in chronicle form the classic Tudor version of the contention of the two houses as fixed by More and Polydore. Richard Grafton at the same time published the rhymed chronicle of John Hardyng with a prose continuation of his own, and six years later he reissued Halle's *Union*. In 1549 Berthelet published *An Epitome of Chronicles*, the work of Thomas Lanquet and Thomas Cooper. With the accession of Mary the publication of chronicles, like the publication of most other things, fell off, but only to be resumed more actively than before at the accession of Elizabeth. From that time on it kept pace with the steady advance of the book-trade. John Kingston began in April 1559 by reprinting Fabyan's chronicle, which had been first printed by Pynson in 1516. William Seres and Thomas Marsh at the same time put out an unauthorized edition, brought up to date by Thomas Crowley, of

[1] Strype, *Annals*, vol. I, 217.

An Epitome of Chronicles, which Cooper immediately countered with a new edition and continuation of his own, called *Cooper's Chronicles*, printed by Berthelet and brought up to date in a new edition in 1565.

The example set by these publications was presently followed by Grafton, but more notably by John Stow and by Raphael Holinshed and his associates as successors to Reynold Wolfe. Grafton had helped to manage the printing of the Great Bible under Henry VIII and had continued to reissue that work until Mary's coming to the throne in 1553. He had also held a patent for printing service-books and, under Edward, the Book of Homilies and the Book of Common Prayer. At the death of Edward he published the proclamation of Lady Jane as queen and lost his privileges, but now with Elizabeth on the throne he was free to resume his activities. In 1563, drawing heavily on Cooper, he published an octavo *Abridgment of the Chronicles of England*, and in 1568 a folio *Chronicle at large*, both printed by Richard Tottel.

Meanwhile John Stow had entered on his long career as chronicler and antiquary. He tells us that about 1563 he was asked by the printer Thomas Marsh to correct 'the old common abridgement, which was first collected [out] of Lanquet and Cooper's epitome, but then much corrupted with oft reprinting'. He is here referring to the unauthorized *Epitome* of 1559. The short-comings of that compilation had prompted Grafton to publish his own *Abridgement*, but Stow approved even less of the latter work, and himself entered the field in 1565 with a small octavo called *A Summarie of Englyshe Chronicles*, which he followed the next year by a still smaller *Summarie of Englyshe Chronicles ... now abridged*. Printed in the first instance by Marsh, these books were frequently reprinted by a succession of other printers and regularly brought down to date by the author.

With Stow the chronicle became a standard literary commodity and the preparation of such works a profession. In 1580 he added to the series a substantial quarto, called *The Chronicles of England* and after 1592 *The Annales of England*, which was regularly brought up to date in succeeding editions by the author and after his death by Edmund Howes. But this was not all. At the conclusion of the 1604 edition of *Annales*, he informed the public that he had also expected 'to publish or leave to posteritie a farre larger Volume' on the history of England, 'long since by me laboured at the request and commandment of the Reverend Father Matthew Parker, Archbishop of Canterbury'. But this project had in the meantime been anticipated by the publication of a work which he describes as 'Raigne Wolfe's collection and other late comers by the name of Raphaell Hollinshead his Chronicles'.[1]

Reynold Wolfe, a German from Strasbourg, had established himself as a printer in London by 1542. He procured the use of the old charnel-house at St Paul's for his shop, and under Henry became the king's printer for the learned languages. Under Edward he published Ponet's Latin catechism and his *Defence of the Marriage of Priests*, Peter Martyr's treatise on the sacrament, Cranmer's work on the same subject and his reply to Gardiner's attack. Under Mary, Wolfe limited his publications to inoffensive subjects, but his name appears high on the list of charter members of the Stationers' Company, and at the confirmation of the charter under Elizabeth he was Master of the company. Regaining his privileges, he printed Jewel's *Apologia* and both of its English translations.

But his devotion to his adopted country and the Protestant cause did not stop at printing. He was acquainted with John Leland, and at the latter's death in 1552 acquired some of his materials and embarked on a project of historical compilation on his own account. Holinshed reports that 'that worthy Citizen Reginald Wolfe meant in his life time to publish an universal Cosmography of the whole world, and therewith also certain particular Histories of every known nation.' Holinshed himself, according to his own statement, was engaged by Wolfe 'to take in hand the collection of those Histories',[2] though according to Stow he was no more

---

[1] Stow, *Survey of London*, edited by C. L. Kingsford (1908), Introduction.

[2] Holinshed, *Chronicles* (1577), Dedication; Stow, *Survey* (Kingsford ed.), Introduction; F. S. Isaac, *English Printing Types of the Sixteenth Century* (1936); E. G. Duff, *Century of the English Book Trade* (1905).

than a hired translator. Wolfe died in 1572, leaving his project unfinished, and Holinshed and his associates, making use of his collections and drawing heavily upon Foxe, went on to compile the work known as Holinshed's chronicle. This was published in two folio volumes in 1577 with the title *The Chronicles of England, Scotlande, and Irelande,* and republished in three volumes ten years later.

Stow supplied the compilers with material and himself contributed to the second edition, but it is doubtful whether his failure to cap his own long series of publications of the same sort with a more comprehensive work was entirely due to his having been thus anticipated. The fact was that his interest had already turned to the antiquarian investigation which found fruition in his unique *Survey of London,* a work which added little to the by that time flourishing national legend.

Stow's contribution to our knowledge of London antiquities, which has given him his greatest fame, came only after he had spent many years supplying his contemporaries with information concerning the national past in the form of chronicles. Holinshed's *Chronicles,* illustrious for Shakespeare's sake, came relatively late in the long series of such compilations by many hands, on which in fact it rested. Any question as to the relative authenticity or value of this or that writer's account of any part of the past with which he may be concerned, or as to the validity of his conception of historical process or method, is here beside the point. The point which concerns us here is that Elizabethan chroniclers, taken all together, put the subjects of Elizabeth into familiar possession of a legend which they could set beside the legend of the chosen people recorded in the Scriptures and which, fabulous as it was, made them aware of themselves as a people having a common past full of meaning for the present.

The two works, however, which were especially designed to make that meaning plain and apply it most directly to the critical situation which arose in the first decade of Elizabeth's reign were Parker's *De Antiquitate Britannicae Ecclesiae,* which has already been discussed, and Foxe's *Actes and Monumentes.* The former was addressed solely to the rulers of the nation, the latter to rulers and people, but both writers were concerned with the same question, namely, as Foxe put it, 'whether the Church of England first received the faith from Rome or not'. His answer to this question was substantially the answer the queen had given to the Catholic bishops ten years before and which Parker and his successors were to go on giving for a long time to come. The true faith had come first to Britain directly from the apostles and only later from Rome, and at a time before Rome had fallen away from the truth.

There were, Foxe argued, 'six or seven good conjectural reasons' for holding this to be true.[1] 'Gildas our countryman' had affirmed that the apostle Philip sent Joseph of Arimathea to Britain in the reign of Tiberius, about the year of the Lord 63, and that Joseph laid the foundation of the faith among the people. Tertullian and Origen were also cited as testifying that the faith had come early to Britain, and Bede that the Britons celebrated Easter after the fashion of the eastern Church, which was taken to indicate whence the faith had come to them. Then there was Nicephorus, who said that the gospel had been carried to those western isles by the apostle Simon Zelotes. And if this was not proof enough, there was the supposedly indisputable fact that the Church had been established in Britain by King Lucius about the year 180. Lucius was said to be the son of King Coilus, the father also of Helena, the mother of Constantine. Mention of such a person occurred in Bede, and Geoffrey of Monmouth supplied a wealth of detail none the less convincing for the fact that no one could tell whence it came. William of Malmesbury elaborated the story still further, linking it to the legend of the founding of the Church at Glastonbury. Polydore repeated the tale with the amused incredulity of a well-bred Italian in 1513, and Fabyan incorporated it in his chronicle in 1515.[2]

As put together out of these sources by Foxe in 1570, the story runs as follows. In the time of the Emperor Commodus, Lucius,

[1] Foxe, I, 305-11.

[2] T. D. Kendrick, *British Antiquity* (1950); J. A. Robinson, *Two Glastonbury Legends* (1926).

son of Coilus, King of the Britons and founder of Colchester, 'hearing of the miracles and wonders done by the Christians at that time in various places,' wrote to Eleutherius, Bishop of Rome, asking to be instructed in the faith. In response to this request the good bishop sent Fugatius and Damian to convert and baptize the king and his people. Lucius thereupon converted all the heathen temples in the realm into Christian churches, the twenty-eight head-priests or 'flamins' into bishops, and the three arch-flamins into archbishops respectively of London, York and Glamorgantia. He also applied to the Bishop of Rome for instruction in the laws of Rome, 'thereby likewise to be governed, as in religion now they are framed accordingly'.

Foxe gives the full text of the Bishop's reply, which, however, later historical scholarship has been able to trace no farther back than the fourteenth century. 'Ye require of us,' Eleutherius is said to have written, 'the Roman laws and the emperor's to be sent over to you, which you may practise and put in use within your realm.' But the answer to this request was that, since the king already has the law and the faith of Christ along with both parts of the Scriptures, he needs nothing more. 'Out of them by God's grace, with the council of your realm, take ye a law, and by that law (through God's sufference) rule his kingdom.' For the king is God's vicar in the realm and the people are his to cherish, maintain, rule and defend in the faith and law of Christ. 'You shall be a king while you rule well; but if you do otherwise, the name of a king shall not remain with you, and you shall lose it, which God forbid.' Foxe clinches the argument with Isaiah XLII. 4: He shall not faint nor give over till he hath set judgment in the earth; and islands shall wait for his law.

Nevertheless the life of the faithful in Britain as elsewhere was to be one of recurring struggle against an enemy working both from without and within. Lucius died without issue, and 'such trouble and variance fell among the Britons (as it happeneth in all other realms, and namely in this realm of England, whensoever succession lacketh) that not only they brought upon them the idolatrous Romans and at length the Saxons but also enwrapped themselves in such misery and desolation as yet to this day remaineth ... For sometimes the idolatrous Romans, sometimes the Britons, reigned and ruled as violence and victory would serve, one king murdering another, till at length the Saxons came and deprived them both.' From this point Foxe's narrative goes on reign by reign as a digest from the chronicles, always returning to the same conception of history and the lessons to be derived from it. Every episode in the contentions of native rulers and people with alien intruders, of Christian Britons with heathen Saxons, of Christian Saxons with heathen Danes, and of Christians in general with defection within their own ranks, is presented as but one more engagement in the spiritual war which fills all time.

At every stage, however, the outcome depends upon the success or failure of rulers in defending the faith and their subjects in the faith. Thus Arthur is introduced not as the fabulous conqueror or the king of romance, whose exploits Foxe declares to be 'more worthy to be joined with the Iliads of Homer than to have place in any ecclesiastical history', but as the godly prince raised up by providence to withstand heathen invaders and give stay and quiet to his people.[1] Vortigern on the other hand, for compounding with Hengist and marrying his daughter, the mother of all the mischief that ensued, is held up as 'an example to all ages and countries what it is first to let in foreign nations into their dominions but especially what it is for princes to join marriage with infidels.' The Britons, princes and people both – here Foxe cites the famous passage in Gildas which turns up later also in Milton's *History of Britain* – bring the judgment of God on themselves, whence it comes that the Saxons swarm over the land and drive the Church into the wilderness of Wales.

Coming then to the Saxons, their kings, their conquests, their conversion, their afflictions in turn under heathen invaders, Foxe finds history having the same lesson to teach. Godly princes defend, ungodly betray the faith, and the people work their own undoing by disobedience. The exemplary king is now Alfred, renowned for his wars against the enemies of Christ and his

[1] Foxe, I, 323.

people, for his laws, for 'the virtuous institution of his life', for his knowledge of good letters and his 'princely desire to set forth the same through all his realm'. These qualities are especially pointed out in order 'to move other rulers and princes in these our days to imitation or else to show them what hath been in times past in their ancestors.'[1]

The method of the preachers whose ministry Foxe proposed to emulate was to choose a case or example from the Scriptures, to explicate and analyse the chosen text according to commonly understood principles, and then to apply both text and doctrine as explicitly as they could or dared to the particular case and circumstances of the auditory. This was also Foxe's method when he came to explicate the lessons of history. Having established the apostolic origin of the faith in Britain and the principle of godly kingship in contrast to its opposite as exemplified by the stories of British and Saxon kings, he went on to recount God's mercies and judgments as exemplified also in the chronicle of Norman and Plantagenet kings from the Conqueror to the end of Edward III. Since this period still fell within the thousand years of peace which ensued to the Church after Constantine, there were as yet no true martyrdoms to be recorded. But since these were the last three hundred years of that millennium, Antichrist was beginning to stir in anticipation of his being set loose again, and the Bishops of Rome were encroaching more and more on the authority which God had vested in civil rulers over all men within their domains.

Hence from this point on Foxe intercalates stories of English kings striving to fulfil their vocation with stories of Roman pontiffs striving to subject kings and emperors to their will, and he does not hesitate to apply these stories to the instruction of Elizabeth, her government and people. 'According to the order which I have begun,' he says, he intends to tell something of each king's reign 'although not pertinent to our ecclesiastical history'. Yet this, he explains at another point, was not really to stray from the subject, but merely to extend its limits in order that 'both kings and such as climb to be about them may take the better

[1] Foxe, II, 21-31.

example by the same, the one to have the love of his subjects, the other to flee ambition and not bear themselves to brag of their fortune and state, how high so ever it be, considering with themselves nothing to be in this world so firm and sure that may promise itself any certain continuance and that is not in perpetual danger of mutation unless it be fastened by God's protection.'[1]

Foxe closes his account of Saxon kings by remarking that their fall showed once more 'what it is for princes to leave no issue or sure succession behind them' and 'what dangers oft do chance to realms public by foreign marriage with other princes'. The record of English kings after the conquest was to yield many more examples of the mutability of fortune when unstayed by divine grace, examples of English rulers faithfully endeavouring or weakly failing to protect themselves and their people against the intrusions of foreign powers and the encroachments of successive popes or their representatives and emissaries upon civil rulers everywhere, but especially in England. This was, of course, the common theme of all Protestant propaganda. What Foxe was doing was to apply the argument to the situation coming to a head in England's relations with the papacy and the Catholic powers in 1570, and to support the charge with what seemed an abundance of irrefragable evidence accompanied by pictorial illustrations of persons, places and events.

The effect in the circumstances which immediately ensued was to fix in the minds of the people, or at any rate of a controlling portion of them at the centre of power and influence, an image of themselves as a nation and of the papal power as the nation's prime enemy, an image which long outlasted the particular occasion. The people were led to think that the crucial test of the fidelity of English kings to their appointed role as defenders of the faith and the people in the faith was this ever recurring challenge to royal supremacy. The test of the people's fidelity was the temptation to rebel when rulers were led to give way by corrupt and ambitious advisers.

Foxe's method was not to tell everything that was known or

[1] Foxe, II, 666–7.

supposed to have happened in each king's reign – he refers his
readers to the chroniclers for that sort of information – but to give
such details as would sustain the moral of each episode and of the
whole sequence. Proceeding thus, he revealed a talent for turning
the material he gathered from sources here and there into seemingly artless narrative which passed presently into the common
stock of popular fable and familiar reference. Hence many of his
stories came to be told and told again, often without regard to his
part in setting them afloat. It was he who brought to the Elizabethan public the timely tale of the humiliation of the Emperor
Henry IV, illustrated by a woodcut of the emperor with his wife
and child waiting for absolution at the Pope's gate at Canossa, and
this tale was quickly followed by another, also illustrated by
woodcut, of the Pope treading on the Emperor Frederick's neck.[1]

It was also Foxe who first popularized the story of Henry II's
contention with Becket. He tells it in such detail and at such length
that he says, 'peradventure I may seem in the story of this one man
to tarry too long', but he offers the excuse that 'the weaker sort,
who have accounted him a saint' have 'in themselves little understanding to judge and discern in the affairs of men'. Foxe presents
the case for Becket with an appearance of fairness but will not
have him to be a martyr. The man died not for the Church but
only for the 'possessions, liberties, exemptions, privileges, dig-
nities, and superiorities' of the Church. 'He was full of devotion
but without any true religion, zealous but clean without knowledge. And therefore as he was stiff and stubborn of nature, so ...
[he] turned to plain rebellion.' Becket disobeyed his own natural
sovereign, obeyed the Pope, and sided with the French against his
own countrymen. Henry did wrong not in proceeding against
him but in not proceeding against him, as any Tudor sovereign
but one would have done, for treason according to law. 'Yet
would I have wished again the law rather publicly to have found
out his fault than the swords of men not bidden nor sent to have
smitten him, having no special commandment either of the prince
or the law so to do.' It was a judgment of the Lord upon Henry

[1] Foxe, II, 189–96; *A. and M.* 1563, 25, 41; 1570, 232, 263.

that he had in the end to abase himself before the Pope and the monks, while the rebel Becket was 'taken up and shrined for a new saint'.[1]

In the same vein Foxe tells Elizabeth and her subjects the story of King John, the classic case of a king of England at loggerheads with the king of France over the succession to his throne and with the Pope over control of the English Church. As the story is here told, John and the realm have been placed under an interdict by the Pope, and the king of France has undertaken to enforce the Pope's sentence, but is repulsed by the English navy. Thereupon the Pope, acting through his agents and emissaries and taking advantage of John's own evil-doing, stirs up strife and confusion among the English barons. Hence the king is led to surrender his crown to the Pope's legate in token of his submission, after which everything goes wrong with him. 'Since I submitted myself and lands, England and Ireland, to the Church of Rome (sorrow come to it) never a thing has prospered with me.' Though the Pope now tries to call off the King of France, the dauphin lays claim to the English crown and invades the realm with the connivance of the English barons. Yet providence has not abandoned England. The barons learn in the nick of time that the French usurper intends, having secured the crown for himself, to execute them for treason and give their estates to his own followers. So the barons return to their allegiance, drive out the French, and, John dying, seat his son upon the throne.

The episode of John's demise serves to drive the point of the story home. While noting that the chroniclers differ in their account of this occurrence, Foxe follows the version of the story which has it that the king was poisoned by a monk of Swinstead at the sacrifice of his own life but with absolution promised by his abbot. A full-page woodcut illustrates the manner of the king's taking off. Here was a timely cautionary tale not soon to be forgotten. Holinshed told it again with additional details in 1577 and 1587. An anonymous playwright put it on the stage at the time of the Armada in a play which Shakespeare found it worth while to

[1] Foxe, II, 196–258.

revive and rewrite. Whether in doing so he also went back to
Holinshed and Foxe as he did on other occasions is immaterial. By
his time four printings of Foxe's book and two of Holinshed had
made the story common property of the Elizabethan public.[1]

Coming to Edward III, Foxe reached a turning point and a
climax in his account of the mercies and judgments which may
befall kings and their people. Edward he presents as, to begin with,
the perfect model of a prince 'renowned for many singular and
heroical virtues, but principally ... for his singular meekness and
clemency towards his subjects and inferiors, ruling them by gentle-
ness and mercy without all rigor or austere severity' and as 'above
all other kings of this realm unto the time of King Henry VIII ...
the greatest bridler of the pope's usurping power and outrageous
oppressions.'[2] And yet, 'as times do change so changeth commonly
the cause and state of man;'[3] Edward falls under the spell of a
concubine and the power of popish bishops. His successor
Richard II, 'starting out of the steps of his progenitors, ceased to
take part with them who took part with the gospel.' Hence his
fall, 'not by the blind wheel of fortune but by the secret hand of
Him who directeth all estates.' That story, Foxe tells his readers,
'is sufficiently contained in Robert Fabyan and in the king's
records in the chronicle of St. Alban's and in other histories at
large.'[4] He himself has now something to tell of more serious and
pressing import even than the falls of kings.

For according to the time scheme revealed in the Apocalypse
the fourteenth century – Edward III's accession occurred in 1327 –
saw the end of the thousand years of freedom from persecution following Constantine's triumph two hundred and ninety-four years
after the death of Christ in the thirtieth year of His age. That is to
say, the year 1300 or thereabout was 'the year of the letting out of
Satan according to the prophecy of the Apocalypse' and so the year
when the persecution of the elect was due to break out anew.[5]

If anyone were inclined to doubt whether this prophecy had in
fact been fulfilled, he had but to consider what had been happen-

[1] Foxe, II, 319–42.   [2] Foxe, II, 806.   [3] Foxe, III, 3.
[4] Foxe, III, 216–17.   [5] Foxe, II, 722–6.

ing in the world since that date. Meanwhile, however, we must note what had been happening to Foxe himself since his return from exile. Having collected and published the stories of a number of victims of persecution under Mary, he had come home to have more such stories put into his hands. Friends and patrons among the newly appointed bishops at Canterbury, London and other places opened episcopal registers and other public records for his examination. Fourteenth- and fifteenth-century chronicles and other materials salvaged from the wreckage of monastic libraries were also made available to him. He had access to the queen's library, and judging from the frequency of the notation 'ex accomodato D. Matth. episc.' in the margins of his book, he had the free run of the great collection of books and manuscripts which Parker was gathering together. Some of these things Foxe would be called upon to edit and John Day to print. Here, besides the printed works of such writers as Fabyan, Polydore and Bale, was a wealth of material for enlarging upon the history of the Church and the monarchy since that crucial prophetic date in the early fourteenth century.

Out of this material Foxe was able to recast and enlarge his account of Wyclif and his successors as it appeared in 1563. Quite truthfully he assured the queen, nothing like his book could have been produced in England under any king since the conquest until the halcyon days of her own rule. What happened therefore to the martyrologist of 1559 should be clear. He became possessed by the kind of excitement which overtakes the historical investigator when he uncovers untouched documentary evidence supporting a view of the past to which he is already emotionally and imaginatively committed. The excitement may be no less genuine and intense when the investigator's motives and standards are something less than pure or correct according to the criteria of a later time.

The excitement of discovery added to partisan zeal meant that Foxe found it difficult to leave anything out, and the result is sometimes something that looks like confusion. Yet he knew well enough what he was about. He was discovering the discrepancy between the facts as we find them – or think we find them – in the primary sources, and the general or summary statements of secondary authorities who may simply be repeating one another. It was not the least of John Foxe's distinctions that he discovered, so to speak, the Public Record Office and the use that could be made of what was to be found there. He acknowledged that he depended upon Fabyan, Polydore, Halle, Grafton, Cooper and other chroniclers for the background of his story, particularly that part not germane to his principal theme, but he was able to claim properly enough that he had gone behind the reports of such writers to the sources by the light of which their statements and conclusions were to be judged. He criticized Polydore in particular on the ground that 'writing of so many things which he never saw, [he] doth not voutsafe to cite unto us those writers of whom he borrowed', and he wondered 'if it be true what I have heard that he ... also burned a heap of our English stories'.[1]

Foxe strewed his own text and margins thick with references to his sources and came near to snowing his readers and opponents under with primary documents. Chronicles were all very well, but one had to consider whence their information came and what purpose they were intended to serve. 'If ye would show out of them the order and course of times, what years [occurred] of dearth and plenty, where kings kept their Christmas, what conduits were made, what mayors and sheriffs were in London, what battles fought, what triumphs and great feasts were holden, when kings began their reign and when they ended, etc.' – as to such things, he says, since it does not matter much whether the statements are true or not or whether anyone believes them or not – 'the chronicler serveth to good purpose and may have his credit.' But not so as to such matters as religion, 'which are to be decided and bolted out by evidence of just demonstration'. On such matters 'the records must be sought, the registers must be turned over, letters also and ancient instruments ought to be perused, and authors with the same compared; finally, the writers amongst themselves one to be conferred with another, with diligence to be

[1] Foxe, III, 750.

laboured and with simplicity, pure from all addition and partiality, to be uttered.'[1]

Whether Foxe lived up in all respects to these professions of scholarly rectitude, whether the evidence he poured forth in such abundance and with such particularity proved what he said it did, are questions which can be answered only on grounds that lie beyond the limits of the present inquiry. Not surprisingly, he made mistakes which his adversaries pounced upon and which in some instances he was at pains to correct. But as to the effect of his approach to the whole subject of authority in religion, there can be no question whatever. It was to bring the subject for better or worse into the arena of public discussion and to put the discussion on an historical or quasi-historical rather than a metaphysical or logical basis.

When he came to the fourteenth century, Foxe found himself with such an abundance of previously untouched documentary material on his hands as no earlier period had afforded. The modern historian, contemplating the same material, sees in it the disintegration of the culture of the high Middle Ages, the decline of the empire, the demoralization of the papacy, the consolidation of the Valois monarchy and the Hapsburg dynastic empire, the advance of an urban, commercial, capitalistic civilization in Italy, the Rhineland and Flanders, the break-up of the feudal system in England under the stress of war, plague, rebellion, dynastic confusion, and the contention of great lords and great prelates with one another for mastery in state and Church.

To Foxe, brooding upon all this by the light of his own time, light that came to him from such writers as Bale, Flacius, the centuriators of Magdeburg, Crespin, Sleidan, and the German and French reformers, the fourteenth century seemed naturally enough the time when Satan had indeed broken loose again to seize upon the see of Peter, persecute the elect, and impose his power upon England. Now popes strove with one another and with kings and emperors for dominion in this world, suborned bishops to oppress the people, and sent forth swarms of friars to corrupt and despoil

[1] Foxe, III, 373-7.

them. Hence the king of England fell into evil ways, his successor betrayed his kingly trust, and a subject usurped his throne.

But Foxe was not content to stop at the conclusion that all the troubles that befell England after Edward III were due simply to this disruption of the law of degree in the state. The cause lay deeper than that, for 'the whole state and condition not only of worldly things but also of religion was so depraved and corrupted' as to be beyond mere human help or remedy. 'The only name of Christ remained amongst Christians, but his true and lively doctrine was as far unknown unto the most part as his name was common unto all men ... Scripture, learning and divinity was known to a few, and that in the schools only, and there also turned and converted almost to sophistry. Instead of Peter and Paul, men occupied their time in studying Aquinas and Scotus and the master of sentence[s].' The Word was forgotten and men were dazzled instead by ceremonies and traditions. 'The people were taught to worship no other thing but that which they did see, and did see almost nothing which they did not worship ... All the whole world was filled and overwhelmed with errors and darkness. And no great marvel, for why, the simple and unlearned people, being far from all knowledge of the holy scripture, thought it sufficient for them to know only these things which were delivered them by their pastors and shepherds and they on the other part taught in a manner nothing else but such things as came forth of the court of Rome.'[1]

At appropriate points in the nearly four hundred pages which Foxe allotted to English kings from Edward III to Richard III, he summarized the events of each reign and returned to the theme of godly kingship. Most of these pages, however, he devoted to instances and contemporary testimonies or reports of the errors and abuses of the unreformed Church. These he presented in what seems a somewhat haphazard order but with an intention consistently enough sustained. Readers could here learn that three centuries before their own time Marsiglio and Occam had each declared that under the law of God popes had no authority over

---

[1] Foxe, II, 792–5.

kings and emperors. They could learn that Dante in his 'canticle of purgatory' and that Petrarch in his epistles had declared the Pope to be the whore of Babylon. 'And if time would serve us to seek out old histories,' Foxe goes on to say, 'we should find plenty of faithful witnesses of old ancient time to give witness against the pope.'[1] If most of these witnesses came from Flacius, that made no difference in the effect on English readers.

Certainly it did nothing to diminish the probative effect of the English documents here brought before them, such as Edward III's letters to the Pope, which Foxe found in the chronicle of Robert Avesbury, 'remaining in the library of J. Stevenson citizen of London', or as 'an old ancient writing intituled "The prayer and complaynt of the Ploughman" ', or as a Lollard tract reprinted from the text published by Tyndale at Antwerp in 1531, or as a popular fable ridiculing the Pope which Foxe alleged that he had found in Froissart, or as an abstract of Archbishop Fitzralph's address to the Pope attacking the mendicant orders, or as Nicholas Cresme's sermon also addressed to the Pope on the sins of the higher clergy.

However, of all these witnesses to the breaking out of Antichrist in the fourteenth century, the most important was Wyclif. Everything that had happened to Foxe since his flight to Germany had served to fix in his mind the conception of this man's role in the providential scheme of things which had been suggested to him first by Bale. 'At what time,' he declares, 'all the world was in the most desperate and vile estate and that the lamentable ignorance and darkness of God his truth had overshadowed the whole earth, this man stepped forth like a valiant champion ... Even,' in the words of Ecclesiasticus, 'as the morning star being in the midst of a cloud and as the moon being full in her course and as the bright beams of the sun, so doth he shine and glister in the temple and church of God ... What time there seemed in a manner to be no one so little a spark of pure doctrine left or remaining, this foresaid Wyclif by God's providence sprang and rose up, through whom the Lord would first waken and raise up again the world.'[2]

---

[1] Foxe, II, 704–23.   [2] Foxe, II, 791–5.

The Lessons of History

This account of Wyclif, evoked by Foxe out of the materials he found at hand in his own time and fitted by him into his version of the traditional Christian view of history, was echoed by Holinshed, who recommended, however, that it be read 'at large' in the pages of Foxe himself. It has not commended itself to historians who have written later on the subject. The Wyclif conceived by the modern historian was a late medieval theologian and disputant in the schools at Oxford who was drawn into service in public life. The public life of his time revolved confusedly about the aged king and the boy who was presently to succeed him. It was a time when the wearer of the crown was having to contend or compound for support in the realm with the ramifying power of the papacy. The great nobles, the rich prelates, and the favourites of the court vied with each other for mastery in the state. Parliament pressed for reform. The secular clergy strove against the mendicant and monastic orders. Fanatics and enthusiasts among the laity and lower clergy attacked the orthodox priesthood, and the peasants and the poor rose up against their overlords and rulers. Wyclif became involved in these contentions when his patron John of Gaunt, Duke of Lancaster, enlisted his abilities in controversy with William of Wykeham, Bishop of Winchester, and William Courtney, Bishop of London, soon to be made Archbishop of Canterbury.

Wyclif began by arguing the case for spiritual equality and religious poverty against the entrenched privilege and wealth of the hierarchy and the monastic orders, backed as they were by Rome. But having embarked on this argument, his own dialectic led him on and on. Presently he found himself urging the authority of the Scriptures and the vocation of preaching against the authority of the priesthood in the administration and discipline of the sacraments, and finally against the doctrine of transubstantiation. At another time and in other circumstances he might have been allowed to expatiate upon such ideas undisturbed in the insulated freedom of the schools, but these were extraordinary times. More ardent and reckless spirits who were anything but academic disputants were soon pressing Wyclif's ideas to more extreme conclusions, and he thus came to appear, perhaps in some degree unwittingly, as the intellectual leader and champion of a popular revolutionary movement which was not, of course, permitted to come off. This was his undoing. He brought upon himself the wrath of Archbishop Courtney, the condemnation of the Pope, expulsion from Oxford, forced retirement to his country living at Lutterworth, and, thanks to Foxe, a secure place in the legend of the English reformation. The movement associated with his name and influence went threateningly on and the champions of orthodoxy and the established order went on arguing against him and his followers for a generation or more after his death, leaving a rich deposit of documentary materials.

The Lollards were put down or driven underground, but their ideas and the story of their activities along with those of their academic inspirer were abundantly put on record by their adversaries. The Carmelite Thomas Netter of Walden or some other member of his order gathered up the principal documents in the dispute extending to 1428. A copy of this work, *Fasciculi Zizaniorum Magistri Johannis Wyclif*, the only copy now extant, came into the hands of John Bale and so of his friend John Foxe. But Foxe also had the use of a manuscript chronicle of events from 1328 to 1388 which he found in the library of Archbishop Parker. This was the work of an anonymous monk of St Alban's and, though hostile to the Lollards and to Wyclif and his patron John of Gaunt, it was full of circumstantial detail.

The story that Foxe put together out of these materials does not present the medieval schoolman entrapped by circumstances in a situation the implications of which were quite beyond his ken. It is the story, told as though it had happened yesterday, of exactly such a victim of persecution as those whose stories had come to Foxe in his exile. It describes Wyclif, moreover, as the first such victim since Antichrist's locking up a thousand years before. Though lacking the usual dreadful climax, it concludes with an episode which suited Foxe's purpose just as well. Forty-four years after Wyclif's death, the Council of Constance condemned him posthumously as a heretic and ordered his remains dug up and cast out of consecrated ground. 'What Heraclitus would not laugh,' Foxe writes, 'or what Democritus would not weep to see these so sage and reverend Catoes occupying their heads to take up a poor man's body so long dead and buried ... and yet peradventure they were not able to find his right bones but took up some other body and so of a Catholic made a heretic.' An accompanying woodcut depicts an archdeacon with his summoner and other officials burning the dead man's bones and pouring his ashes into the stream beside Lutterworth church.[1]

From this point on *Actes and Monumentes* in 1570 served as a history of the Protestant Reformation designed for the subjects of Elizabeth I – not, of course, for later readers with other ideas as to how history should be written or what course reformation should have taken. Foxe was as certain as Aylmer that Wyclif begot Huss, Huss begot Luther and Luther begot truth, but it did not occur to him that England should wait for truth to come to her from Germany. It had come to England straight from the apostles and had remained there ever since through all vicissitudes. Foxe's account of the Reformation included the struggle of the elect everywhere, but it was chiefly occupied with the struggle of one English ruler after another to keep the faith pure and defend the people in the faith. This was the central engagement in the whole age-long struggle of Christ and Antichrist. With a mind full of the anxieties of the present crisis of that conflict in England, Foxe went on to reap the fresh harvest of stories and of details pertaining to the stories he had already published to be yielded by the records now available to him in the collections of Parker, Bale and other friends, and in episcopal registers, royal archives and parliamentary rolls, always taking pains to stress the authenticity of his texts.

Thus from episcopal registers at Canterbury, Hereford and Norwich, Foxe was able to give verbatim reports of Lollards who had been examined by authorities of the Church in the reigns of Richard II, Henry IV and Henry V. He printed what purported to be William Thorpe's own account of his examination by Archbishop Arundel exactly 'as we received it, copied out and corrected

[1] Foxe, III, 95–6.

by Master William Tindall', who had indeed published the story somewhere on the Continent about 1530. Foxe wished that 'for the more credit of the matter' Tyndale had printed the report in the writer's 'own natural speech wherein it was first written', but in default of that he assured his readers that he and his printer had Master Whitehead's word that he had seen 'the true ancient copy'. Foxe drew his account of John Purvey, next on his list, from that person's own writings as reported by his adversaries in *Fasciculi Zizaniorum*, and he went on to give 'a certain godly and most fruitful sermon' by one Wimbledon, preached about the same time at Paul's Cross and now printed in the very language in which it was written in an old worn copy belonging to the Archbishop of Canterbury.

To William Sawtrey and John Badby he assigned a place of special significance in his bede-roll of Lollard martyrs. Each of these men, for disputing against his superiors concerning the doctrine of the Mass, had been condemned and handed over for punishment by the civil authorities under the newly adopted statute of 1401, *de heretico comburendo*. A single-column woodcut depicted Sawtrey in billowing flames with 'Jesus have mercy' coming from his lips. A more realistic and dramatic picture showed Badby calling on Christ while penned in a cask on a heap of burning faggots at the centre of a vigorously drawn group of men on foot with flaming brands, a gentleman on horseback directing proceedings, and rows of clergy with folded hands looking on. Some pages farther on the picture of a poor man with a bundle of straw on his back illustrated the manner in which recanting heretics were required to do penance. Finally Foxe rounded out his account of the Lollards with the story of Sir John Oldcastle, which Bale had originally put together out of *Fasciculi Zizaniorum* and the chronicles. In the meantime Nicholas Harpsfield,[1] the ejected Archdeacon of St Paul's, now a prisoner in the Fleet, had attacked certain inaccuracies in the previous edition of Foxe's book and argued against the claims of the Lollards to be considered martyrs, and Foxe concluded his account of Oldcastle

---

[1] Alanus Copus (pseud.), *Dialogi Sex* (1566).

with a vigorous reply and a statement of his standards and procedures as an historian.

But he was not forgetting that Wyclif had begotten Huss. As
the true faith had in the beginning started up first in Britain and
spread thence to other lands, so it had done again in the fourteenth
century. Hence into his history of Yorkist and Lancastrian kings
Foxe interjects an account of Huss and his followers on the Continent and of the Councils of Constance and Basle. How much of
this he drew from Cochlaeus's *Historiae Hussitarum*, Aeneas
Sylvius's *Commentarii* and the other authorities so freely displayed
in the margins of his book, and how much from the compilations
of the indispensable Flacius, it is not necessary to inquire. It was
enough for Foxe's public that, in addition to the seemingly unanswerable proof of his position drawn from English records, he
also brought forward a seemingly overwhelming array of testimony to the struggles and sufferings of reformers on the Continent
drawn from the most impressive continental sources, including
Catholics themselves.

Neither did Foxe forget that he was also writing history for the
instruction of the queen and her subjects in their mutual responsibilities as ruler and ruled. He gave no detailed account of the
contentions of York and Lancaster, but left no doubt as to his
opinion of the outcome. Richard II was a lawful king unlawfully
deposed. After him came 'three wrong kings in a row, under
whom all the noble blood was slain up and half the commons
thereto', and the wrong was later compounded by the murder
of the Protector, Duke Humphrey, 'a true-hearted Prince'.[1]
Edward IV, while not wholly given over by God, was properly
chastened for his wantonness and for trusting too much to the
inconstant people. Richard III was a usurper justly overthrown,
and Henry VII was a true prince sent by providence to put things
right again. All this was in close enough accord with the Tudor
party line, which with the accession of Elizabeth became also the
Protestant party line, but, so far as Foxe was concerned, with a
significant variation.

[1] Foxe, III, 216–21; I, 93–4.

The Lessons of History

The commonly understood moral of the story was that all the troubles that befell the realm after the deposition of Richard II were a judgment on rulers and people for that violation of the universal law of subordination in the state. We have been told that belief in the existence of such a law was a fixed element in what has been described as the Elizabethan world view. The philosophic historian must, however, resist the temptation to suppose that the generations he writes about were more philosophical, more consistent in their ideas, and more given to living up to them than men commonly are in any time we know anything about. If the Elizabethans had at all times subordinated every other consideration to the obligation to respect the law of degree in the state, the outcome would have been very different from what in fact it became – different for Elizabeth, still more for her successors. The law of degree was one thing, but there were practical conditions it could not be made to fit, angles to the Elizabethan view of the world which pointed another way, offences of other sorts on which divine justice must also be expected to fall. There were implicit and unacknowledged but inescapable restraints on the authority supposed to be vested in rulers in the nature of things, limitations upon the obedience that might in fact be safely demanded of subjects. These things were not usually mentioned to Elizabeth, who understood them anyhow without being told, but Foxe made them explicit enough in a cautionary way in his version of the history of her predecessors.

Granted that the Lord required every man to be content with the station in life to which he had been called under the government of Church and state, it was also understood that the Lord required his vice-gerent in the state to defend the faith and preserve the people in the faith. But what could be the function of an historian if it was not to expound the judgments of the Lord upon rulers as revealed in the record of the past? The principle of degree in the state Foxe assumes to be axiomatic, but he says little about it. In his view of the matter, the deciding reason for the judgment which overtook Richard II was his yielding to the dictation of the Pope in the suppression of Wyclif and the gospel. The king's giving way to evil counsel gave occasion to evil doing on the part of his subjects, and the lesson for other rulers was plain. 'What danger it is for princes not to have knowledge and understanding themselves but to be led by other men's eyes and especially trusting to such guides who through hypocrisy both deceive them and devour the people.' Not that Richard's offence excused Henry's, who proved to be a king 'to the godly ... ever terrible, in his actions immeasurable, of few men heartily beloved.' He was, Foxe says, 'the first of all English kings that began the unmerciful burning of Christ's saints'. Consequently judgment overtook him too; an evil conscience, the rebellion of subjects, death by strange disease.[1]

Coming to Henry V, Foxe was aware that a legend had sprung up about that monarch's exploits which ignored the judgment supposed to follow from father to son, but he declined to meddle with that story. He told instead the story of Henry's betrayal of Oldcastle, the friend of his youth. 'This king in life and all his doings was so devout and serviceable to the Pope and his chaplains that he was called of many the prince of priests.'[2] With that Foxe goes on to Henry VI, who, he says, was 'a good and quiet prince, if he had not otherwise been abused by some'. His ruin 'came not without the just appointment of the Lord either for that Henry of Lancaster's house were such enemies of God's people and for the burning of [Sir John Oldcastle] and many others or else for the unjust displacing of King Richard II or else, thirdly, for the cruel slaughter of Humphrey the good Duke of Gloucester, his uncle.'[3] The burning of still another of Wyclif's followers in the reign of Edward IV is noted with the observation that 'since the time of King Richard II there is no reign of any king to be assigned hitherto wherein some good man or other hath not suffered the pains of fire for the religion and true testimony of Christ Jesus.'[4]

Coming to the close of Henry VII's reign, Foxe sums up the lesson to be learned from the history of all the English kings since the Conqueror. Though worldly prosperity is more often the lot

[1] Foxe, III, 229.   [2] Foxe, III, 579.
[3] Foxe, III, 753.   [4] Foxe, III, 755.

of the wicked than the godly, yet history shows that 'such princes as have most defended the Church of Christ committed to their governance from injury and violence of the Bishop of Rome have not lacked at God's hand great blessing and felicity.' Rulers who have not shielded the faithful from persecution at the behest of foreign tyrants have on the other hand been denied God's favour, 'so that either they were deposed or, if they flourished for a while, yet they did not long continue.' The Henries II and III and the Edwards I and III were rulers of the one sort; Edward II, Richard II, the three Henries who followed, and Richard III were of the other.

As for Henry VII, it was to be wished that that otherwise prudent and temperate prince had checked the Papists' rage against the flock of Christ, for 'when the Church of Christ beginneth to be injured with violence and to go to wrack through misorder and negligence, the state of the commonwealth cannot long endure without some alteration and strike of God's correction.' So it might have happened in this king's reign, but just as persecution was beginning to grow hot under his rule, God called him away, and his posterity made up for this his one defect.[1]

So much as to the duty of princes as exemplified by the history of English kings. But Foxe was still intent upon having his readers see their own history within that universal frame revealed by St John and the prophets. Consequently, before going on to relate what happened under Henry VII's posterity, he introduced an account of the contemporaneous advance of the Turks, recapitulated his account of the progressive betrayal of the Church by the papacy, and linked the two by a restatement of his apocalyptical conception of historical chronology.

In the contention of Catholic and Protestant powers in Europe, the advance of the Turks was a complicating as well as a profoundly disturbing factor. Solyman died in 1566 and Foxe heard of the event while his book was being printed. Out of an array of sources which he cited in text and margin he had by that time probably compiled his spirited account of the Ottoman Turks

[1] Foxe, IV, 131–3.

from their rise about 1300 to their taking of Constantinople in 1453, their siege of Vienna in 1529, and their subjugation of Hungary. The remarkable thing from his point of view about these astounding occurrences was that they fitted exactly the time-scheme he had deduced from Revelation. He admitted that 'although touching the precise points of years and times it is not for us to be exquisite therein', nevertheless, 'where diligence and studious meditation may help to our knowledge, I would not wish negligence to be a pretence to ignorance'. The beast in the Apocalypse bore the number 666, and in the year of the Lord 666 arose 'the detestable sect of Mahumet'. The year 1300 was the thousandth year after the chaining up of Satan in the time of Constantine, the year in which Satan was to break out again, and the year in which Ottoman, the first of the Turkish conquerors, began his reign. But it was also, as Foxe had already demonstrated, the time when the corruption of the visible Church which began with Hildebrand reached its completion with Boniface VII. Obviously, therefore, the Turk and the Pope were but the two faces of Antichrist broken loose again for the testing of God's elect, and thus prophecy was confirmed twice over in a revelation redoubled of God's purpose in history.

But this raised a disturbing question. Why should God appear to be thus forsaking His own? Why was it that nothing had sufficed so far to halt the infidel's advance? The Bishop of Rome had spared no effort, princes had spared neither expense nor courage, to withstand him. Yet they had lost the whole of Asia and were scarce able to defend the little of Europe that was left to them. To these questions Foxe gave, of course, the right Protestant answer. The danger now threatening Christendom was the same danger which English saints and English kings had often confronted and overcome. Nothing happens in this world without forewarning. Let no one suppose 'that such a great alteration and mutation of kingdoms, such a terrible and general persecution of God's people ... cometh without the knowledge, sufferance and determination of the Lord before.' The whole power of Satan 'goeth with the Turk' and man has no power of his own to stand against him. Nothing can suffice 'but only the name, spirit, and power' of the Lord 'going with us in our battles'.

That is, nothing but the Word. 'He that presumeth beyond the promises in the Word expressed goeth not but wandereth he cannot tell whither ... He that made us without our counsel did also redeem us as pleased him. If he be merciful, let us be thankful. And if his mercies surmount our capacities, let us therefore not resist but search his Word, and thereunto apply our will; which if we will do, all our contentions will soon be at point.' The Turks are an affliction sent by the Lord to teach us to trust only in Christ thus revealed. 'Let us not presume to admix His majesty with any of our trumpery. He that bringeth St George or St Denis as patrons to the field to fight against the Turk leaveth Christ, no doubt, at home.'[1]

What with all the new material he had turned up in this place and that, Foxe's book had now grown to two volumes, and he brought Volume I to conclusion in a remarkable statement entitled, 'The proud primacy of Popes paynted out in Tables, in order of their rising up by little and little, from faithfull Byshops and Martyrs, to become Lordes and governours over kynges and kyngdomes, exalting themselves in the Temple of God, above all that is called God. etc. 2 Thes. 2.' This was a concluding indictment of the papacy drawn up out of decrees and pronouncements of popes themselves. It was accompanied by twelve 'tables' or pictures, one to a page, depicting successive stages in the degeneration of the Church. They begin with a pagan emperor torturing Christian saints, followed by Constantine embracing the Christian bishops and in the next picture advancing them to a seat beside himself. But after that they show an emperor kissing the Pope's toe, Henry IV prostrate being crowned by the Pope's foot, kept waiting in the snow at Canossa and finally surrendering his crown. Then comes King John giving up his crown to Pandulph, Henry III kissing the legate Langton's knee, the Emperor Frederick 'shent' for holding the Pope's stirrup on the wrong side, the Pope mounted on his mule with the emperor on foot at the beast's head

[1] Foxe, IV, 21, 93–122.

and kings marching before him, the Pope in his litter borne high on men's shoulders, again with kings on foot preceding him. Here was the graphic epitome of Foxe's polemic history of the papacy, published for the edification of the queen and her subjects on the morrow of the Pope's bull of excommunication against her and placed in the book at the conclusion of Volume I where no one could miss it.

The Book of Martyrs had now grown to two volumes, and the second volume was given a separate title, framed in the same representation of the two Churches at the last judgment which appeared in the first: *The second Volume of the Ecclesiasticall history, conteynyng the Actes and Monumentes of Martyrs, with a generall discourse of these latter persecutions, horrible troubles, and tumultes, styrred by Romish Prelates in the Church, with divers other thynges incident especially to the Realme of England and Scotland, as partly also to all other foreine nations appertaynyng, from the tyme of K. Henry the VIII to Queene Elizabeth our gratious Lady now reygnyng.* A woodcut on the first page of the text showed Henry VIII on his chair of state with his council in a circle about him. Another woodcut farther on in the book showed the king seated, sword in hand, with Pope Clement under his feet, Cranmer presenting him with the Bible, Cromwell standing by, and Pole and Fisher interceding frantically for the prostrate pontiff.

The latter picture, which replaced the former at the beginning of the volume in later editions, expressed the dominant theme of the work from this point on. Everything in its account of the Church and of British and English kings up to this point had been planned to lead up to Henry VIII. Everything from this point on was intended to lead to Elizabeth. This is the case though the second volume, like the first, may seem to the impatient modern reader to be a heaping together of disparate parts and materials. But if we consider the work as a whole, giving due attention to the author's comments in text and margin, his explanation of his apocalyptical time-scheme, his running heads, his references to sources, and his woodcut illustrations, we shall see the work coming more and more sharply into focus upon Elizabeth and the situation which after 1570 closed in more and more threateningly upon her.

A scant four hundred pages had sufficed for Foxe in 1563 to cover the reign of Henry VIII. He took at least a hundred and sixty more than that in 1570, the pages being a third larger. He presented much of the same material but rearranged, edited, and extended with fresh information drawn from printed and written sources and from personal reports. He began with a few notorious cases of persecution early in the period, and then went on to sum up the progress of reformation on the Continent after Huss. Drawing upon Luther, Melancthon, Sleidan, Flacius, Crespin, Pantaleon and similar sources, he supplied the English public with its first comprehensive printed account of Luther and the German reformers, Zwingli and his successors at Zürich, the reformers and martyrs of the Rhineland and Switzerland, including – though briefly – Geneva, and of France, Piedmont and Italy. In the nineteenth century this account came in for severe criticism by writers with greater information and a different point of view, but again we are concerned here with what was known and thought in the time not of Victoria but of Elizabeth.

Having thus brought his readers up to date concerning the state of the Protestant cause on the Continent, Foxe was ready to go on with his account of the war against Antichrist in England, where the records were particularly rich for his purpose and where the danger had again become particularly acute. Everything depended more than ever on Elizabeth's continuance at the head of the state, on her adherence to the role of godly prince and defender of the faith, and on the loyalty of the people to her person. There could consequently be no letting up in his endeavour to instruct both her and her subjects in their obligations under the law of God as exemplified in history and scripture. Elizabeth needed especially to be taught the lessons of her father's case and indeed to have various matters in the history of his reign explained, or at any rate explained away.

Foxe provided an account, therefore, of the great alterations made by Henry in Church and state, following the outline of

events supplied by Halle's chronicle and filling in details from
official documents and other contemporaneous sources. As before,
however, this part of the story had to be handled circumspectly.
Henry was the queen's father; yet he had sent her mother to the
block and at one point disinherited Elizabeth herself. He had
liberated Church and nation from subjection to the Pope; yet he
had sanctioned the persecution of undoubted saints. He was, in a
word, a prime example of the godliness to be looked for in princes
but also of the human propensity to err, to which even the
godliest princes were liable. The paradox was, of course, an all too
familiar one, and Foxe resolved the difficulty in the usual way by
putting the blame for Henry's misdeeds upon his advisers. 'If
princes have always their counsel about them, that is but a
common thing. If some time they have evil counsel ministered,
that I take to be the fault rather of such as be about them than of
princes themselves.' When the king had good counsel, he did
much good; when wicked counsel prevailed, then 'how much
religion and all good things went prosperously forward before, so
much on the contrary side all revolted backward again.'

Thus whatever wrong the king did was reduced to the venial
error of following wrong advice, and Foxe was able to turn the
story of Henry's reign into another cautionary tale for princes, for
one prince in particular, illustrating the endless war waged by
Antichrist upon the realm of England and its rulers. Here, moreover, was not simply a pious tale, but an authentic history of real
persons and well-remembered events. The central character was,
of course, Henry himself, described as a prince 'of his own nature
and disposition ... so inclinable and forward in all things virtuous
and commendable that the like enterprise of redress of religion
hath not lightly been seen in any other prince'.[1] But always the
greater the inclination to the good, the fiercer the onslaught of the
enemy both within and without. This universal condition of
man's spiritual life explained the vicissitudes of royal policy,
swayed now by good, now by evil counsellors. Of the latter sort
the first was Wolsey, 'this glorious cardinal ... more like a prince

[1] Foxe, V, 605.

than a priest ... making (in a manner) the whole realm to bend to his beck and to dance to his pipe', all that he might keep the king subject to the church and the church to himself.[1] So it came about that, when conscience compelled Henry to seek the annulment of his marriage to his deceased brother's wife, he fell victim to Wolsey's schemes for getting himself made pope. But providence ordering otherwise, Wolsey's machinations were discovered, and Henry, acting now with the advice of all the learned men of Christendom, freed the realm and the Church from their subjection to Rome and himself from the quandary of his marriage. 'Seeing this Gordian knot would not be loosed at Rome, he was driven even against his will (as God would) to play the noble Alexander himself and with the sword of his princely authority knapt the knot at one stroke clean asunder, loosing as it were with one solution infinite questions.'[2]

The special instrument of providence for the accomplishment of this happy solution was the 'mother to our most noble queen now', the 'comforter and aider of all the professors of Christ's gospel'. And Foxe goes on to say of Anne, 'principally this one commendation she left behind her that during her life the religion of Christ most happily flourished and had a right prosperous course.' The causes which led the king to harden his heart against her are dismissed as groundless. For there was 'secret practising of the papists against her' and Gardiner 'was not altogether asleep'. Her vindication came in 'the evident demonstration of God's favour in maintaining, preserving and advancing the offspring of her body, the lady Elizabeth, now queen'.[3] And besides that, notwithstanding Henry's wrong-doing in her respect, providence directed him to the choice of another godly consort and the begetting of a godly prince to be his heir.[4]

Yet the war of Antichrist against the defender of the faith still went on. More and Fisher, Gardiner and Bonner sought to gain sole command of the king's ear in the hope of displacing Cromwell and Cranmer from his counsels. Foxe claimed to have many

[1] Foxe, IV, 589.   [2] Foxe, V, 55.
[3] Foxe, V, 62-4.   [4] Foxe, V, 137.

THE POPE SUPPRESSED BY HENRY VIII

informants still alive 'who are witnesses of these things which we report and greater things also than these'.[1] Among them surely were Bale, whose patron Cromwell had been, and Ralph Morice, who had been Cranmer's secretary. With information derived from such sources, Foxe produced a lively account of Cromwell's career as faithful counsellor to the king and providential instrument of reformation. 'For indeed such was his nature that in all his doings he could not abide any kind of popery or false religion ... and less could he abide the ambitious pride of popish prelacy, which, professing all humility, was so elated in pride that kings could not rule their own realms for them.'[2] However, 'these snuffling prelates' could as little abide Cromwell, and so it came about that Gardiner by traducing him to the king procured his fall. Nevertheless (here Foxe is drawing upon the reports of Henry's last days relayed to him by Cranmer's secretary), the struggle which always went on within the king's breast took one more saving turn before the end. Wishing Cromwell were alive again, he thwarted Gardiner's machinations against Cranmer and intended, if he had lived, 'to have repurged the estate of the church ... so that he would not have left one mass in all England'.[3]

The lesson Foxe would have Henry's daughter deduce from the story of her father's doings was plain. 'Such malicious makebates about princes and parliaments,' he declares, 'never lacked in commonwealths,' and the lesson is enforced by a string of historical instances including Edward II, Richard II, Duke Humphrey, the queen's own mother 'falsely condemned', and herself 'as falsely disinherited'. And the lesson is further driven home by stories interspersed here and there with woodcut illustrations of martyrs who had suffered during Henry's reign at the hands of his evil counsellors. Some of these stories had already been independently printed. Some had appeared in less detail in Halle. Some Foxe had himself published in earlier editions of his work. But he was now able to add more stories and more details, many of them furnished by living witnesses.

Thus in his account of Thomas Bilney, put together out of

[1] Foxe, V, 369. [2] Foxe, V, 398–9. [3] Foxe, V, 692.

information drawn from Latimer's sermons, surviving members of Latimer's circle, and Archbishop Parker, Foxe established the legend of that protomartyr of the new religion. In his account of Tyndale, drawn from Tyndale's own writings, the printed attacks of More, the notice in Halle, and the reminiscences of Bale and others, he established the story of that sainted hero's struggle to get the Word translated and put into print. In the account which he obtained from 'ancient and credible persons' of 'Master Garret, curate of Honey-lane London', who was prosecuted for peddling Tyndale's New Testament and other forbidden publications among the scholars at Oxford, he told a lively tale which shows what difficulties the government encountered in trying to suppress both the agents and the products of the printing-press. In his account of John Lambert, based on a tract by the man himself and the testimony of someone identified only by initials, Foxe tells a story which illustrates a pattern of behaviour which was to have many followers and cause much trouble. It is the story of a born agitator and fanatic determined to win attention for himself and his cause by putting his inquisitors and superiors in the wrong in a noisy public scene, even at the cost of getting himself burned for heresy in the market-place.

There was also the notorious case of four men prosecuted at Windsor, Foxe says 'for righteousness sake and for the gospel', but really for suddenly drawing back the curtain on the future which the circulation of books in vernacular print was preparing for statesmen in Gardiner's position and with his convictions. The story had been recorded briefly by both Fabyan and Halle and somewhat inaccurately by Foxe himself in 1563. However, he had now received a vivid and full account of the affair from John Marbeck, who, he says, 'was also then a party to the said doings and can testify the truth thereof'. Marbeck had been organist at the royal chapel of St George and, though no scholar in the strict sense of the word, he was an assiduous student of his English Bible and a self-taught theologian of sorts. The men prosecuted with him were a chorister of the chapel who, it was said, smelt of the new learning and was given to ridiculing common practices in the Church as superstitious and idolatrous; a tailor and church-warden, who remonstrated at the blasphemous absurdity of a sermon preached by the vicar of his church; a common priest, who had been drawing large crowds to hear him preach the gospel.

What Marbeck's story reveals concerning these men and himself is that recent changes in the Church, but especially the circulation of the Bible, had set all sorts of people in town and chapter speculating and pronouncing on subjects supposed to be beyond their competence and to disputing with persons not accustomed to having their own pronouncements called in question. When the conservative reaction of Henry's closing years set in, the authorities presently took the situation at Windsor in hand, with the result that these four, having had the ill luck or the indiscretion to call particular attention to themselves, were arrested on suspicion, examined, convicted of heresy, and sentenced to be burned.

Marbeck, however, was pardoned by the king and lived to tell the story and, assuming that Foxe printed it exactly as it came to him, to tell it extremely well. Marbeck's account of his own part in the affair is particularly revealing of the effect which the Bible and the books now springing into print relating to the Bible were having on ordinarily unheard-of and unheard-from people. Though he understood Latin, as he said, 'but simply', Marbeck was obviously a man of considerable native intelligence. The authorities upon arresting him found him possessed of a collection of books and papers which they regarded as surprisingly large for a man of his standing and profession. Asked why he had made such a collection, he replied, 'for none other cause ... but to come by knowledge, for I, being unlearned and desirous to understand some part of the scripture, thought by reading of learned men's works to come sooner thereby.' When the Matthews Bible came out, he borrowed a copy and began transcribing it for his own use, and Richard Turner, a chantry priest at the royal college at Windsor and a fellow of Magdalen College, later a Marian exile, suggested that he might also transpose into English a Latin concordance to the Bible.

By the time of his arrest he had got as far as the letter L. But

Gardiner and the others who examined him refused to believe that a man who knew so little Latin should have accomplished what Marbeck claimed to have done without assistance. He demonstrated to them how he had used the English text to find his way around in the Latin, but they were still incredulous, and Gardiner was aghast that such a thing should be attempted at all. 'What a devil made thee to meddle with Scriptures?' 'If such a book should go forth in English, it would destroy the Latin tongue.' Convinced that someone with greater learning as well as heretical ideas must be behind Marbeck – there were in fact two persons against whom they hoped to get sufficient evidence to warrant an arrest – the bishop and his associates pressed the accused and his wife with alternate threats and promises to reveal their collaborators and instigators. But this, Marbeck saw clearly enough, meant that for him to clear himself, if that were possible at all, he must inculpate others in an offence to which he would not himself admit and of which his accusers could produce no proof other than the admission he refused to make. They finally gave up the attempt and secured his conviction on his admission that he had once transcribed at request an epistle of Calvin's against the doctrine of the Mass. Reprieved from the stake without recovering his papers, he began all over again and published his concordance in 1550 with a dedication to Edward VI.[1]

Such stories as these, whatever else may be said about them, reveal the growing apprehension which overtook men of conservative temper in Henry's government along with the extraordinary difficulties they encountered when they endeavoured to keep the process of revolutionary change from disrupting the established order. Gardiner was appalled at the idea of an English concordance to the Bible because he feared that, if the vulgar dialect were permitted to displace the universal language of the Church, England would be cut off from the life of Christendom at large and the authority of the Church in England would be completely subverted. The result could only be confusion of counsel, disregard of all due precedence, proliferation of error.

[1] Foxe, V, 474–97.

Wilful and unwary men would assume that the spiritual equality of all men before God meant that they were free to question the authority of their natural superiors. They would assume that the doctrine of election by grace meant that they were themselves already elected to salvation here and now with no further need for mediation on their behalf by the Church. They would assume that the anticipated final advent of the Redeemer meant that their deliverance from the necessary limitations put upon them by their natural superiors in this world was imminent. And all these errors went back to the cardinal erroneous notion that the salvation of mankind had been accomplished once for all by Christ on the Cross, that all anyone needed in order to partake in the fruit of that atonement was to believe in its sufficiency, and that all one needed in order to believe in its sufficiency was the Word, read in a book or heard from the pulpit.

It was, of course, not to be denied that the spread of such ideas on the Continent had led to profound disturbances in the established order accompanied by outbursts of revolutionary violence. It was not unreasonable to suppose that their unabated continuance in England would lead to similar results. But the difficulty in which Gardiner and others of his way of thinking now found themselves was to know how and at what point to halt the process of change they had themselves had a hand in starting. Unable to stop the issuance and circulation of the Bible and the flood of printed books which followed in its wake, they thought to offset their disruptive effect by insisting upon strict, explicit adherence to the doctrine and discipline of the sacrament as they understood it. The Act of Six Articles made deviation in that regard a capital offence. The Act *ex officio* gave the government authority to question suspected persons under oath. The Act *De heretico comburendo* prescribed the punishment. With these statutory implements at their command, the defenders of the ancient order in Henry's closing years and again under Mary undertook to uproot the seeds of subversion and expose its agents. The result was the series of hearings, trials and executions of which the only record to come down to us is in most cases that published by Foxe and based upon the reports of the accused and their friends, who were understandably in no state of mind to do justice to the intentions or the arguments of their examiners and judges.

Yet whatever the merits of their case, the champions of the old order were under a serious misapprehension and made a disastrous miscalculation. What they were attempting to do was to control by legal action under the authority of the state the thoughts, utterances and personal associations of persons who were not in the usual sense lawbreakers at all and who did not regard themselves as such. They were not, as in certain notorious cases on the Continent, typically uprooted peasants or unemployed labourers deluded by dreams of the millennium. No one of consequence in England objected to suppressing such people, usually stigmatized as Anabaptists. Foxe himself merely objected to their being burned. The men under attack in England could claim to be loyal subjects of the Crown with pretensions to literacy and respectability if not to learning and gentility, and they were able to count on a measure of agreement and support from many higher in the social scale. The government, having authorized the publication of the Bible in the common tongue and its setting up in churches, seemed to be saying to these people that they must not think or talk about what they read.

Under these conditions the government's proceedings against them and their responses fell into an all too familiar pattern. People were held on suspicion supported only by reports of informers or the tittle-tattle of neighbours and acquaintances. Charged with no specific offence against the law, they were required to answer on oath questions concerning their beliefs and associations which, they apprehended, were designed to make them expose themselves or their friends to prosecution for what offences they could not tell and were not told. They were pressed to save themselves by informing on others. And if they held back, they were required to answer precisely and correctly certain questions concerning the doctrines of the Church, intended, they believed, to entrap them into making statements which would lay them open to accusations of heresy. They for their part demanded to be told what they were being held for and who were their accusers. They demurred at having to swear in advance to testify concerning any matter whatever their inquisitors might choose to ask them about. They complained of being forced into making compromising and incriminating statements. They showed a strong repugnance to inculpating other persons. Pressed to declare what they believed concerning controverted points of faith, they asserted the authority of the Scriptures. Threatened with punishment, they appealed to the laws of the realm. Thus every examination, as Foxe reports it, tended to wind up in a dramatic scene in which an honest believer was shown pitting the plain truth of the Word against the super-subtle sophistries of hypocritical churchmen and a loyal subject of the Crown was shown asserting his rights as an Englishman against a popish prelate.

In such stories as these Foxe in effect set a pattern for common people to follow whenever government should invade what men were learning to think of as their rights. Then, after bringing his readers up to date regarding the progress of reformation in Scotland and the interdiction of both Luther and Henry by the Pope, he went on to 'the acts and things done in the reign of Edward VI'. Drawing upon the godly divines who had had the instructing of the boy king, Foxe told the story of his precocity, his egregious saintliness and his edifying early death. It was a story ready-made for setting before Elizabeth the pattern of behaviour she was expected to follow. It began with a woodcut of the young Josiah restoring the Bible to his people and sending the Papists packing back to Rome, purging the temples, burning the images, and promoting the preaching of the Word and the setting to rights of the font and the holy table.

Edward was depicted as 'a prince although but tender in years yet for his sage and mature ripeness in wit and all princely ornaments' superior to all but few. 'And first to begin with that which is the chiefest property of all extern things in a prince to be considered, that is, to be loved of his subjects ... never came prince in this realm more highly esteemed, more amply magnified, or more dearly and tenderly beloved of all his subjects, but especially of the good and learned sort ... and as he was entirely of his subjects beloved, so with no less good will he loved them again.' To these virtues he added 'skill and knowledge of tongues and other sciences, whereunto he seemed rather born than brought up'.[1] There were few sermons at which he would not be present taking notes. He could reason out of the Scriptures with the learnedest divines. He had all the gifts and graces necessary for the government of both state and Church. He was expert in affairs of exchange, skilful in the entertainment of ambassadors, attentive to poor men's suits.

But the feature of Edward's reign which Foxe singles out as unique is that 'he always spared the life of man'. Like Josiah he silenced the makers of idolatrous sacrifices and turned them out of their places, yet killed none of them. 'Amongst the whole number of the popish sort, of whom some privily did steal out of the realm, many were crafty dissemblers, some were open adversaries ... there was not one man that lost his life.' Merciful even to heretics, the young king argued with John Cheke for tolerance and pleaded with his council and with Cranmer himself against burning the Anabaptist Joan Boucher. 'What my lord,' Foxe reports him to have said, 'will ye have me send her quick to the devil in her error?' There were also, to be sure, the Dutchman George 'who died for certain articles not much necessary here to be rehearsed', and Thomas Dobbe, arrested early in the reign for speaking against the Mass, who died in prison. But besides these 'there was none else in all King Edward's reign that died in any manner cause of religion ... The rage of persecution ceasing and the sword taken out of the adversaries' hands, there was now no danger to the godly, unless it were by wealth and prosperity, which many times bringeth more damage in corrupting men's minds than any time of persecution or affliction.'[2]

Over against this portrait of the godly prince and the stories of such persons as Anne Askew and John Marbeck Foxe placed his running characterization of Stephen Gardiner, their common adversary, as the perfect image of the proud, overbearing, inter-

[1] Foxe, V, 699.   [2] Foxe, V, 698–704.

fering, time-serving, lordly prelate. The picture of Gardiner offered us by the judicious modern historian is that of the conscientious conservative statesman endeavouring to hold fast by established principles and institutions even while moving with the times. He had gone along with the king in rejecting the pretensions of the papacy, and he had supported up to a point the changes that followed. But the time came – sooner, to be sure, with him than with some others – when it seemed that the process of change had gone far enough and must be halted lest it go too far, as indeed it did or threatened to do when, at the accession of Edward, Gardiner's rivals took over the direction of reform. He then took a position of conscientious objection and stoutly maintained it until the accession of Mary, when he was vested with the chief responsibility for instituting a counter movement which soon began going to the opposite extreme. As Lord Chancellor Gardiner did his duty as he saw it in suppressing the leaders of the resistance to the queen's government, but as a humane man of moderating temper he appears to have been soon revolted by the excesses of his own partisans. He did not live to witness the disaster to his cause which he had been unable to prevent.

The Gardiner of the judicious modern historian bears little resemblance to the Gardiner whom Foxe impressed upon the imagination of his countrymen in the next reign. His animus was in the first place an expression of the resentment he took over from Bale against the supplanter of Cromwell and the prosecutor of Anne Askew. This was confirmed by the stories of the other victims of Gardiner's conscientiousness and by the records of both Gardiner's and Bonner's resistance to the changes put into operation by Cranmer and Ridley under Edward. Under Mary, Foxe saw in Gardiner the chief inquisitor and most impressive personality in the examination and prosecution of John Rogers, John Bradford and Roland Taylor. At the same time he saw in Bonner, whose lot it was as Bishop of London to examine and prosecute John Philpot and numerous other suspected persons, Gardiner's chief lieutenant and coadjutor.

But unfortunately for the reputation of both men, it could now more than ever be said, *litera manet*. The heretics it fell to them to proceed against on behalf of the old faith were men of spirit and ability who wrote particularly vivid and dramatic accounts of their experience in defending themselves and their cause, of their bearding these great churchmen in their pride, riddling all their arguments, and defying all their power, and once John Foxe had put the martyrs' stories into English print, there was nothing for a long time that could be done to retrieve the reputation of the men who sent them to the stake. It may well be that Gardiner withdrew in revulsion from participation in these affairs as the situation got out of hand, and that Bonner was the more or less reluctant agent of a policy he regretted. Nevertheless, it was natural enough that Foxe, with such materials at hand, should have pilloried both 'bloody Bonner' and 'wily Winchester' as the chief agents of Antichrist in Mary's unhappy reign.

Gardiner, however, for having in addition to everything else sought the destruction of the princess Elizabeth, was the prime offender.

> He was of a proud stomach and high-minded, in his own opinion and conceit flattering himself too much, in wit crafty and subtle, toward his superior flattering and fair spoken, to his inferiors fierce, against his equal stout and envious, namely if in judgment and sentence he anything withstood him.[1]

> Here hast thou (good reader) this stout prelate of Winchester with all his properties, doings, and qualities as in a certain anatomy proportioned out unto thee, whereby thou mayst boldly judge and nothing err in thy judgment what is to be esteemed of him by his fruits, as who was neither true protestant nor right papist, neither constant in his error, nor yet steadfast in the truth, neither friend to the pope, and yet a perfect enemy to Christ, false in King Henry's time, a dissembler in King Edward's time, double perjured and a murderer in Queen Mary's time, mutable and inconstant in all times.[2]

[1] Foxe, VII, 585.   [2] Foxe, VII, 603.

CHAPTER VI

The Dreadful and Bloody Regiment

༄

HAVING thus set forth the lessons of history for the edification of the queen and her subjects, in particular of the history of the Church and realm of England, Foxe came back on page 1,567 to 'the dreadful and bloody regiment' of Queen Mary. The remaining 736 pages were devoted to the stories of that time which he had been gathering, editing and enlarging upon in the successive editions of his book. They were, of course, the primary reason for the book's existence, and they continued to be its most memorable feature. But they were not the whole book. As more and more disturbing events followed hard upon one another after Mary's death, the occurrences of her brief unhappy reign came to seem not less but more significant, and the chroniclers who sprang up again on Elizabeth's accession promptly added the annals of those years to their compilations.

But Foxe did what no chronicler attempted. In 1563 and more extensively in 1570, he framed the stories of the Marian martyrs in a coherent account of the actors and events of Mary's reign sharply focussed on the single overriding issue of religion and keyed to the rapidly developing national crisis. Whether the facts and the meaning of the facts were in every respect what he made them out to be, we need not inquire. The historical importance of what he did lies in this, that his account of Mary's reign was the fullest, the most cogently conceived, and the most absorbing which reached the Elizabethan public, and that it was at once accepted as the most convincing and authoritative. Here was what ordinary Protestant Englishmen for generations to come were going to believe had happened at that crucial point in their national history.

The Dreadful and Bloody Regiment

The story as Foxe told it began with the evil omen of Mary's broken promise of toleration to the Suffolk men who had supported her claim to the throne, 'for though a man be never so puissant of power, yet breach of promise is an evil upholder of quietness, fear is worser, but cruelty is worst of all.'[1] From this he went on to Mary's successful assertion of her hereditary right, the repulse and fall of Northumberland, the repression of preaching and printing, the reinstatement of the Mass, the ejection of the reformed clergy, the annulment of their marriages, the debate in convocation concerning the sacrament, the preparations for the Spanish marriage, Wyatt's rebellion, the queen's speech at Guildhall, the execution of Lady Jane Grey, the harassment of the Princess Elizabeth, and, as the crowning event of Mary's first year on the throne, the arrest of Cranmer, Ridley and Latimer, their imprisonment in the Tower, their arraignment in a great disputation at Oxford in April 1554, followed by their condemnation and imprisonment. From this point Foxe goes on in his narrative to the queen's coronation, her marriage and false pregnancy, the arrival of Pole as papal legate, and the submission to and reconciliation with Rome.

But along with these events he also tells of the manifesto issued by a group of preachers under arrest in London, protesting against the treatment which their three leaders had received at Oxford and demanding for themselves the opportunity to argue for their cause under fair and free conditions. These men had been notable preachers under Edward and were being held in various London prisons in the hope, it would seem, that they would presently set an example for their followers by submitting and conforming. They chose instead to defy the government and argue their case on such grounds and in such a temper that Gardiner and his associates were left with no recourse but to prosecute them as heretics.

Yet strangely, as it seems to us, they still managed while in prison to communicate with their friends. How the stories of Rogers and Bradford got into circulation, we have already seen. Laurence Saunders, when deprived of his benefice at All Hallows,

[1] Foxe, VI, 387.

Bread Street, retailed his wrongs and his sufferings in letters to his wife and friends. John Hooper, when deprived of his bishopric, also told his story in letters to his friends. Rowland Taylor was sent to the King's Bench prison for resisting the intrusion of a priest into his church at Hadley, but his wife and a devoted servant saw to the recording of the fracas and its consequences. These were the earliest victims of the policy which Gardiner set in motion in January 1555, and their stories reached Foxe at Basle in time to be included in the Latin version of his book in 1559. He transposed them into English in 1563 with the accrual of more details. In 1570 he placed them in the context of his narrative of Mary's reign just after the notorious disputation at Oxford and the hollow triumph of the queen's Spanish marriage and the Catholic restoration.

But the queen and her government, having committed themselves to extreme measures by the execution of these leading preachers of heresy and conscientious disobedience, soon found that there was no stopping with these few, even though Gardiner may have been inclined to draw back. And Foxe, having begun by printing the reports which reached him in exile of Rogers, Bradford and the rest, gathered up many more such reports after his return home. Hence, along with the stories of the three high-ranking prisoners awaiting their fate at Oxford and the five preachers going to theirs from their London prisons, he went on in 1570 to tell the stories of some sixty-odd other persons burned in 1555, artisans, husbandmen, tradesmen, apprentices and the like in addition to a bishop, a number of persons classed as gentlemen and a few former monks and friars who had taken to preaching. This material with accompanying woodcuts took up the two hundred and sixty pages which brought the narrative to its next pivotal episode, the second arraignment and final condemnation and execution of Ridley and Latimer at Oxford in October 1555.

Foxe had been able to present that story in 1559 only in summary form. On his return from exile, having joined forces with John Day, he was able to make use of letters and other writings of both men, the reports of George Shipside, who had attended

Ridley, his brother-in-law, right up to the end, of Augustine Bernher, who had done the same for Latimer, and no doubt of other witnesses whose names are not known. Hence in 1563 Foxe was able to give a detailed account of each man's career, accompanied by texts of his letters and other writings, and to relate his appearance, demeanour, words and actions before the commission appointed by Pole as papal legate to examine and try them both. The story concluded with a circumstantial account of the things said and done in the denouement at the stake. In 1570 Foxe reprinted the story with a few insignificant changes and omissions and one memorable addition. The result, whatever one may think of it as history, was a vivid narrative presenting the English Protestant position on the two crucial issues of the Word as opposed to the Mass and of royal – which is to say national – supremacy as opposed to papal, and centring in two sharply differentiated and brilliantly characterized heroic figures.

The action of the story begins with the lord bishops of the commission taking their high seats in the divinity school, 'being then fair set and trimmed with cloth of tissue and cushions of velvet'. Ridley is brought in first and at once causes a great to-do by refusing to lift his cap or bend his knee at the naming of the Pope, though ostentatiously ready to show due obeisance to the queen. He is still every inch an Anglican bishop, still the resolute, resourceful dialectician, parrying every charge or argument brought against him until his inquisitors are moved to adjure him, 'Master Ridley, consider your state; remember your former degree, spare your body; especially consider your soul, which Christ so dearly bought.' Let him recant and repent, be reconciled and again joined to the Church like so many of his former associates. 'My lord,' he replies, 'I acknowledge an unspotted Church of Christ in the which no man can err, without the which no man can be saved, the which is spread throughout all the world, that is the congregation of the faithful.'[1]

Latimer, who has been kept waiting all this time in an anteroom, appears next and immediately interjects a personal com-

[1] Foxe, VII, 517–29.

plaint designed to embarrass his judges and win sympathy for himself. 'My lords,' he exclaims, 'if I appear again, I pray you not to send for me until you are ready. For I am an old man, and it is a great hurt to mine old age to tarry so long gazing upon the cold walls.' And though the presiding bishop apologizes for having kept him waiting, there is still no reasoning with him or stopping him from playing to the gallery. He scorns any role but that of mere preacher of the Word, and he has the preacher's sense for an audience, the preacher's confidence that he can make even a hostile audience attend to what he says and what he represents.

In the course of the discussion which now ensues, he refers to a certain book which, he says, makes the claim that scripture proves that the clergy have authority to rule all things as they will, and he appears not to know that the author of the book, the Bishop of Gloucester, is present as one of the commission. He exclaims at any rate, 'what a gelding of scripture is this, what a clipping of God's coin!' Whereat, we are told, the crowd of people standing by smiled, and in the rapid interchange that followed, with Latimer taking quick-witted advantage of his adversaries, the people laughed and then laughed again. Whereupon he turns on them with, 'Why my masters, this is no laughing matter. I answer upon life and death. *Vae vobis qui ridetis nunc, quoniam flebitis,*' showing that he could still manage a bit of Latin when it served his turn. Nevertheless the Bishop of Gloucester, nettled by the laughter, breaks in to say, 'Hereby Master Latimer everybody may see what learning you have,' and Latimer, not to be put down, blazes out with what is in effect another appeal to the audience, the audience beyond the walls of the divinity school as well as that within.

Lo, you look for learning at my hands, which have gone so long to the school of oblivion, making the bare walls my library, keeping me so long in prison without book or pen and ink, and now you let me loose to come and answer to articles. You deal with me as though two were appointed to fight for life and death, and over night the one through friends and favour is cherished and hath good counsel given him to encounter with his enemy. The other for envy or lack of friends all the whole night is set in the stocks. In the morning when they shall meet, the one is in strength and lusty, the other is stark of his limbs and almost dead for feebleness. Think you that to run through this man with a spear is not a goodly victory?[1]

The story goes on to their sentencing, their degrading, their handing over to the magistrate, their last conferring with such persons as are permitted to come to them, their marching severally to the place of execution. Ridley goes before like a bishop in square cap and fair black gown and tippet, both furred. Latimer comes after in his worn Bristol frieze frock with a buttoned cap and a kerchief on his head, his shroud hanging over his hose to his feet. Men's hearts were stirred, we are told, 'beholding on the one side the honour they sometimes had, and on the other the calamity whereunto they were fallen'. Ridley, as he passes the prison where Cranmer lay, looks up hoping to see his friend at the window, but Cranmer is inside, held in dispute by a Spanish friar set to badger him. Then Ridley, looking over his shoulder and seeing Latimer behind him, calls out, 'Oh be ye there?' and Latimer calls back, 'Yea, have after as fast as I can follow.'

Arrived at the stake, they find a great crowd awaiting them and have to submit to being preached over and charged with being Lutherans, Oecolampadians and Zwinglians. Ridley attempts to reply, but the vice-chancellor claps his hands over his mouth. Finally, after the usual preparations by the victims and the executioner, Foxe tells us, 'then brought they a faggot kindled with fire, and laid the same down at Dr Ridley's feet', and in 1563 the story goes directly on to its harrowing climax. In 1570, however, Foxe added that at this kindling of the fire Latimer cried out, 'Be of good comfort, Master Ridley, and play the man. We shall this day light such a candle by God's grace in England as I trust shall never be put out.'

[1] Foxe, VII, 529–34.

The Dreadful and Bloody Regiment

It is hard to believe that Latimer did not actually speak these long-to-be-remembered words, but whether in fact he did so and someone remembered them in time for Foxe to insert them into the story fifteen years after the event, or whether Foxe or someone else had the genius to put words so fitting to the man and the occasion into Latimer's mouth, there is no telling. One can only marvel, here as at other points in Foxe's book, at the unfailing gift which all sorts of English people in that time seem to have had at command for appropriate, expressive, dramatic speech.[1]

The death of Gardiner shortly after that of Ridley and Latimer enabled Foxe to add as epilogue to their story a concluding account of the character and career of their great adversary and so to fix upon the latter the stigma he was long to bear in public esteem. Next, after the stories of John Philpot and some lesser martyrs burned at Smithfield, came the story of Cranmer's final agony at Oxford in April 1556. The circumstances of the case, as well as the eminence of the sufferer, made this the most famous of the proceedings of the Marian government against the leaders of opposition, and ensured that there would be no lack of reports of what happened on the occasion for Foxe to make the most of for his purpose.

Henry VIII's archbishop was naturally enough the person whom the queen and the men bent upon doing her will held to be peculiarly responsible for the former rejection of herself and her mother and the lapse of the English Church from its historic obedience. Hence, after condemning him but before sending him to the stake, they sought to induce him to recant as publicly as possible. In the interval between the passing and the execution of sentence upon him, they subjected him to a prolonged working-over which left him without will or power to resist.

The result is not difficult to understand. He broke down, as men did and still do under such treatment, and put his name to a series of statements prepared for him to sign in which he apparently retracted everything he had come to stand for in the public eye. He was a man entrapped in the dilemma to which the beliefs

[1] Foxe, VII, 547-51.

of so many men of his age seemed to lead. He had formerly found it according to his conscience but also to his interest to put obedience to the ruler of the state above obedience to the Pope. Now the ruler of the state, whom he had bound himself to obey, repudiated the authority he had argued to be hers and required his return to the obedience he had rejected. But his prosecutors went too far. In sudden revulsion at the last moment, he seized the opportunity which they themselves imposed upon him to recant all his recantations in a resounding scene in St Mary's church, and to signalize what he had done by a dramatic gesture at the stake destined to be long remembered together with Latimer's last words.

Such, at any rate, was the story that Foxe put into circulation at the accession of Elizabeth. The Marian authorities, not wishing to be balked of the effect they had hoped for, published the recantations Cranmer had signed and an account of the circumstances. But enough of these reports reached Foxe at Basle to enable him to tell the story from his own point of view, including Cranmer's prayers and speeches at St Mary's, the most significant of the recantations which he had subsequently retracted, and a circumstantial account of his putting his offending hand first into the flame in the final scene. In 1563 Foxe drew upon official records for additional details, and in 1570 he rounded out the story with an account of Cranmer's career based upon the recollections of the archbishop's former secretary, Ralph Morice, which were compiled at the instance of Archbishop Parker.[1]

With the execution of Cranmer the Marian regime disposed of all the principal leaders of opposition to the restoration of the old religion who had not made good their escape to the Continent or found secure hiding at home. But as the difficulties and disappointments of the regime continued there was no stopping the prosecution of those who failed to conform to its demands. The last two years of the reign saw the burning of both the books and the bones of Bucer and Fagius at Cambridge, as well as the execution of several scores of lesser gentry, minor clergy, artisans,

[1] Foxe, VIII, 3–91.

husbandmen, housewives and the like. The stories of people such as these served to assure Foxe's readers that what great and famous personages had endured through faith in the Word, common people like themselves had also endured, and would still be having to suffer if providence had not intervened in their behalf by calling Elizabeth to the throne.

Drawing thus towards the close of his huge book, Foxe told again the story he had told in 1563 of Elizabeth's safe deliverance from the persecution she had shared with others of the faithful during her sister's reign, but he added now an account of Mary's last days and 'A briefe declaration shewing the unprosperous successe of Queene Mary in persecuting God's people, and how mightily God wrought against her in all her affairs'. The story of Elizabeth as princess showed her steadfastly enduring all the perils of the godly in those evil days. The story of Mary showed her committing all the mistakes that Elizabeth as queen was to be warned against. For Mary had made every possible mistake that an English ruler could commit. She had followed evil advisers; she had submitted to the Pope; she had married a foreigner and a Catholic; she had suppressed God's Word and persecuted His saints. Consequently He had confounded her in all her doings in less time and more completely than any of her predecessors except Richard III. He had 'so turned the wheel of her own spinning against her that her high buildings of such joys and felicities came to a castle-come-down'. 'And thus much,' Foxe concludes, 'touching the unlucky and rueful reign of Queen Mary, not for any detraction to her place and state royal, whereunto she was called of the Lord' but only that 'all readers and rulers may not only see how the Lord did work against her therefore but also by her may be advertised and learn what a perilous thing it is for men and women in authority upon blind zeal and opinion to stir up persecution in Christ's Church to the effusion of Christian blood.'

Yet though he speaks more than once of 'the dreadful and bloody regiment' of Queen Mary, of bloody Gardiner and bloody Bonner, he never applies the notorious legendary epithet to the queen herself, and in the end he writes of her with a certain commiseration for her personal tragedy. Defeated in all her plans, disappointed of all her hopes, she seemed, he said, 'neither to have the favour of God nor the hearts of her subjects nor yet the love of her husband'. It is indeed to Foxe that we owe the well-known story of Mary on her deathbed mourning 'for the king's majesty her husband, which was gone from her', but also telling those about her, 'when I am dead and opened, you shall find Calais lying at my heart.' The story came, Foxe says, from the queen's own attendants, 'Master Rise and Mistress Clarencius (if it be true that they told me which heard it of Master Rise himself').[1] Holinshed took it over word for word with due acknowledgment in 1587, along with the rest of Foxe's concluding account of Mary.

Such was the final full-blown design and make-up of the book which Foxe addressed so pointedly to the queen and her people in the crisis of 1570, issued again with a few changes and additions in 1576 and yet again with a few more in 1583. Our concern in these pages, let us not forget, however, is not with Foxe's short-comings as an historian but with the view of history, especially of recent history and the immediate predicament of England, which he put before readers in his own time. At no point in the work, huge as it was, did he lose sight of its purpose or falter in its design. He presented the stories of the Marian martyrs in what he took to be the true context of events in Mary's 'unlucky and rueful reign', and in the context of universal church history and the history of the English Church and monarchy since their beginning. History he conceived in terms of that age-long conflict between Christ and Antichrist within the breast, and of the two Churches within the world and within the Church itself.

Considered in this perspective, Foxe's Marian martyrology is seen to be not a mere heaping up of sensational and revolting stories, but a coherent whole centred on the traditional theme of the spiritual war which fills all time. The whole sequence of stories with its containing narrative is seen to revolve about the successive episodes in the spiritual struggle of the three leaders of the new faith as prisoners, disputants and martyrs in the Tower

[1] Foxe, VIII, 624–8.

and at Oxford. Closely linked to these key stories of Cranmer as the patriarch, Ridley as the militant advocate, and Latimer as the apostle of the religion of the Word, we have the stories of their immediate followers, the London preachers, whose stories were the earliest to reach Foxe for publication in 1559. But intermingled among all these in roughly chronological order we have the usually briefer accounts of other persons of various ranks which kept coming to Foxe's hands after his return to England. And finally, as the climax of the whole sequence, we have the story of the providential escape of Elizabeth herself from the same fate.

It was, of course, essential that these stories should conclude with a burning, and it was the burnings and the pictures of burnings which still stuck in people's minds when the disputes which led to such dreadful conclusions no longer seemed important or were but dimly understood. But those disputes and their implications are not to be passed lightly over or ignored if we seek to understand what the book meant to the people for whom it was intended. The reports of the Marian martyrs let us see at least a little way into the state of mind, the ideas, the motives and the modes of expression, also the illusions and prejudices, of the general run of people living at the time, of such people as do not usually get into the record of history as well as of such as do.

The experiences of the Marian martyrs as Foxe reports them revolve characteristically about a conflict of wills, repeated over and over again in varying detail, between a single individual certain of his direct, subjective knowledge of what he takes to be true and right, and the representatives of power in Church and state, demanding his instant explicit submission to constituted authority. Every story poses the same question in another set of human circumstances. Was a man bound at all times to stand by his own notion of his own condition as he had come to understand it through discourse by whatever channel, spoken, written, and – which now made all the difference – printed? Or was he obliged, putting all this aside, to behave and believe as he was told by authority, whose responsibility it was to direct him in such matters? Discussion of the question, however, always resolved itself into a dispute proceeding at cross purposes into semantic confusion concerning the nature of Christ's presence in the sacrament of communion. Jewel, as we have seen, had presented the Protestant position on that question in the dialectic of the schools. Foxe brought it before his readers in dramatic narratives about people they knew or knew about, people who might have been themselves.

Every story in his collection might be expected to conclude with the scene at the stake, but that scene was only the climax for which the reader was prepared by a series of scenes in which the martyr, assured by the Word of election to salvation and reassured by persecution, stands up for what he knows against an array of inquisitors drawn from the top-ranking members of the hierarchy. They for their part ply him with subtle, equivocating questions, designed to convict him of heresy out of his own mouth, an imputation he resents and a crime he abhors. He for his part riddles their arguments, assails their motives, and challenges their authority with what purports, as anyone may read for himself, to be plain truth in plain English from scripture. This done, he marches triumphantly off to testify before clouds of witnesses at the stake, having in the meantime usually seen to it that his own account of the affair should be conveyed in writing to his friends and sympathizers. Nothing could have been better calculated in the event to put his judges at a polemic disadvantage or to promote public interest in men like himself and in the Bible.

There was, of course, much behind that crucial question concerning the sacrament which finds no expression in Foxe's book and which he and his martyrs were in no state of mind to comprehend, namely the whole mystery of the atonement as the Church had been re-enacting it for ages past in the ritual of the Mass, setting it forth by means of chant, processional, drama, fable and the other arts, formulating it didactically and rationalizing it philosophically in doctrine. Who was to say that the redeeming, civilizing power of this great complex of ideas, beliefs and usages was no longer to operate in the Church and through the Church in the community at large? Certainly not Mary and such high-spirited counsellors of hers as Gardiner and Pole. To deny the validity of the sacrament as they conceived it was for them no venial error, but a deliberate attempt to subvert both Church and state. And by the same reasoning the debacle which was soon to overtake their well-meant endeavour to forfend disruption seemed no less inexplicable than appalling. For while the minds of men obsessed with their own notions of the meaning of the Word were closed to everything which justified the questions their inquisitors pressed so insistently upon them, their inquisitors for their part failed to comprehend what lay behind the answers their questions elicited.

The martyrs replied that, to all who acknowledged the atonement Christ had performed for them once and for all on the Cross, Christ was indeed really present in the sacrament of communion, present, that is, in spirit, which was all that mattered. These were the elect, and the communion of the elect was the Church. Whence had they got these ideas? Their adversaries said from Luther and Zwingli (seldom Calvin). They themselves said from the Scriptures and the fathers nearest to the Scriptures in time. In all this there was, needless to say, nothing new. The new thing which made all the difference was their having the Bible to read and refer to in English. For the experience of reading the Bible for oneself in the common tongue had been happening to increasing numbers of people in the last twenty years, while the Mass was being allowed to fall more and more under eclipse. As for the fathers, the one who meant the most to evangelists of the Word was Augustine, who took them back to St Paul, who taught them not only that a man may be born again, but also how he might know that the rebirth Paul taught him to look for had actually come to pass.

But what could seem more like the experience of Paul awakening to Christ in his vision than this awakening to what they took to be Christ speaking to them from the printed page? Well might Gardiner be taken aback at the thought of what the multiplication of books in the national vernacular might portend for the religion as well as the language of the universal Church. For to people disposed to respond to biblical legend, prophecy and poetry as presented to them in the language of Tyndale and Coverdale, the rites and the arts of the Church, dulled by use and abuse, even more the abstractions of medieval theology and metaphysics, would soon be emptied of meaning. More than that, the exciting experience of discovering the book and themselves in the book drew its devotees together in an intimacy more personal and intense than anything they had lately been accustomed to in the Church itself. Sacramental grace would seem to inhere not in oblation having to be continually renewed, but in the sense of having been mystically singled out from the general run of fallen men for salvation, and in the association with others sharing or striving to share in the same experience.

But this grace was something that had actually happened to them, not something to be argued about. Consequently every attempt of the representatives of authority to argue the question of the real presence with the man before them got nowhere, and, failing to convince him of his error by the ordinary processes of their dialectic, they could only demand his instant submission as a subject of the queen in her capacity as head of the civil state. Upon that the discussion would veer away from the question of the sacrament to the question of the nature and limits of authority in both the civil and the ecclesiastical realms, the relations of those jurisdictions to one another, the reciprocal rights and responsibilities of rulers and ruled in each.

The effect was not to break the impasse at which these discussions invariably arrived, but to shift the discussion to another ground on which the devotees of the Word could argue not merely from the assumption that they were members of the spiritual communion of the elect, but also with the consciousness of belonging to the community of Englishmen and the conviction that merely to be English was to be someone in particular, with particular claims to consideration.

What they would have to say on this ground to the accusation brought against them by the Marian regime was clearly forecast in the supplication which the London preachers addressed to the king, queen, and parliament in January 1555. Anticipating their fate under the newly re-enacted law for the punishment of heretics, they avoided so far as they could any argument over the sacrament, and defended their position on grounds of law and constitutional right. They had shown themselves, they said, under the late king to be 'true, faithful and diligent subjects ... in the sincere ministering of God's holy word as in due obedience to the higher powers'. They had acted 'as the laws of God at all times and the statutes of the realm did then allow'. Notwithstanding which, the present government has cast them into prison, deprived them of their livings, possessions and books, and slandered them as heretics. All this has been 'contrary to the laws of justice, equity and right'. Now, since their accusers appear both as witnesses against them and judges over them, they beg that they may be allowed to answer the charges brought against them before king, queen and parliament or before impartial arbiters. They beg the privilege of answering 'either by mouth or writing in plain English tongue', and of having 'free use of all their own books' and opportunity of 'conference among themselves'. This was in a word to demand the privileges which Englishmen would soon be laying claim to as their ancient constitutional rights. 'Which things being granted,' they conclude, it will presently appear that they are no heretics, but rather true believers and faithful subjects, wrongfully accused by the queen's evil counsellors.[1]

The signers of this supplication could hardly have expected the Marian government to accede to their request. They were writing for the record, which Foxe was to see should be laid before the English public. For what they were doing was to impugn the queen's authority to proceed against them on the ground that she was herself in effect impugning the authority of the sovereign who preceded her on the throne. This was, of course, to expose the anomaly which plagued the queen's policy from the beginning. If subjects were to be prosecuted by one ruler for acts legally performed under a former, what surety could there be in law for anyone at any time? And this was to raise the perplexing

[1] Foxe, VI, 550-53, 589-90.

question to which these discussions always led as to where the responsibility of decision in affairs of state might be supposed to lie when one absolute authority commanded one thing and another the opposite. Granted that the ruler was subject only to the commands of God, was he authorized to revoke the commands of a former ruler, also issued, as must be supposed, in accordance with God's will? And where was the revelation of God's will to be looked for: in the dictates of the Church as voiced by the hierarchy, or in the Word as found in the book and expounded by the pulpit? The London preachers charged with heresy made no explicit attack on the right of kings to rule as they would, but there was no need for them to do so. They had but to impale their adversaries on the horns of a dilemma that would not down, see to getting their stories told in their own way, accept the glory of martyrdom, and so shift the moral burden of proof to their opponents.

How the constitutional debate concerning sovereignty and subjection was rendered into the dramatic terms of conflict between opposing personalities is to be seen in the story of John Rogers, the first on Foxe's bede-roll of Marian martyrs. Here was the true saint with only God on his side standing up for the true faith against an overbearing, hypocritical, sophistical Lord Chancellor with a pack of time-serving sycophants at his heels. When after a few preliminaries they come to the question concerning the sacrament, the bishops all stand up and take off their caps, but Rogers scornfully refuses to be drawn into debate on the subject. He tells them flatly that their attempted distinction between real and substantial on the one hand, and corporeal on the other, is incomprehensible.

But he is no meddler in such matters. It was enough for him that 'even as the most part of your doctrine in other points is false and the defence thereof only by force and cruelty, so in this matter I think it be as false as the rest.' This was to beg the question, but it was also to counter the imputation of heresy with a charge of inhumanity compounded by illegality. They have kept him in prison for almost a year and a half and let him have no penny of income from his church livings. They reply, thus letting him change the subject, that he has no just title to those livings because Ridley who bestowed them was a usurper. 'Was the king therefore a usurper,' he demands, 'which gave Dr Ridley the bishopric?' His questioner, before he can think what he is saying, answers yea and then tries to hedge. But this only brings the discussion back to ground on which, as the story goes, Rogers has his inquisitors at a clear disadvantage.

Conformity to the long-accepted doctrine of the sacrament, to the apostolic Church, to the celibacy of the priesthood, to the use of Latin, and to all that these things implied in respect to the established order of society – here was the rock to which Gardiner had held through all the changes of three troubled reigns. Obedience to the Pope, on the other hand, he had been willing, like Henry and many another, to forswear with no sense of breaking irretrievably with the past. Royal supremacy under Edward, however, had entailed heterodoxy and revolution, and Gardiner had been put into the invidious position of having in obedience to conscience to deny obedience to constituted authority, and this, embarrassingly enough, was precisely the position taken by the man now before him.

There is no telling whether, if royal supremacy had continued under Edward to support orthodoxy on the sacrament, Gardiner would have continued to abjure the papacy, or whether, having learned his lesson, he would in any event have returned to his former obedience. But to the martyrs this question was not germane. He and the bishops who stood with him under Mary, some of whom had, unlike him, accommodated their consciences to the Edwardian dispensation, were now open to the accusation, just or not, that they had been moved to return to the obedience they had lately forsworn by the basest of motives and were only seeking to justify what they had done by persecuting better men than themselves for not doing likewise.

Of this equivocal aspect of his adversaries' position, Rogers took full advantage. The question which, as he tells the story, provoked the liveliest altercation between them was whether he would obey the queen, seconded now by an Act of parliament, and acknowledge the supremacy of the Pope as head of the Church in England. His answer is that he has always obeyed the queen and never dissented from the true Catholic Church. What, they demand, not when he acknowledged King Henry to be the Church's head? Never the head in spiritual things, he replies, but only Christ. 'Yea ... if thou hadst said so in his days (and they nodded a head at me with a laughter) thou hadst not been alive now.'

But Rogers let that pass in order to ask, did they really believe what they now professed, seeing that, with parliament agreeing, they had been preaching and writing the contrary for twenty years past? 'Tush,' says Gardiner, 'that parliament was with most great cruelty constrained.' 'With cruelty,' Rogers exclaims, 'why then I perceive that you take a wrong way with cruelty to persuade men's consciences.' At this another inquisitor explains that what the Chancellor means is that the present parliament has greater authority than the former because 'more condescended to it', and this sets Rogers off on another tack. 'It goeth not, my lord, by the more or lesser part, but by the wiser, truer and godlier part,' but Gardiner will not let him go on. They have ten more out of Newgate to examine. What does he propose to do, 'enter into one church with the whole realm as it is now, or not?' And Rogers gives the right Protestant answer. 'No, said I, I will first see it proved by the Scriptures.'

Let him have pen, ink and books and he will show them the truth. 'But still the lord chancellor played on one string.' 'Should, quoth he, when a parliament hath concluded a thing, one or any private person have authority to discuss whether they have done right or wrong?' 'I answered shortly that all the laws of men might not, neither could, rule the word of God, but that they all must be discussed and judged thereby.' So the story goes on, 'taunt upon taunt, check upon check,' until it comes to the last exchange of gibes on the second day. 'If Henry VIII were alive,' Rogers tells them, 'and should call a parliament and begin to determine a thing (and I would have alleged the example of the act of making the queen a bastard and of making himself the superior head, but I could not, being interrupted of one, whom God forgive) then will ye (pointing to my Lord Chancellor) and ye and ye and so ye (pointing to the rest of the bishops) say, amen and it like your grace, it is meet that it be so enacted.'

Here my Lord Chancellor would suffer me to speak no more, but bade me sit down mockingly, saying that I was sent for to be instructed of them, and I would take it upon me to be their instructor.

My lord, quoth I, I stand and sit not. Shall I not be suffered to speak for my life?

Shall we suffer thee to tell a tale and to prate, quoth he.'[1]

Yet this, as we have seen, was exactly what the Marian government could not, or at any rate did not, prevent. Rogers was but the first of a succession of such characters who, when pressed with the question concerning Christ's presence in the sacrament, summarily rejected the traditional explanation of that mystery and went on to press upon their inquisitors the hardly less difficult question concerning authority in Church and state. None of these men, however, told a more circumstantial or dramatic story of the series of examinations and encounters to which he was subjected than John Bradford. 'Would we had all other remains of the martyrs,' Foxe wrote to Grindal, 'brought together with equal care.'

Judging from this account and the additional details supplied by Foxe himself, Bradford proved a formidable antagonist when baited with the usual question. Not for nothing had he read law in the Inner Temple, been converted by Latimer's preaching, studied divinity at Cambridge under Martin Bucer, and been picked by Ridley for a fellowship at Pembroke, a prebend at St Paul's, and a royal chaplaincy under Edward. Mary's government had clapped him into prison but had not kept him from preaching to his fellow-prisoners or from pouring out spiritual comfort to people outside. We see him in Foxe's pages pitting his

[1] Foxe, VI, 591–612.

wits, his command of words and his knowledge of the Scriptures against the authority of high-ranking ecclesiastics whom he treats as scapegoats for the Crown's mistakes. And in his account of his appearances before Gardiner and the rest, we see him directing his efforts less to refuting his adversaries' arguments than to scoring off them for effect upon the public.

He reports that his examiners began by offering him the queen's pardon, 'if so be you will with us return, and if you will do as we have done,' and at his refusal, 'the said Lord Chancellor something snuffed.' 'I know thou hast a glorious tongue,' Bradford is told, 'and goodly shows thou makest, but all is lies.' So they proceed quickly to the crucial question, 'what say you by the ministration of the communion as now you know it is?' and he is ready with the usual evasion and the usual challenge. 'I have been six times sworn that I shall in no case consent to the practising of any juris-diction or any authority on the Bishop of Rome's behalf within this realm of England. Now before God I humbly pray your honour to tell me, whether you ask me this question by his authority or no?' 'Tush,' says Gardiner, 'Herod's oaths a man should make no conscience of.' Bradford, he continues, has been writing letters from prison contrary to the queen's command, and yet the queen offers him her pardon if he will confess and con-form. His reply is to thank her for her mercy but deny wrong-doing. He wishes to live 'as a quiet subject without clog of con-science', and 'if otherwise I behave myself, then I am in danger of the law. In the mean season I ask no more than the benefit of a subject, till I be convinced of transgression.'

A little later he adjures the Lord Chancellor, 'seek no guiltless blood, nor hunt by questions to bring into the snare them which are out of the same. At this present I stand before you guilty or guiltless; if guilty, then proceed and give sentence accordingly; if guiltless, then give me the benefit of a subject, which hitherto I could not have.' Gardiner objects, 'thou goest about to deny obedience to the queen, who now requireth obedience to the Bishop of Rome,' and he is met with the usual rejoinder that Bradford will give 'ensample of all most humble obedience to the queen's highness so long as she requireth not obedience against God'.

By this time Gardiner had said that the doctrine taught in King Edward's day was proved wrong by the fact that it had ended in treason and rebellion, and Bradford had come back at him with, 'Ah, my lord, that you could enter into God's sanctuary and mark the end of this present doctrine that you so magnify.' But other questioners take up the attack, some of them old acquaintances. Among them is Nicholas Harpsfield, who shifts from the question how one knows Christ in the sacrament to the related question, how one can know the true Church. Bradford's answer is that to know the Church 'we must put on such eyes as good men put on to see and know Christ when He walked here on earth.' 'But what if you be deceived?' Harpsfield interjects, and the answer comes in a flash, ' "What if you should say the sun did not shine now?" and the sun did shine through the window where they sat.'

Next come the two Spanish friars, who fly into such a rage that 'the whole house rang again, chafing with *om* and *cho*'. 'If Bradford had been anything hot,' we are told, 'one house could not have held them.' So in the end there is nothing to be done but turn him over to the sheriff. Gardiner's concluding exclamation is, 'Oh Lord God! what a fellow thou art! Thou wouldst go about to bring into the people's heads that we – all the lords of the parliament house, the knights and burgesses, and all the whole realm – be perjured. Oh what heresy is this!' A final touch is given to the story by showing Bradford going to the stake with a youthful apprentice who has been condemned for believing as he had learned from Rogers and Hooper. Bradford exhorts the lad, 'Be of good comfort, brother, for we shall have a merry supper with the Lord this night.'[1]

But besides being the hero and author of one of the most striking tales in the whole Book of Martyrs, Bradford also left materials which enabled Foxe to present him as a prototype of all the physicians of the soul who would presently be undertaking the spiritual direction of more and more of Elizabeth's subjects.

[1] Foxe, VII, 143–92.

During the eighteen months of his imprisonment he poured forth epistles, meditations, and expostulations to his wife, mother and friends, to troubled souls who applied to him for comfort, to others who, he thought, needed to be admonished for being less troubled than they should have been, to the people of London, Cambridge and Manchester, to Cranmer, Ridley and Latimer, to the king, queen and parliament. Of these writings a few reached Foxe at Basle in time to be included in the Latin version of his book, more became available for the English version of 1563, and still more in 1570. A large number also appeared in the collection of martyrs' letters published by Day in 1564 with an introduction by Coverdale. The significance of these writings was unmistakable. The martyrs as reported by Foxe were setting the example and defining the themes of discourse to be followed by the swarm of preachers who sprang up under Elizabeth and supplied the inspiration and energy behind the Puritan movement. What Bradford did in these so-called letters was what Greenham and Richard Rogers and the long succession of 'spiritual' preachers would soon be doing.

In a time that tried men's souls, they set up to be physicians of the soul, concerned above everything else with individual cases, their own to begin with. If the martyrs, in responding to the questions directed at them in their examinations by the council or its representatives, eschewed discussion of abstract theological or metaphysical matters, it was in order to demand instant attention to their own personal grievances on grounds of right and justice, representing their own cases as one with the common lot. They were more concerned with the analysis and determination of individual predicaments involving moral choice and requiring decision than with the systematic organization of ideas or conformity to established rules and concepts. The question which preoccupied their minds to the exclusion of all others was, what must a man do to be saved? And their answer to that question was belief in the possibility of one's election to salvation by prevenient grace. The advantage of that belief was that it settled the question once for all and left a man free to apply the doctrine to the resolution of individual problems one by one. To that end, the farther the vernacular Bible extended its hold upon the popular mind, the more it served the preachers as a means of extending their function and influence.

The most appealing way to present the Bible to popular apprehension was as a body of case histories covering the whole range of spiritual experience. For the physician of souls could testify that what had happened in his own case was no more and no less than what had happened to Paul and many another in the Scriptures. What had happened to himself and to Paul could happen to anyone if God chose, and who could say that God was not free to choose whom he would? But besides the story of Paul, the Bible offered a multitude of stories exemplifying the countless trials and uncertainties, ardours and ordeals, which the spirit of man is heir to. Hence, while the traditional apparatus of the Church for the spiritual comfort and discipline of men's lives was falling into neglect and disuse, the ministers of the Word were showing men how to find surcease for their troubles by looking into the Scriptures and their own breasts.

It is the way of the physician of souls in any age to treat every patient's case as a case by itself while knowing that no case is beyond the purview of the law that covers all. Bradford's assumption, the continuing assumption of the spiritual brotherhood, was that every soul since the fall of man is involved in the same predicament. Each is involved in the war of the two Adams within the breast, of the two Churches within the Church, of the two realms within the realm. The only hope for anyone is to find himself on the winning side of this conflict, a thing which, though it does not happen to everyone, may happen to anyone whatever at any time and cannot be prevented by man or devil. These were the elect, and their election, while not subject to their command, was within the compass of their knowledge and experience.

It was therefore for the physician of souls to teach the people how to watch for and respond to grace when it came, and naturally grace generally did come to souls thus alerted. Naturally, too, the fate of those whom grace passed by was of no personal concern to the elect beyond the duty of letting them know what might be in store for them. This is not hard to understand, for to people whose desperate need was to know what to think and where to turn in such a period of violent change, it was the positive effect of the doctrine of election upon their own predicament which chiefly mattered. If some were left out of Zion, it was no doing of the elect. They were free. They would have to endure the trials, even to martyrdom, which are the lot of the elect, but they had only to endure in order to gain certain evidence of their election and ultimate reward.

Thus in the writings which Bradford managed to send to his friends from prison while waiting to play out his role as one of the elect, we have the classic themes and images of the saga of spiritual pilgrimage and war which were soon to resound from a hundred pulpits. 'Again,' he says, 'consider that this world is the place of trial of God's people and the devil's servants, for as the one will follow his master whatsoever cometh of it, so will the other.'

Let no man deceive himself, for he that gathereth not with Christ scattereth abroad ... So doth the husbandman in ploughing and tilling set before him the harvest time; so doth the fisher consider the draught of his net rather than the casting in; so doth the merchant the return of his merchandise; and so should we in these stormy days set before us ... the coming of our Saviour Christ to judgment, the fire that shall burn the wicked and disobedient to God's gospel, the blast of the trump, the exceeding glory prepared for us in heaven eternally ... Consider where you be, not at home but in a strange country. Consider among whom you are conversant, even in the midst of your enemies ... and then I trust you will not much muse at affliction, which you cannot be without, being as you be God's children ... But now I write my farewell to you in this life indeed upon certain knowledge. My staff standeth at the door. I continually look for the sheriff to come for me, and I thank God I am ready for him. Now I go to practise that which I have preached. Now am I climbing up the hill; it will cause me to puff and blow before I come to the cliff. The hill is steep and high, my breath is short, and my strength is feeble. Pray therefore to the Lord for me, that as I have now through his goodness even almost come to the top, I may by his grace be strengthened not to rest till I come where I should be.[1]

We see Bradford laying bare his soul for the edification of other souls in need of spiritual comfort. In the story of Rowland Taylor we see the same character from the point of view of one of his devoted flock. We see the parson of a town, the good shepherd, living dutifully among his people, giving himself to the study of the Scriptures, fulfilling the charge upon him to feed the Lord's sheep. But upon Queen Mary's accession Taylor not only continued to play his part as before, but also offered physical resistance to the officiant who came to say Mass in his church. So we have the usual story. Taylor is arrested, brought before Gardiner, questioned as to the sacrament, charged with disobeying the queen's commands, accused of treason, condemned for heresy, and sent to prison, where he proceeds to write up his own account of the treatment he has received up to this point. But then his man, John Hull, takes up the story, and in artless but vivid and precise detail tells of the martyr's triumphant progress from his prison in the Compter in the Poultry, through Essex and Suffolk villages all the familiar way to Hadley, the stake at Aldham Common, and so to glory.

The writer does full circumstantial justice to the final scene, but not before he has brought the character who is his subject before us in his habit as he lived. The preacher's wife and son dine with him on his last night in prison, and he gives the one an English prayer book and the other a book of martyr stories out of Eusebius. He is summoned at two in the morning and led through the dark streets to the Woolsack Inn at Aldgate without. His wife and children have been waiting for him in the porch of St Botolph's church, and as he and the guard draw near, his wife cries

---

[1] Foxe, VII, 252–5.

out, 'Rowland, Rowland, where art thou?' For, we are told, 'it was a very dark morning, that one could not see the other'. The sheriff's men would have hurried on, but the sheriff bids them stay, and the prisoner and his family kneel down on the stones and say the Lord's prayer. In the morning the sheriff of Essex comes and carries him off on horseback. At Brentford a former servant, not knowing what has happened, greets him, but is rebuked by the guard and threatened with arrest. 'I cry you mercy,' says the man, 'I thought it none offence to talk to a true man.' Whereupon the sheriff, seeing how the people feel towards his prisoner, puts a mask on him so that no one should know him.

'All the way Dr Taylor was joyful and merry,' speaking such notable things as to cause his attendants, all but one, to weep. At Chelmsford the sheriff of Suffolk takes charge, but before starting on the next stage of their journey, they all have supper together and the company do their best to persuade the good parson to conform and save his life. 'For ye are well beloved of all men as well for your virtues as for your learning, and me think it were great pity you should cast away yourself willingly.' At that, the sheriff and all the yeomen of the guard drink to him. He seems to ponder the question for a while, and then tells them that there are many who will be deceived of their expectation when he arrives at Hadley. At that the company rejoice, thinking he intends to give way, until it occurs to the sheriff to ask what he means by this, and he tells them, 'I am as you see a man that hath a great carcase,' and the worms in Hadley churchyard 'which should have had jolly feeding upon this carrion' will 'lose their bait and feeding that they looked to have had of it.'

He is held two days at Lavenham, 'and thither came to him a great number of gentlemen and justices upon great horses' with promises of pardon and promotion, 'yea a bishopric', if he would but relent and recant, all to no avail. So there is nothing for it but take him on towards Hadley. When they come near that place, he asks to be allowed to alight for a certain purpose and, his need satisfied, 'he leapt and set a frisk or twain as men commonly do in dancing'. He rejoices, he says, 'for now I know I am almost at home. I lack not past two stiles to go over, and I am even at my father's house'. At Hadley the people line the way on both sides, 'saying one to another, there goeth our good shepherd from us that so faithfully hath taught us ... Good Lord strengthen him and comfort him'.

At Aldham Common, where he is to suffer, he is forbidden to speak to the people, but still manages to cry out, 'I have taught you nothing but God's holy word.' When he kneels down to pray, a woman kneels and prays with him, though 'they thrust her away and threatened to tread her down with horses.' A butcher refuses the order to set up the faggots, and his place is taken by one who is 'for his virtues a very hangman', assisted by another said to be 'a very drunkard', a third who had lost an ear in King Edward's time for seditious talk, and a fourth who, we are told, still plays the vice in stage plays and interludes. When a bystander throws a faggot at the victim, the latter cries, 'Oh friend, I have harm enough, what needed that?'[1]

So far the stories of the Marian martyrs here discussed came from university-trained, clerical intellectuals such as were in the next reign to find their natural place in the pulpit but also to keep the book-trade busy. Yet as the Marian regime floundered on in deeper and deeper frustration, it kept finding others, not of this group but not necessarily less articulate or vocal, whom it could not but suspect of heresy and prosecute for seeking to subvert the established order. And as Foxe went on from edition to edition, more and more stories of such people turned up to be fitted into his book. What he himself may have contributed to this material in preparing it for publication, one cannot precisely say. He insists now and again that he printed it just as it came to him. In printing the story of Richard Woodman, for example, he tells us that 'for as much as the matter is something strange and will peradventure scarce stand credit upon my narration ... ye shall hear himself speak and testify'.[2] Certainly many of these stories give unmistakable evidence of having come from persons actually involved in them as principals or witnesses. They express the usual attitude

[1] Foxe, VI, 676–703.   [2] Foxe, VIII, 333.

towards the two questions concerning the sacrament and the authority of the queen to require obedience to the Pope, and they tell what is in outline and outcome the usual story of persecution. They tell the story, however, in many instances with a fullness of circumstantial detail reflecting the common life and common speech of men and women in village, town and countryside which leaves little doubt of their authenticity.

A few of the subjects and presumed authors of these stories appear to have been younger men of some formal education who had barely had time to get started as preachers when they were caught in the backdraught of reaction against the new religion. Others were persons of little education, many of them workers in one branch or other of the cloth-trade, who, having been captivated by the Bible, found themselves under an inner compulsion to go about telling other people what had happened to them and what it meant, undeterred by any doubt as to their own understanding of the truth revealed in the Word. Many, women as well as men, were simple folk who, besides discovering the Bible, had incurred the suspicion of neighbours and local officials by talking too freely, by absenting themselves from church or by some other form of imprudent behaviour.

All such people would soon be having more and more printed books of various sorts put in their way, but meanwhile they still lacked much book-learning beyond what they may have got for themselves from the one all-important book which the efforts of Tyndale, Coverdale and Rogers had brought within their ken. This did not mean that they were lacking in imagination or intelligence, but it was still true that the spoken rather than the written or the printed word was their most immediate source of mental stimulation and their primary mode of self-expression. It was after all preaching which got them started on the Bible in the first place, and the excitement that came from the Bible was in large part the excitement of discovering all the things that, knowing no language but their native English, they now had to think and talk about, things that it much concerned them to understand concerning themselves and their own souls.

The Dreadful and Bloody Regiment

Needless to say, there is much too much of all this in Foxe for modern taste, jaded by a plethora of print and talk. Yet there is also much that the student of English life and letters on the eve of the Elizabethan age may well give ear to, not a little to remind him that the intoxication of these people with the sound of their own voices speaking all manner of things in their own language would in the next generation break out in poetry and drama as well as in martyr tales and sermons, in parliament and the press as well as in the pulpit.

There is, as we have seen, drama enough in the accounts of the Marian martyrs of rank and influence which were the original stuff from which the Book of Martyrs grew, but the same gift for expressive speech and action comes out in the stories of less notable persons, both men and women. Take, for example, George Marsh, who suffered at Chester in April 1555, and whose story reached Foxe through the martyr's brother. Here we have a young man, ordained under Edward and called up by his bishop soon after Mary's accession to be examined as to his views concerning the body and blood of Christ in the sacrament. The usual set-to follows – the bishop calling on the young man, in terms that mean nothing to him, to acknowledge as true a statement he rejects as incomprehensible to common sense, and on the other hand a self-centred, opinionated young man standing fast by his own notion of the truth because he has worked it out for himself in the only language he really knows. When they press him further, he merely begs them not to ask such hard, unprofitable questions, 'whereby to bring my body into danger of death and to suck my blood'. Offended at his thus turning those two highly charged words back upon them, his examiners protest that they intend nothing but to make him a good Christian man.

So they keep at him with their questions, which only provoke him to more and more defiant answers. The scene closes, as do so many of these scenes, with *non disputandum est cum haeretico*. The final scene is the final sentencing. The bishop draws the document out of his bosom and begins to read. The chancellor calls on him to stop, for if he goes on it will be too late for the accused to save himself by repenting. Priests and bystanders, among them 'one Pulleyn a shoemaker', beg him to give way. They kneel and pray for him, and he does the same for them. But though he admits to desiring the queen's mercy and 'did love her grace as faithfully as any of them', he will not budge.

'Then the bishop put his spectacles upon his nose' as though to go on with reading the sentence. Again the chancellor interrupts 'with a glavering and smiling countenance'. Again the bishop pauses, and takes off his spectacles. Again the bystanders pluck the accused by the sleeve and beg him to save himself while he can. Still he refuses. 'So the bishop read out his sentence to the end,' saying that now he will pray for the condemned man no more. The jailor, however, bids his prisoner, 'Farewell, good George, with weeping tears.' 'So he went all the way unto his death with his book in his hand, looking upon the same, and many of the people said, "this man goeth not unto his death as a thief or as one that deserveth to die." ' But at the stake the sheriff says to him, 'George Marsh, we must have no sermoning now.'[1]

Marsh, who had studied at Cambridge, was a martyr of some education. But oftentimes, we are told, 'the will and pleasure of God is to beautify and adorn His kingdom with the weak and simple instruments of this world such as in the Old Testament Amos was, who with many other of obscure and unknown names were called from the herds and fields to the honour of prophets.' 'Wherefore,' the story goes on to say, 'George Eagles is not to be neglected for his occupation.' This man was a tailor, who 'being eloquent and of good utterance, gave and applied himself to the profit of Christ's church' by going about the country, preaching the gospel to such effect that he was known by the legendary name of Trudgeover.[2]

Another character of the same sort was Rawlins White, a fisherman, who in King Edward's time had his little boy learn to read the Bible so that he could also instruct his father. The result was that the latter left off his fishing in order with his boy's help to instruct others in the gospel. When Mary came to the throne,

[1] Foxe, VII, 39–68.   [2] Foxe, VIII, 393–7.

naturally he was had up before the bishop to be reasoned with, but the bishop's kind of reasoning was beyond his comprehension. 'My lord,' he says, 'I am a Christian man, and I hold no opinions contrary to the Word of God, and if I do I desire to be reformed out of the Word of God, as a Christian man ought to be.' 'The chief cause of his trouble,' we are told, 'was his opinion touching the sacrament of the altar,' but on that subject nothing the bishop could say could make any impression on him. 'Proceed in your law a God's name … but for an heretic you shall never condemn me while the world standeth.' 'Rawlins ye left me, and Rawlins you find me, and by God's grace Rawlins I will continue.'

And as so often in these stories, full dramatic advantage is taken of the final scene. 'In going towards the stake he fell down upon his knees and kissed the ground, and in rising again, the earth a little sticking on his nose, he said these words, "earth unto earth and dust unto dust, thou art my mother and unto thee I shall return." ' But with his back to the stake, he says to the friend who reported the tale to Foxe, 'I feel a great fighting between the flesh and the spirit, and the flesh would very fain have his swinge, and therefore I pray you, when you see me anything tempted, hold your finger up to me, and I trust that I shall remember myself.'[1]

There is also the story of William Hunter, a silk-weaver's apprentice, who is found by the summoner reading the Bible in church. 'What meddlest thou with the Bible?' the young man is asked, 'Knowest thou what thou readest and canst expound the Scriptures?' Upon his answering that he reads only for his own comfort, the summoner exclaims, 'It was never merry since the Bible came abroad in English', and bustles off to fetch the vicar. The vicar comes and demands, 'Sirrah, who gave thee leave to read in the Bible and expound it?' and when William disclaims expounding but dares to suggest that the vicar ought to be doing just that, the latter upbraids him for a heretic, saying, 'it is a merry world when such as thou art shall teach us what is the truth.'

The lad flees the neighbourhood, is pursued, caught and brought

[1] Foxe, VII, 28–33.

before the local justice of the peace. 'Thou naughty boy,' the squire tells him, 'wilt thou not take things as they are but expound them as thou wilt?' He is sent up to London to be quizzed by Bonner, and Bonner, saying, 'I like thee well', offers to make him free of his trade and set him up in business if he will conform, but to no avail. At the stake, as the fire is being laid to the faggots, the victim casts the psalter he has been carrying to his brother, and the brother says, ' "William, think on the holy passion of Christ and be not afraid of death," and William answered, "I am not afraid." '[1]

Women in these stories are as stout of mind, ready of speech, and quick to act as men. We hear of Elizabeth Folkes that when she came to be burned she plucked off her petticoat and would have given it to her mother, but 'the wicked there attending would not suffer her to give it. Therefore taking the said petticoat in her hand, she threw it away from her, saying, "farewell the world, farewell faith, farewell hope, and so taking the stake in her hand, said, welcome love." '[2]

We hear of Alice Driver talking down the two learned churchmen set to convince her of her errors. 'Have you no more to say?' she exclaims when she has apparently dumbfounded them with her vehemence.

> God be honoured. You be not able to resist the spirit of God in me a poor woman. I was an honest poor man's daughter, never brought up in the university as you have been, but I have driven the plough before my father many a time, I thank God. Yet notwithstanding, in the defence of God's truth and in the cause of my master Christ, by his grace I will set my foot against the foot of any of you all in the maintenance and defence of the same, and if I had a thousand lives, it should go for payment thereof ... and so went she to prison again as joyful as the bird of day, praying and glorifying the name of God.[3]

Some of these stories, however, are not without touches of

[1] Foxe, VI, 722–9.   [2] Foxe, VIII, 393.   [3] Foxe, VIII, 493.

something like comic relief. We are told that when the watch came to search for Agnes Wardall they had to knock three times before an attendant looked out of the bay window beside the door. She excuses the delay by saying that she is a stranger here and has heard say 'that there be spirits walking about which, if a man do answer at the first call or the second, he stands in great danger, and I was never so afraid in my life.' The men laugh, but before they can get in, the woman they are after has time to hide in a secret closet. They withdraw, she escapes through a gap in the garden palings, and lies low among the nettles in a ditch with her buckram apron over her head. Her pursuers draw near, but one of them, 'a simple, honest, plain man ... espying where she lay gave a hem and made a noise with his bill.' Next day he sends her word that next time she should hide farther off.[1]

We hear also of Peter Moone, a tailor whom the bishop is about to let go, since he seems a timorous, weak man. However, someone standing by says, 'But my lord, he hath a perilous woman unto his wife.' Peter, being ordered to bring her in, objects, 'I am as able to command her to come before my lord as ye are to command the worst boy in your house.' Nevertheless, he does bring her in after dinner, and the bishop begins examining her. He is interrupted, however, by the chancellor leading in a whole new flock of heretics and Anabaptists from the cloth country. Peter and his wife are told to stand aside, and the woman sees her chance. She has posted her baby in the yard below, the baby begins to cry, she begs leave to go and give it suck, and so in the upshot they get away.[2]

More grim and more characteristic but not less dramatic in its outcome is the story of Roger Holland, with which it will be as well to conclude this brief consideration of the martyrs more or less submerged in the later pages of Foxe's huge compilation. The story begins on what was to become a familiar theme. Its subject is an idle apprentice turned from his evil ways by a maid in his master's household who saves him from disgrace, gets him to read the Bible, and so wins him to the true faith and a life of godly

[1] Foxe, VIII, 219–22.   [2] Foxe, VIII, 223–5.

devotion and business enterprise. He marries her, all goes well with him, he rises to be a merchant tailor of London, and at that point in the happier time to come, the story would have ended. But now Roger is called up before Bonner, and we have another lively scene in which the defender of the passing order is outfaced by the upstart of the age to come. Again the bishop has to hear it said, ' ... as for your Latin service, what are we of the laity the better for it? ... wherein shall a young man direct his ways but by the Word of God, and yet you will hide it from us in a tongue unknown.' At the stake in Smithfield, this young man prophesied that 'after this day in this place shall there not be any by him put to the trial of fire and faggot.' At this Bonner cried out, 'Roger, thou art, I perceive, as mad in these thy heresies as Joan Bocher. In anger and fume thou wouldst become a railing prophet.' Foxe adds the observation that 'after this day there was never none that suffered in Smithfield for the testimony of the gospel.'[1]

For the time was running out for the unfortunate queen. Foxe fills the next few pages with the stories of the few remaining martyrs burned in places outside London in the last weeks of the reign, and of divers others saved at the last moment by the providential calling of Elizabeth to the throne. This brings him to the crowning story of his book, the story of Elizabeth herself, set off by his account of Mary's unhappy end. He concludes the whole with a brief pronouncement of God's judgments on the agents of the late queen's policy of persecution, and a prayer for the shortening of the days of the kingdom of Satan and the early coming of the kingdom of Christ on earth.

* * *

Here then was the much expanded Book of Martyrs which John Foxe and his publisher brought before the public in 1570, not long after the Catholic uprising had been put down in the north and not long before parliament convened on April 2nd in a frenzy of loyalty and apprehension. Never had such a work on such a scale appeared in English before, certainly never at such a

---

[1] Foxe, VIII, 473–9.

moment. It was received at once as the one authoritative account of the whole chain of events in the history of the Church and the nation which had brought on the perilous situation in which both now found themselves. The mayor and corporation of London, prompted by the Archbishop of Canterbury and the Bishops of London and Ely, immediately ordered the book to be set up for all to read in city orphanages and the halls of city companies.[1] Convocation issued canons, which John Day soon put into print,[2] ordering bishops to make available in hall or chamber for the use of strangers and servants 'the holy Bible in the largest volume as it was lately printed in London and also that full and perfect history which is entitled Monuments of Martyrs and other such like books'. Deans were to provide the same in cathedrals for the use of clergy and people. Deans, archdeacons and resident canons were to do the same, 'everyone for his own family'.

The Book of Martyrs was also soon to be found in parish churches and Oxford and Cambridge colleges. In 1572 John Whitgift of Trinity College commended it to the attention of the Puritan author of *An Admonition to Parliament*. Foxe presented a copy to his college of Magdalen and received a reward of £6 13s. 4d. In 1573 the parish of St Michael's Cornhill bought a copy for £2 2s. 6d. to be kept 'tied with a chain to the great eagle of Brass'.[3] By 1577, we learn from William Harrison, 'every office at court had either a Bible or the book of the acts and monuments of the church of England or both, besides some histories and chronicles.'[4] Drake took a copy with him in 1577 when he set forth on the voyage which was to take him round the world, and on occasion plied his Spanish prisoners with it and whiled away dull days at sea by colouring the pictures.[5] After his victory at Cadiz in 1587, he wrote to Foxe to thank him for his prayers.[6]

[1] Arber, *Transcript ... Stationers' Register*, I, 496.
[2] *A Booke of certaine Canons ... Printed by John Daye* (1571).
[3] Mozley, *John Foxe and his Book*, 147.
[4] Harrison, 'Description of England,' Holinshed, *Chronicles* (1577), 84.
[5] Z. Nuttall, *New Light on Drake*, Hakluyt Society, ser. II, vol. xxxiv, (1914), 19, 348, 354–8.
[6] Quoted in Mozley, *John Foxe and his Book*, 101–2.

The Dreadful and Bloody Regiment

The Catholic revolt of 1570 was quickly crushed, but the fear of Catholic counter-revolution and foreign invasion continued to haunt the adherents of the new regime and the new religion. Parliament had no sooner dispersed in 1571 when another plot was discovered, involving the Queen of Scots, the Pope, the Duke of Norfolk, Philip of Spain and his lieutenant Alva in the Netherlands. For twenty years there would continue to be plots and rumours of plots against Elizabeth's life, wars and rumours of wars against Protestant rulers and peoples everywhere. The Pope would egg Catholic rulers on to enforce the Church's decrees against schismatical England and its heretical queen. Catholic writers would expatiate on the doctrine of tyrannicide. In Scotland a party would hold out in Mary's support, and there would be no telling into whose hands the young king might fall or what line he would eventually take. In France, Catherine de Medici and her son, leagued with Mary's Guise relatives, would stir up the Paris mob to massacre Huguenots. In the Netherlands Alva would carry on a war of persecution against Philip's Protestant subjects, and at sea and in the new world the Spanish would block the passage of English ships and prosecute English seamen and traders for heresy. A papal force would invade Ireland, and finally Philip would send the Armada to invade England itself. And all this time no one could tell how many Catholics and Catholic sympathizers there would be within the realm conspiring with a foreign invader, no one could tell how many Jesuits and seminary priests seeking to corrupt the queen's faithful subjects.

Or so at any rate the queen's faithful subjects believed, all the more confidently for having Foxe's great book to convince them that this, or something so like this as to make no difference, had always been the case in England. If any of them did not or perhaps could not read the book for themselves, they could at least look at the pictures and listen while their preachers retailed the book to them. For so long as the outcome of the struggle with the Catholic powers remained uncertain, the book lost none of its timely relevance, and Foxe and his enterprising publisher took advantage of the fact. In 1576 they put out a third edition, substantially unaltered though more cheaply printed. In 1583 they issued a fourth edition with some added matter, printed on the same scale as in 1570. Not only that, but many stories from *Actes and Monumentes*, including the story of Elizabeth's experiences under her sister's rule and the account of Mary's last days, were incorporated word for word with due acknowledgment in Holinshed's *Chronicles* in 1577 and again in 1587. Day died in 1584, Foxe in 1587, surviving just long enough to hear of the execution of the Queen of Scots but not long enough to hear of Drake's exploit at Cadiz. In 1589, in the wake of the Armada, Timothy Bright published *An Abridgement of the Booke of the Actes and Monumentes of the Church*, a quarto of 792 pages, which, omitting or condensing much of the documentary material of the original, presented the substance of Foxe's historical narrative and most of the stories by and about the Marian martyrs in all their essential details. 'There is not a book,' the compiler assured his readers, 'under the scriptures more necessary for a Christian to be conversant in ... Here mayst thou read not only what hath been suffered of the old fathers of the Church who have with their blood purchased unto us this freedom of the gospel, but of late times what thy father, thy mother, thy brother, and thy friend have suffered for the like testimony, whereby the sincerity of the gospel standeth at this day.' In 1596 Day's successor in business issued a fifth edition of the book itself, the last to appear in the lifetime of the queen.

CHAPTER VII

The Elect Nation

〜〜〜

WHAT John Foxe's *Actes and Monumentes* did to justify the place accorded to it in its own time beside the Bible should now be clear. By the time James came to the throne the Book of Martyrs and the stream of annals, chronologies and histories in similar vein had gone far to establish in the public mind a familiar legend of the nation's history, of the part which its rulers had played in the working out of its destiny, and so too a quite definite conception of the part rulers might be expected to play henceforth. Foxe, of course, had not originated this legend, certainly not single-handed, but he had put the current elements of the legend together in a single connected narrative which the Elizabethan regime and its supporters accepted at once as the most convincing statement of their position in their continuing struggle with the powers opposing them at home and abroad. The book provided a circumstantial account of the events which had led directly to the queen's accession. In the stories of the Marian martyrs, with Elizabeth's own story for climax, it presented in the most vivid dramatic terms the essence of the faith presumed to have been established in the national Church by her authority.

It framed these stories in an account of ecclesiastical history which purported to show that this faith was the same for which the martyrs of the primitive Church had died, the same which had been brought uncorrupted to Britain in the beginning directly from the apostles. This account of Church history the book also linked to a history of the long succession of native rulers down to Elizabeth, shown as owing their authority directly to divine appointment and prospering or not, and their people with them, according as they heeded their vocation to defend the faith and the people in the faith, or suffered themselves to be misled by false counsellors, or overborne by misbelieving usurpers and invaders. And to conclude, the book made plain that by all the signs to be found in scripture and history the will of God was about to be fulfilled in England by a prince perfect in her obedience to her vocation, ruling a people perfect in their obedience to her authority.

That is to say, Foxe set the apocalyptical conception of England which he brought back from exile at the death of Mary in a valid historical perspective focussed on the place and function of kingship now devolving upon Elizabeth. The course of events in Elizabeth's long reign, not least her own dazzling performance in the role appointed her in the Book of Martyrs, impressed that conception more and more deeply on the public mind. Elizabeth, who probably did not need Foxe to instruct her in the lessons of history, exploited the gifts of personality and the arts of showmanship at her command to counteract the disruptive effects of religion among her subjects by attracting their devotion to herself as queen and exciting their pride in being, like herself, above everything else English. The effect was to make them, in spite of their religious differences, more conscious of England as an entity by itself and of themselves as a people set apart from all others.

It was also to give greater meaning to that body of fact and fable concerning the national past which a thriving book-trade was putting into print for all to read. A succession of scholars, collectors and antiquaries, following up the work of Leland, Bale, Foxe and Parker, grew fascinated by England itself, its history, language, customs, topography, local monuments and antiquities. Scholars such as these, to be sure, as they went on accumulating knowledge, came to have their doubts about this or that feature of the legend which now passed for history – about Brute and Arthur and the fabled kings of Britain, about Joseph of Arimathea, King Lucius and Pope Eleutherius, even about such a matter as the poisoning of King John by a monk of Swinstead – but they did not question the general outlines or the essential truth of a legend so apposite to the continuing crisis in which Elizabeth and her people found themselves.

The Elect Nation

From the anticipations bred by that legend and the conception of the nation's history and destiny which it expressed sprang much of the enthusiasm with which the people greeted Elizabeth's successor on his coming to the throne. Gunpowder Treason, coming shortly after his accession, reawakened all the old apprehensions: hence parliament imposed a more stringent oath of allegiance on the king's subjects, directed especially against Catholics, and the Stationers' Company issued a new edition of *Actes and Monumentes*. This appeared in 1610 with the addition of an account of the massacre of Protestants in France, introduced by an epistle to the reader by Edward Bulkeley. James himself, who had already expounded in print the teachings of scripture and history on the rights and responsibilities of kings, challenged Cardinal Bellarmine to debate the subject and in 1610 published in London his own collected writings on that and other questions. Lancelot Andrewes as court preacher would also expatiate on the subject in years to come on the anniversary of Gunpowder Treason and other appropriate occasions, not omitting to remind the king from time to time that God had chosen England above all other nations for His special favour.

Yet though James was all too ready to explain as well as embrace the role left to him by his predecessor, he was less than ready to cope with the conditions entailed upon it at her death. He participated personally in the conference which he presently called to discuss Puritan proposals for further reform in the Church, pronounced the rule of 'no bishop no king', and talked of harrying the Puritans out of the land, but he authorized a new translation of the Bible, and took no effective measures to stop the spread of preaching or impede the growth of that unacknowledged brotherhood of the pulpit which was making itself the most influential instrument for the direction of public opinion. Not only that, but he soon stirred up old suspicions and prejudices by making overtures to Spain for peace and a Spanish wife for his son, while failing to stand by his daughter and her husband when assailed by the Catholic powers in Germany.

The dissatisfactions he thus provoked were compounded for

him and his son by their antagonizing of parliament, and they were fatally exacerbated by Charles's elevation of Laud to the primacy and Laud's challenge to the very existence of the brotherhood of preachers, supported as it was by many of the Protestant gentry and their kinsmen and allies in London and the great towns. The result was a new exodus of preachers of the Word and their flocks which in the next ten years took, it is estimated, some 40,000 subjects of the king to the Continent and 20,000 to North America, fleeing what they chose to regard as the renewal of persecution by papistical bishops contrary to scripture and the laws and customs of the realm.

There also followed in 1632 a new edition, the seventh to be issued in English, of *Actes and Monumentes*, published by the Stationers' Company in three volumes with additions supplied by Nathaniel Holmes. To the prefatory matter of the first volume as it appeared in previous editions, Holmes added a topical outline and chronology for the further enlightenment and encouragement of readers. To the third volume, containing the stories of the Marian martyrs, he added, along with a separate title-page, a long section called 'A continuation of the Histories of Foreign Martyrs: From the happy reign of the most renowned Queene Elizabeth to these times. With sundry Relations of those bloudy Massacres in the Cities of France in the yeare 1572. Whereunto are annexed the two Deliverances of our *English* Nation: the one from the *Spanish Invasion* in 88. The other from *Gunpowder Treason* in the yeare 1605. Together with the Barbarous cruelties exercised upon the Professors of the Gospell in the Valtoline, 1621.' The writer introduced his account of these events with 'A Treatise of afflictions and Persecutions of the Faithfull, preparing them with patience to suffer martyrdome', and he concluded his account of the Armada with a report, attributed to a Spanish spy, of Elizabeth's appearance before her army at Tilbury and a free but lively translation of the poem which Beza addressed to the queen from Geneva on the occasion of her great victory.

With the striking down by parliament in November 1640 of Laud's power over pulpit and press, the exiles were free to come home, and preachers and their followers were free to renew their agitation for getting on with that more perfect reformation which, they held, had been prevented since Elizabeth's passing by papists and prelates. They conveniently forgot, of course, all that Elizabeth herself had done to prevent such a reformation in her own time. In 1641 the Stationers took the occasion to issue still another edition of *Actes and Monumentes*. To the work as it had appeared in 1632, they added a portrait of the author, engraved by George Glover, and a life in Latin and English by Foxe's son Simeon. All editions up to this time had included the woodcuts which had first appeared in 1563 or 1570, but the original blocks from which they had been printed had become so battered and so riddled by worms that they were now replaced by new blocks crudely copied from the originals.

Whether any successor to Elizabeth could have played the part he took over from her to the general satisfaction of his subjects in the conditions that followed her reign of forty-four years may well be doubted. Yet however that may be, as the difficulties that James and Charles ran into in their endeavour to play the part steadily multiplied and deepened, the figure of their great predecessor and the legend associated with her memory loomed larger and larger in the public mind, kept alive by successive editions of the Book of Martyrs and the abridgements, annals, chronicles, histories, sermons and other publications which followed after it, drew upon it, and helped to perpetuate the legend and the lesson it conveyed. The most enduring and dependable annalist of Elizabeth's reign was John Stow, and after his death, which occurred not long after that of the queen herself, Edmund Howes continued his work of keeping the people informed concerning former times as well as their own down to 1632.

Meanwhile, the growing interest in national origins and antiquities, which found expression in the 'Description of Britain' which William Harrison contributed to Holinshed's *Chronicles* in 1577, was taken up by William Camden, and the work begun by Parker of collecting books, manuscripts and other records relating to the English past was taken up by Sir Robert Cotton. Camden published the first edition of his *Britannia*, an octavo dedicated to Lord Burghley, in 1587, and the fifth and final edition, a folio dedicated to King James, in 1607. In 1610 appeared an English translation of the work by Philemon Holland. Camden supplied readers with a detailed description of the geography, topography, and local antiquities and monuments of the realm, introduced by a summary account of national origins and subsequent events before the Norman Conquest. The author offers acknowledgment in passing to Bale, Parker and Foxe for their diligence in establishing proof for the story of the early planting of the Christian faith in Britain.

Burghley, shortly before his death in 1598, proposed to the author of *Britannia* that he undertake the writing of a history of the queen's reign, and in 1615 Camden published *Annales Rerum Anglicarum et Hibernicarum, Regnante Elizabetha*, covering events down to 1589. Devoted though he was to Elizabeth's memory and the way things had been done in her time, Camden wrote in Latin, withheld publication of the latter part of his work, and refused to permit its translation into English. But there was no keeping his account of the great queen from the vernacular public indefinitely. The final section, covering the years from 1588 to the accession of James, was published in Latin in 1627, six years after Camden's death. Meanwhile, however, in 1624 P. de Bellegent, a French Protestant living in England, translated the first three parts of the work into French and published them in London, and the next year Abraham Darcie, a Genevan also domiciled in England, published an English translation of de Bellegent's French. The latter had dedicated his version of the book to James as the story of 'the happy and magnificent reestablishment of evangelical truth and purity, the first and sovereign cause of your majesty's glory, and the prosperity of your people'. Darcie dedicated his retranslation to Charles, asking to whom else he could 'commit the story of her who, whilst she lived, was the joy of England, the terror and admiration of the world'. He also fitted his book out with an engraved title-page picturing the victories of her reign and followed by an explanation, an injunction to 'Here read the days when Britain's ground With blessings all was compassed round', and a portrait of the queen. In 1629 Thomas Browne of Christ Church, Oxford, domestic chaplain to Laud himself, translated the fourth part of Camden's narrative, and in 1630 Robert Norton, son of the zealous Puritan of Elizabeth's time, Thomas Norton, published a fresh translation of the whole.

Camden's account of Elizabeth's reign opens with a brilliant summation, following the main outlines of the story laid down by Foxe and the chroniclers, of the course of events and the points at issue in the struggle over the Church from Henry VIII to the death of Mary. Henry is presented as 'a magnanimous prince ... in whose great mind were confusedly mixed many eminent virtues with no less notorious vice', one who 'raged against the Papists by hanging, drawing and quartering and against Protestants by burning them alive'. Edward is depicted as a saintly reformer, in whose time, however, 'ambition and emulation among the nobility, presumption and disobedience among the common people, grew so extravagant and insolent that England seemed to be as it were in a downright frenzy'. Mary is commended for her piety, commiseration towards the poor, and munificence towards the nobility and the clergy, but her reign is described as a time ill spoken of 'by reason of the barbarous cruelty of the bishops', who are said to have burned more Protestants of all ranks in five years than Henry had done in thirty-seven, or than all English kings since John. Against this background Camden gives us the picture derived from Foxe of the Princess Elizabeth as a prodigy of studious, steadfast, modest devotion to Protestant principles.

That Camden's annals of Elizabeth, culminating as they did in the story of the great triumph over the old enemy in '88, should have been published just as James was negotiating with that enemy for peace and another marriage alliance, was significant enough. Even more significant was it that Norton's translation should have appeared just when Laud was reasserting the authority of bishops with the king's approval. For Camden, though no Puritan as well as no papist, was a sound Protestant whose book expressed the point of view of a man who remembered what bishops were supposed to have done when they ruled the Church in the reign of Queen Mary, and whose idea of the Church and how it should be governed was formed in the reign of Elizabeth. Elizabeth, he tells his readers in his opening pages, at once restored the Protestant religion, replacing the bishops of her sister's regime by 'the learnedest Protestants that could be found'. 'What manner of men they were,' he tells us after listing their names, 'and what they suffered, being exiles in Germany in the reign of Queen Mary or else hiding in England', he leaves to 'the Ecclesiastical Historian', meaning of course Foxe.

He goes on to record the activities of fugitive papists but also those of over-zealous Protestants who, professing a more sincere religion, sought to have all things reformed according to the pattern of Geneva. 'Incredible it is how much the followers of this sect increased everywhere through a certain obstinate wilfulness in them, indiscretion of the bishops, and secret favour of certain noblemen who gaped after the wealth of the Church, which sect began presently to be known by the odious name of Puritans.' Archbishop Grindal, however, he commends as a grave, learned and religious man whose fall from the queen's grace was due to the machinations of his adversaries, not to his favouring of Puritans. Whitgift he also commends as an excellent and learned man whom he credits with restoring the doctrine and discipline which had been established in the Church by the authority of parliament but had been 'run out of square' by the connivance of prelates, the obstinacy of Puritans, and the influence of some of the nobility, while the papists stood by and laughed.

But the central figure in Camden's story as it unrolls from year to year and as Norton puts it into English words in 1630 is the great queen with her motto *semper eadem*. 'The Protestant religion,' he begins on his first page, 'being now by authority of parliament established,' the queen's first care was to defend it against the practices of its enemies. 'Neither did she suffer the least innovation therein.' 'Her second care was to hold an even course in her whole life and all her actions,' to provide for the safety of her people and 'purchase herself love amongst her subjects, amongst her enemies fear, and glory amongst all men.' What she accomplished, 'let present and future ages judge by those things which with uncorrupt faithfulness shall be delivered out of the very commentaries of the kingdom.' Some six hundred pages later in Norton's version of the book readers of the time of Charles I were told that 'no oblivion shall ever bury the glory of her name, for her happy and renowned memory still liveth and shall for ever live in the minds of men to all posterity "as of one" ' – here he lets it be known that he is quoting from King James (*Basilikon Doron*, London, 1603) – ' "who in wisdom and felicity of government surpassed," without envy be it spoken, "all the princes since the days of Augustus." '

What Camden did was to compile the fullest contemporary of the late queen for the generation which immediately followed her and still remembered the great accomplishments of her reign. But even before the publication of his *Annales*, veiled as it was in Latin, his example had inspired his friend and associate John Speed to put the legend of England and the great queen before the public in English. This he did in 1611 in two handsome folio volumes totalling over nine hundred pages and dedicated to the queen's successor. The first was entitled *The Theatre of Great Britain: Presenting an Exact Geography of the Kingdome of England, Scotland, Ireland, and the Iles adjoyning*, and the second, *The History of Great Britaine Under the Conquests of ye Romans, Saxons, Danes and Normans. Their Originals, Manners, Warres, Coines & Seales: with ye Successions, Lives, Acts & Issues of the English Monarchs from Julius Caesar to our most gracious Sovereigne King James*. By giving her subjects occasion to grow fascinated with herself, Elizabeth had given them occasion also to fall in love, so to speak, with England, the land in its various parts and features as well as its history. But since 1559, when John Aylmer had poured out the nostalgia of the home-bound exile in his *An Harborowe for Faithfull Subjects*, no writer had expressed that love with quite such exuberance as Speed in 1611.

Let me crave thy acceptance where I have done right and
thine assistance to correct me where I miss ... thy love with
mine being alike obliged unto this our native land. Whose
beauty and benefits, not afar off, as Moses saw Canaan from
Pisgah, but by mine own travels through every province of
England and Wales mine eyes have beheld, and whose
climate, temperature, plenty and pleasures make it to be as
the very Eden of Europe (pardon me I pray if affection pass
limits) for the store of corn in the champian, and of pasturage
in the lower grounds, presseth the cart under the sheaves to
the barn and filleth the coffers of the possessors. Neither are
the faces of the mountains and hills only spread over with
infinite herds and sorts of cattle, but their entrails also are in
continual travail and continually delivered of their rich pro-
genies of copper, lead and iron, marble, crystal, jet, alabaster,
yea most wonder-working lodestone, to say nothing either of
cannel and seacoal as rich for profit and as needfull for use, or
of the goodly quarries of choicest stone as necessary for
strength as estimable for beauty. Her seas and rivers so stored
with fish and her fells and fens so replenished with wild fowl
that they even present themselves for ready prey to their
takers. Briefly, every soil is so enriched with plenty and
pleasures as the inhabitants think there is no other paradise in
the earth but where themselves dwell.

Speed's description of this paradise in his *Theatre* was followed
in his *History* by another rendering of the often repeated story
which began with the legendary founding of the monarchy and
the Church in Britain. A contemporary of Camden, he had early
become one of the group of men interested in the national past
who in the closing years of Elizabeth's reign clustered about
Sir Robert Cotton, the greatest collector since Parker of English
books, manuscripts and public records. 'I have put my sickle,'
Speed said, 'into other men's corn and have laid my building
upon other men's foundations.' His book, like previous books of
the same sort, was a compilation of materials drawn from the

same sources, to which it makes frequent acknowledgment, but it was a compilation on a grand scale and in a heightened tone. It tells us that the climax of the long succession of native rulers and defenders of the faith came when the long-dead stem of ancient British kings put forth five princes of the Tudor name, 'the first of them the richest and the wisest king of this western world, the second the sorest wounder of the papal authority, the third the forwardest in all pious actions, the fourth the ferventest for the religion of Rome, and the fifth a maiden queen the most famously renowned among the world's monarchs.' Speed's account of Mary's reign, of the Marian martyrs, and of Elizabeth under Mary's rule amounts to another abridgement of the Book of Martyrs with frequent injunctions in the margin to 'see Foxe at large'. The whole concludes with the trials and triumphs of Elizabeth as queen, 'who for her royal actions and princely qualities of mind ... may be singled out for an *Idea* of an absolute prince ... of all the princes of her time the most exact observer both for action and ceremony of true regal deportment and magnificence.'

One cannot help reflecting on how tired Elizabeth's successors must have grown of hearing about her magnificence and the glories of her reign. For it was not only learned historians who kept singing her praises. Thomas Heywood took the occasion of her death to put the story of her experiences under her sister's rule as narrated by Foxe into a play, *If you know not me you know nobody: Or the troubles of Queen Elizabeth*, which some unauthorized hand presently took down in the theatre and in 1605 put into print.[1] About the same time Heywood also produced a play, drawing heavily on Foxe and the chroniclers, which was called *The Famous History of Sir Thomas Wyat* and published in 1607. The play on Elizabeth, which saw its fifth printing in 1623, was revived on the stage not long after the accession of Charles I and was reprinted again in 1632, and again in a somewhat ex-

[1] Edited by Madeleine Doran, Malone Society Reprints (1935); E. K. Chambers, *Elizabethan Stage*, III, 342; G. E. Bentley, *Jacobean and Caroline Stage*, IV, 372.

panded version with prologue and epilogue by the author in 1639. Prologue and epilogue had been printed in a separate collection in 1637. But this was not all. In 1631 Heywood turned his play into a prose narrative, called *England's Elizabeth: Her Life and Troubles during her Minoritie from the Cradle to the Crown*. In 1639 he turned it into 'heroicall verse' and gave it the title *The life and death of Queen Elizabeth from the Womb to the Tomb*. In 1640 he opened his *Exemplary Lives and Memorable Acts of Nine the most worthy women of the World* with the story of Deborah and concluded it with that of Elizabeth. Finally, in 1641 he incorporated his account of the reigns of Mary and Elizabeth, depending so largely on Foxe, in the work he called *The Life of Merlin* and described as containing the pith and marrow of Holinshed, Polychronicon, Speed, Fabyan and other books of giant-like bulk and binding.

Thus on the eve of the revolution which was permanently to disrupt what Elizabeth had made of the monarchy and the Church, a popular playwright and hack writer was still finding it worth his while to exploit the legend of the great queen. But he was not the only one to leave evidence of the spell she continued to exercise over the popular imagination, or to echo the legend of which she was the climactic figure. In 1650 a certain Sir Anthony Weldon, who had held a minor post in her household, had been ousted and disgruntled under James, and had taken parliament's side in the civil war, published a tract called *The Court and Character of King James* in which he ridiculed the king and his Scottish attendants and celebrated 'that most glorious sun that ever shined in our firmament of England, the never to be forgotten Queen Elizabeth of happy memory'.

Sir William Sanderson, who served Charles at court and in the war and later wrote a history of his reign and the reigns of his father and grandmother, defended James's memory, but even in doing so still did obeisance to the memory of Elizabeth. 'She hath,' he said, 'been highly valued since her death, the best of any former sovereign over us. She was fitted for fortune's darling but with some imprisonment to mould her for the rule and sovereignty of a kingdom ... she showed her justice and piety as a precedent to posterity ... She was magnificent comparitivè with other princes, which yet she disposed frugally, having always much to do with little money.' There was in contrast not much that even this loyal gentleman could think magnificent about James.

James's reputation was being vindicated at about the same time by Godfrey Goodman, High-Church bishop and crypto-Catholic, but in his case, too, the memory of the queen still overshadowed that of her successor.[1] Writing about 1650, Goodman recalled seeing her sixty years before as she came from court by torchlight in great state after the Armada victory, the people crying 'God save your majesty', and she, a woman ravaged by age but magnificent as ever, replying 'God bless you my people'. 'This wrought such an impression upon us,' Goodman adds, 'that all the way we did nothing but talk what an admirable queen she was.' Though men grew weary in her last days, he continues, of being ruled by an old woman and looked forward to great things with the coming of their new king, nevertheless, 'after a few years, when we had experience of the Scottish government ... the Queen did seem to revive; then was her memory much magnified – such ringing of bells, such public joy and sermons in commemoration of her, the picture of her tomb painted in many churches and in effect more solemnity and joy in memory of her coronation than was for the coming in of King James.'

For the truth was that after the Armada the great redemptive climax towards which history was supposed to have been moving since Wyclif had not come off, not at any rate to the satisfaction of the brotherhood of preachers and those listeners to their preaching whose disappointment with Elizabeth's successors had been exacerbated by the pretensions of the Laudian episcopate. Hence, with the strategic check to the king's proceedings which came in 1640, the preachers invoked the old familiar legend concerning England's appointed place in the designs of providence. Since in England Antichrist was destined to meet his final doom, in Eng-

[1] Goodman, *The Court of James I* (1839); G. I. Soden, *Godfrey Goodman* (1953).

land he had always put up his fiercest resistance, but if parliament would heed the call which the preachers now again voiced, the victorious consummation of the historic process set in motion in the reign of Elizabeth but frustrated since would finally be accomplished.

One of the first things parliament did after assembling in November 1640 was to appoint a day of fasting, humiliation and prayer to prepare itself for the work before it. There were to be services with preaching morning and afternoon for the members of the House of Commons at St Margaret's, Westminster. The day fixed for the occasion was, as it happened, the anniversary of Elizabeth's accession, and Cornelius Burges, preaching in the morning, assured his hearers that, whether or not they had remembered the significance of the day, providence had surely directed them in their choice. 'Remember and consider,' he said, 'that this very day ... eighty-two years sithence began a new resurrection of this kingdom from the dead.' That is to say, 'our second happy reformation of religion by the auspicious entrance of our late royal Deborah ... into her blessed and glorious reign'.[1] In the afternoon Stephen Marshall again reminded the members that 'this day eighty-two years agone the Lord set up His gospel among us.'[2]

Both preachers were as certain as Lancelot Andrewes had been twenty-five years before that the English were a people singled out by the Lord for special favour. In Marshall's words, 'we have been hitherto kept as another Land of Goshen where light hath still shined when all others have been in darkness'. But parliament must understand what God expected of a people so favoured. Whenever the Lord bestows some special favour upon a people, Burges said, it is a sign that He is willing to make a covenant with them to grant still more. 'Where He once opens His hand to take a people into His protection, He opens His heart to take them

[1] *Sermon Preached to the Honourable House of Commons ... November 17, 1640* (1641).

[2] *Sermon Preached before the Honourable House of Commons ... November 17, 1640* (1641).

into His bosom.' But this does not mean that they have nothing to do but enter at once and take their ease in Zion. 'He that hath obtained most and greatest deliverances will ere long stand in need of more.' If a people is to go on drawing deliverances upon itself, the one thing necessary is that it should on its part 'enter into a solemn covenant with the Lord upon consideration of what he hath done already'.

This teaching Burges and Marshall explicated out of the history of the chosen people of the Old Testament, and Burges in particular went on to explicate it further out of the history of the elect people of England. He tells the members of parliament – what surely they must often have been told or have read for themselves – how Henry VIII had delivered his people out of Babylon and cast out the Pope, how Edward VI had for a time cast out popery itself, how Mary had brought it back 'to drink drunk of the blood of our ancestors', and how finally Elizabeth, 'that glorious Deborah ... although her heart was upright and loathed the idolatry of the former reign, yet found ... work enough to restore anything at all and to make any beginning of a reformation ... having such a strong party of stout popelings to grapple with at home and such potent and dangerous abettors of them to cope withal abroad.' Not only that, but her endeavours were also thwarted, it was said, by the addiction of returning exiles to the forms of worship and discipline they had practised at Frankfurt.

This was a version of the history of Elizabeth's reign which would have astonished that lady herself, could she have heard it, lying near by in her tomb in the Abbey. It was meant, however, to impress upon the men gathered at St Margaret's on that anniversary the idea that they were bound by covenant with the Lord to complete the work which had been left unfinished at her death and prevented ever since by the bishops, who were still keeping the Lord's people from perfecting the reformation she had begun.

This appeal was presently seconded by John Milton, bringing to the preachers' support an unremitting temper, an extraordinary energy of mind and imagination, and an equally extraordinary power of verbal expression. Up to this point there had not been much to mark him outwardly as greatly different from other men of his time and station who had been reared in the Protestant tradition for a career in the pulpit. But having entered Cambridge in the year of Charles I's accession, he had during his seven years in the university seen Laud's rise to ascendancy in the Church, and concluding himself 'church-outed', he had turned to poetry as his vocation and the study of history as essential to his preparation. Poetry he conceived as the supreme technique for teaching men how to overcome the consequences of man's original fall. History he conceived as the record of the recurring lapses and recoveries of men on their way to that final decisive recovery which was destined to bring redemption to God's chosen people. With ideas and intentions such as these, Milton went to Italy in 1638 to complete his preparations for the career he had chosen, and he got back to England on the eve of the Long Parliament with plans for undertaking an English heroic poem in emulation of Virgil and Tasso. Virgil had written of the founding of a new Troy after the fall of the old, Tasso of the recovery of Jerusalem from the infidel. He would write a poem for his fellow-countrymen in the mother dialect embodying the same theme of recovery after fall in a fable drawn from legendary British history.

But before he got far with that project, the far-off consummation he had intended to foreshadow and celebrate in his heroic poem suddenly came, or seemed to come, within reach of achievement. So he wrote not an Arthuriad but a series of revolutionary tracts intended to persuade parliament to proceed at once to the completion of that long-delayed reformation initiated three centuries earlier by Wyclif, reformation of Church government, but also, as he went on, of marriage, of education, of the laws for the regulation of printing – the reconstitution, in fact, of the whole framework of Church and state into a species of puritan Utopia or humanist New Jerusalem. But the series of revolutionary tracts which concluded with *Areopagitica* began with *Of Reformation Touching Church-Discipline in England and the Causes that hitherto have hindered it.* The argument, which concluded with the vision of England, 'muing her mighty youth and kindling her undazzled eyes at the full midday beam, purging and unscaling her long abused sight at the fountain itself of heavenly radiance', started with a reassertion of that view of the English past, of that account of the progress of reformation in England since Wyclif, which had been first fixed in the English mind by the Book of Martyrs.

By 1640 Milton had, to be sure, read many historians besides Foxe and had learned to distinguish critically among them. He realized, as indeed Foxe himself had done, that there were elements in the familiar story which were rather for poets to use than for historians to credit. He made plain, when a few years later he essayed himself to write a history of Britain, that he held the monkish chroniclers on whom so much of the story depended in contempt and found only the Roman writers credible and indeed admirable. He inferred that some of Foxe's martyrs, notably the bishops among them, may have died for something less than the truth. He knew too well what Whitgift, with the queen's support, had done to suppress reform to believe everything that Foxe or Camden or Speed wrote in her praise, and he was chary of mentioning her name even while glorifying the accomplishments of her reign. Yet in the great contention which came to a head in 1640, not many Englishmen, whichever side they took, were able to think about the issues at stake in their time, let alone express their thoughts, without the use of that familiar parallel code of reference to the saga of the chosen people of the Old Testament and the elect people of England which had come down to them in English print from the days of Elizabeth.

Certainly not Milton, his imagination taking fire at the events which followed his return from Italy with plans for a poem doctrinal to the nation on a theme from the nation's history. He addressed the Long Parliament with nothing less than the same apocalyptical fervour with which Foxe, Jewel, Aylmer and other returning exiles had hailed the accession of Elizabeth some eighty years before. Parliament and the English people must be made to understand that the will of God, revealed in scripture and history, was still directing events to an appointed end. Divine purpose, having come thus far, was moving to perfect fulfilment, and the people of England, having often before served as its agents, were to be the agents of its next advance.

After many dark ages reformation had 'struck through the black and settled night of ignorance and anti-Christian tyranny', and England had been appointed to 'set up a standard for the recovery of lost truth and blow the evangelic trumpet to the nations'. All succeeding reformers had lit their tapers at the light of Wyclif's kindling. Popes, prelates and tyrants had laboured to stifle the light, but in Elizabeth's time God had made a covenant with England, freed her from bondage, built up her Britannic empire with all her daughter islands about her, and scattered her enemy over the northern ocean even to the frozen Thule. With all the world to choose from, He 'hath yet ever had this island under the special indulgent eye of his providence'. Heaven has appointed England 'to give out reformation to the world'. It has been her people's glory and wonted prerogative to be 'the first asserters of every great vindication'. Let her not forget 'her precedence of teaching nations how to live'. 'Lords and commons of England,' he tells them, 'consider what nation it is whereof ye are and whereof ye are the governors.' For now that God is once more decreeing 'some new and great period in His Church, even to the reforming of reformation itself, what does He then but reveal Himself to His Englishmen; I say as His manner is, first to us.'

The preachers' sermons on November 17th, 1640, followed as they were by Milton's addresses, calling upon the Long Parliament to complete the reformation begun at the accession of Elizabeth eighty-two years before but left unfinished at the close of her reign, may be said to bring the story of the Book of Martyrs to a period, though not to its conclusion. What came, however, of the effort so long persisted in by the Puritan wing of the reform party in England for a still more perfect reformation, what became of Milton's apocalyptical vision of an England reformed according to his humanized conception of reformation, what became of the Book of Martyrs after the final disruption of the historic Church in the Puritan Revolution, all this is another story.

As things turned out in the reign of Elizabeth, the religion of the Word and the Protestant view of the Church prevailed in England, and Englishmen took, like other Protestants, to arguing endlessly among themselves about the meaning of the Word, especially in its application to practical questions of government in Church and state. Yet important though the differences were which presently rose among them, no less important were the unspoken assumptions which the English of that age continued to hold in common and which kept them, in the long run, more alike than they were different in their way of responding to the widening experiences which awaited them in the age to come.

To these ideas the Book of Martyrs gave immediate, dramatic expression, confirming the conception of individual spiritual experience set forth by the pulpit and adding the support of an account of the universal process and design of the whole history of mankind. The example of martyrs, the lessons of history, and the teachings of the pulpit led men to suppose that they might expect the coming of a great change which would set them free from the weakness and uncertainty which flesh is heir to and, whatever happened to the generality of fallen souls, would give their own souls assurance that they had nothing to fear here or hereafter.

Such assurance was not to be invoked at will, but neither was it dependent upon chance or circumstance. It did not come to everyone – that was obvious – but it might come at any time to anyone whatever, and since it came by God's will and election alone, no power on earth could stop it. This conception of the working of man's inner life was, of course, not original with the English, and they added little of note to its systematic or speculative elaboration. Yet its impact on the English people at this stage in their history was not on that account less far-reaching in its effect. Conditions in England – the fact of its being an island placed as it was on the map of Europe, the stage it had come to in the development of its institutions, the emergence of London as a metropolitan centre, the character of the people, the state of their language, the genius and personality of their ruler – all this meant not only that England would follow a course peculiar to itself but that Protestantism would there follow a course peculiar to England. It would produce not reformers and theologians of the stature of half a dozen or more continental figures, but a plethora of preachers, writers, poets and public men, adventurers and statesmen, speculators and politicians, explorers and planters of colonies, men with an overweening and often unreflecting confidence in themselves and the rectitude of their own intentions.

The prime enterprise which had evoked the creative energies of English reformers was the translation of the Scriptures into the common tongue and their circulation among the people. The thing which more than anything else gave vitality to the idea of an inner spiritual change leading to a new life and a new way of life became for the English the encounter with that extraordinary book, brought thus within the compass of ordinary experience. They were led to conclude, naturally enough, that by the lively apprehension of the Word in their own familiar speech, heard from the pulpit and read in print, was to be gained a knowledge which would settle everything once and for all. Such a conviction was the easier to embrace since in the book that same familiar speech seemed itself to spring into new life. For in fashioning their version of the book the succession of translators which began with Tyndale managed to weld the divers elements of that speech into an instrument of extraordinary evocative power.

Given the nature of the Bible itself and what the English translators made of it, one can understand how men so possessed by the passion for utterance which it inspired came to erect the book into a religion. Persecution confirmed them in the assurance of election conveyed by their experience; martyrdom provided a hallowed occasion for testifying to their experience; exile convinced them that only such as were able to testify to such an experience as theirs could claim to be of the true Church. For, having been turned out of the visible Church as re-constituted under Mary and turned in upon themselves by banishment, they naturally took

The Elect Nation

recourse in the idea that not the body which had cast them out but they themselves were the true Church, that the true Church had always been such a company of chosen spirits as themselves, that the condition of the true Church in this world had always been to be rejected and persecuted.

This condition, to be sure, was to last for the Marian exiles only so long as the Marian regime lasted, and some of them, when their own footing in the new establishment was made secure, were content to take their ease in Zion. But the time for the process of history to terminate and the elect to cease from struggling was really not yet. For the accession of Elizabeth settled none of the issues which had flared up in the clash of the Marian government with the Marian martyrs, and the situation which followed her accession merely gave added force to the ideas which the martyrs' disciples brought home with them. What was more, the increasing pressures which the Catholic powers brought to bear against Elizabeth over the succeeding years, gave these ideas still greater force and meaning for her subjects in general. The idea of a pre-destined salvation reserved for the elect, of the Church as a com-munion of elect souls beset in all ages by enemies without and within, of the progression of the elect from age to age towards an apocalyptical vindication – these conceptions assumed in many minds a meaning and an application which went beyond their merely religious context.

One did not need to share in all the manifestations of the new religion or endorse all the demands of the reformers and their supporters in parliament in order to accept without question the explanation put forward by the preachers and by Foxe in his book of the dangerous predicament in which the queen and the nation found themselves, or to embrace the hope and the solution which they expressed. The prolonged uncertainties of the time rendered many an otherwise sober mind susceptible to the dream of an impending change which would end all uncertainty at a single stroke. One could hardly remain totally impervious to the ex-pectancy with which the evangelists of the Word continued to look to the queen even when she hung back from the perfect ful-

fulment of the reformation to which they believed she was necessarily committed.

For the Church as they conceived it appeared now as one with the nation, and for many, besides the champions of a still more perfect reformation, the nation itself assumed something of the nature of a mystical communion of chosen spirits, a peculiar people set apart from the rest of mankind. The continued attacks of the nation's and the Church's adversaries served not only to fortify the godly in their sense of election, but also to persuade many besides – those especially, perhaps, whose interests depended most immediately upon the security of the regime – that there must be something special about being English, that the English were being subjected to the unusual trials now afflicting them because they were nothing less than an elect people called to play a particular part in the designs of providence. This conviction, which received something like official support with the official recognition of Foxe's book in 1571, grew with every one of the queen's narrow escapes from the attacks of her enemies, and when Antichrist finally came sailing up the Channel in 1588 and the wind, as Milton reminded the Long Parliament in 1641, scattered him over the northern ocean even to the frozen Thule, it was natural to conclude that, as Aylmer had said in 1559, God was indeed English.

What the queen thought about all this in her private mind, especially what she thought about herself in the role of God's appointed instrument for executing His design for England, one would not dare to say. She may have more than half believed, as she was told over and over again, that He had really cast her for the part. Certainly she played the part for all it was worth whenever her cue came. In the language affected by courtiers and poets she might be addressed as Cynthia or Gloriana, but in the language she herself used in dealing with parliament, the language of politics, she spoke of herself as the nursing mother of Israel. Yet she never allowed her judgment to be captivated or betrayed by her own facility of utterance. She had seen what troubles her sister had let herself in for by permitting one set of ecclesiasts to rule the roost in the name of true religion. She was wary of letting those of any other persuasion attempt the same. A Protestant theocracy operating through an untrammelled pulpit might prove as difficult to keep in hand as a Catholic hierarchy answerable to Rome. She would play nursing mother in Israel as occasion might require, but she would have no synod of divines running the Church, and no faction of their supporters in parliament telling her how the Church should be constituted and governed.

It was not, considering the danger in which they as well as she stood, that they were unable to make out a case for a more positive policy and an end to temporizing with subjects who failed to conform to the religion established by law. Knowing as we do what happened in the end, it is easy to say that the queen was wiser in her generation than those who kept pressing her for what they called a more perfect reformation and for more drastic action against recusant Catholics. If she resisted their importunities, it was not that she had any compunctions about doing whatever seemed necessary to meet any challenge to her authority in either the ecclesiastical or the civil realm, but neither had she any to prevent her leaving religious questions to be dealt with as occasion might require and circumstances permit.

Religion, it was still generally assumed, was the bond of union in the state, but the fact was that the general revival of the religious spirit fomented by reformers, Catholic no less than Protestant, was promoting not civil union but civil contention, and the problem of rulers was to preserve the unity of the state in spite of religious dissension and notwithstanding the winds of doctrine blowing ever more violently from the pulpit and the printing press. Few men supposed that such a condition of affairs was to be regarded as proper, natural and irremediable. Most men expected that by some dialectical or disciplinary process dissension would be brought to an end, unity of faith restored, and all men brought together again in one true Church. The Roman Church, but also each of the derivative branches of the historic Church, looked forward not to being merely tolerated by the others but to becoming itself the one, all-embracing, universal communion. Yet no matter how zealously the missionaries and evangelists of one faith or the other laboured to convert all men to their way of thinking, and no matter how conscientiously civil rulers endeavoured to compel everyone to conform, the effect was not to restore unity to Christendom and union to the state, but to promote and perpetuate the disintegration of the historic Church which all parties deplored in principle but promoted in practice.

At the moment that Elizabeth came to the throne in England her fellow-rulers in France and Scotland and in Spain and the Netherlands, though at bitter odds with one another, were nevertheless making war on their subjects in the vain hope of restoring the unity of faith assumed to be the bond of civil union. But the English people were as deeply divided in religion as any other, the danger was as great that their differences would lead to civil disruption, and if Elizabeth had done as other rulers, she would have used her authority to enforce general conformity to the settlement of religious matters adopted at the outset of her reign. She did nothing so simple and straightforward as that, and if she had, the outcome would doubtless have been what it was on the Continent: civil turmoil and religious war.

Her way of meeting the problem presented by the seemingly irrepressible religious strife of the age is to be seen in her way of administering what has ever since been known as the Elizabethan settlement of religion, a settlement no more remarkable for the things it settled than for those it left unsettled, or to be settled, if at all, at some other time. It settled that there would be a national Church with a liturgy in the vernacular keyed to the vernacular Bible, a body of doctrines judiciously vague on controverted points, and a hierarchical government responsible to the Crown. To this settlement the queen's subjects were required by law to adhere, and the queen was disposed to enforce the law as strictly as in her judgment seemed necessary. But how strictly that might be depended on circumstances. Anabaptists would be burned for heresy, Catholic missionaries hanged for treason, and Puritans kept from undermining the authority of bishops by the device of Presbyterian 'classes', but the law was more or less tempered for peaceable subjects of whatever persuasion who might be slack in subscribing to all the doctrines and conforming to all the practices of the religion by law established.

Yet though the queen resisted Protestant demands for more rigorous laws in respect to religion and stricter enforcement of the laws against recusants, she remained aware that she needed Protestant support to counterbalance Catholic opposition backed by foreign power. Able and dependable men more inclined than she to the Protestant view of things were retained for years as trusted servants and counsellors. The universities were allowed to go on educating young men for the Protestant ministry. Sir Walter Mildmay and the Countess of Sussex were permitted to found new colleges for them at Cambridge. Persons of means were allowed to retain them as tutors and chaplains until benefices or pulpits could be found for them. Patrons, vestries, Inns of Court, town councils and voluntary groups were allowed to pay them for lecturing on the Bible.

Hence the class of educated, articulate, professional intellectuals of idealistic temper which the Marian government had endeavoured so desperately to bring under control continued to grow in numbers and influence under Elizabeth, and the English people by the end of the reign were thoroughly committed and habituated to the religion of the Word. The Puritans were effectually prevented from taking the government of the Church out of the hands of bishops responsible to the Crown, but William Perkins and the brotherhood of spiritual preachers, so long as they were content not to meddle with questions of government, were allowed to set forth the doctrines and the way of life they deduced from the Bible and to have their teachings put into print. And all this time, as we have seen, Foxe's great book was kept before the public with its dedication to the queen and the official endorsement of the Church itself.

Thus the national Church became fixed under Elizabeth in a position which enabled it in the long run to hold its ground at the centre of national life against both the revolutionary and the counter-revolutionary forces of the time, while the dynamic impulses set in motion by the religion of the Word were left sufficient liberty to proliferate as they might in the age to come. What followed was not the new dawn and the last age envisioned by Bale, Foxe, Aylmer, Jewel and other survivors of the reign of Mary who hailed the accession of Elizabeth, but a new age none the less, not the New Jerusalem but a new England, not a visible communion of elected saints awaiting the millennium but a people with a strong sense of their identity as a nation set apart from all others, aware of what they took to be a common past, and intent on what they took to be their appointed place and destiny in the world.

The consequences were to be far-reaching, for presently the world was all before them to go where they chose, taking with them their sense of election and their expectation of great things to come bred by the religion of the Word. The Word, however, and the spiritual attitude and way of life that sprang from it were more easily transportable than the established Church. The multiplication of printed books, the popularization of the Scriptures, the classics and the literature of Reformation and Renaissance, the coming together of English and Scottish peoples, of the Church and the Kirk, under the Crown, their involvement with the recalcitrant Irish, and the hiving-off of all three together, speaking the same language and bearing the same seeds of difference, to North America with the expectation of finding or founding the New Jerusalem, Utopia or perhaps only El Dorado, all this made the hardly won predominance of the ecclesiastical frame established under Elizabeth at the centre of things in England but a single factor of diminishing importance in the development of a civilization, Elizabethan in its inception and English, but not Anglican, in character.

It would remain much of a piece and not to be mistaken for any other in the world. But its common character would be due not to the unity of all its members in the Church of England or in any other Church, but in the use of the English language, English books, English law, and a religion centred on the individual apprehension of whatever might be taken to be the truth revealed in the English Bible. Yet though the Bible would go everywhere with these people and take its place in the life of every English-speaking community, no single segment of the historic Church would ever realize its expectation of imposing itself on the multiplicity of personal, local, denominational beliefs, opinions and practices springing from the Elizabethan settlement as administered by the great queen.

That such would be the outcome of that settlement so administered, Foxe had perhaps a kind of premonition. In 1570, besides a new dedication to the queen, he added an address 'To the True and Faithfull Congregation of Christ's Universal Church with all and singular the members thereof wheresoever congregated or dispersed through the realm of England.' He concluded this address by exhorting his countrymen to wait patiently upon the Lord and edify one another in all humility.

And if there cannot be an end of our disputing and contending one against an other, yet let there be a moderation in our affections. And for so much as it is the good will of our God that Satan thus should be let loose among us for a short time, yet let us strive in the meanwhile what we can to amend the malice of the time with mutual humanity. They that be in error, let them not disdain to learn. They which have greater talents of knowledge committed, instruct in simplicity them that be simple. No man liveth in that commonwealth where nothing is amiss. But yet because God hath so placed us Englishmen here in one commonwealth, also in one Church, as in one ship together, let us not mangle or divide the ship, which being divided perisheth, but every man serve in his order with diligence, wherein he is called.

APPENDIX

'Fox's Book of Martyrs'

◦∾ᵂᵂᵂ∾◦

Foxe was always more preoccupied in *Actes and Monumentes* with the necessity of preventing the English Church from being again subjected to Catholic authority than he was with the need to make it instantly more Protestant than the queen would allow. This continued to be the case, though in his personal convictions he inclined to the Puritan side. Hence his book continued to be regarded as the quasi-official defence of the Church of England so long as the Catholic powers seemed to threaten its security. As the threat receded, the book signified less and less to all parties as a defence of the established Church against its external enemies, while the evangelical party within the Church and dissenters of all degrees looked to 'Fox's Book of Martyrs' for evidence of the oppression which the truly faithful have always had to suffer at the hands of one established hierarchy or another. This change in the book's position in public esteem is reflected in the later history of its publication.

The Stationers' Company issued one more edition of *Actes and Monumentes*, the ninth, in 1684, in anticipation of the coming of James II to the throne. This edition, the most sumptuous of all, reproduced the edition of 1641 but printed the entire text for the first time in roman and italic type, and the illustrations, recopied from the originals, from copper plates. It also supplied a new frontispiece portrait of the author, engraved by John Sturt. This was the last edition to reproduce the original in its entirety with reasonable fidelity until we come to the edition launched in the interest of the evangelical cause by S. R. Cattley in 1837, and reissued several times thereafter by Josiah Pratt.

Meanwhile various hands had been exploiting *Actes and Monumentes* with far less respect for the original. In 1732 appeared a

251

work entitled *The Book of Martyrs: Containing an Account of the Sufferings and Death of the Protestants in the reign of Mary the First. Illustrated with Copper Plates. Originally Written by Mr. John Fox: And now revised and corrected by an Impartial Hand.* This version of Foxe's book appeared again in 1761 and several times thereafter, 'revised and corrected with a recommendatory preface' by Martin Madan, a noted Wesleyan preacher, who in 1776 added a second volume similarly derived from Foxe, entitled *The Lives of the Primitive Martyrs from the Birth of our Blessed Saviour to the Reign of Queen Mary.* By that time Wesley himself in his *Christian Library* in 1750 had printed four hundred pages from Foxe in which he gave condensed versions of the stories of the Marian martyrs, revising the language to make it, he said, more intelligible, and omitting 'all the secular history' as well as everything 'which contained nothing particularly affecting or instructive'. In 1784 another Methodist divine, Paul Wright, went much farther in adapting Foxe's book for similar purposes, calling the result of his effort *The New and Complete Book of Martyrs, or an Universal History of Martyrdom: being Fox's Book of Martyrs, Revised and Corrected, with Additions and great Improvements.* After that came many other versions of something still called 'Fox's Book of Martyrs', continuing down to the twentieth century and bearing less and less resemblance to the work which the original author addressed to Elizabeth I in 1563. In 1954 the Protestant Truth Society in Fleet Street was still circulating something called by that title.

What we see in these later versions of Foxe's book, many of which in the eighteenth and nineteenth centuries were published to be sold by subscription in separate numbers, is the progressive corruption and vulgarization of the original for the propagation of an increasingly narrow evangelical Protestant piety. Foxe's whole account of ecclesiastical and national history, by which he sought to make his contemporaries understand what happened in Mary's reign and its bearing on the situation in which they found themselves under her successor, dropped completely out. The book opened now with the stories of the sufferings inflicted on

Appendix

Protestants in the days of 'bloody Mary', so described apparently for the first time by Paul Wright, and went on to retail other stories drawn from other sources of the persecution of true believers in other times and places by the established powers of state and church. The woodcuts of the original editions, especially those depicting burnings and other horrors, were copied and re-copied, and many more sensational pictures added of the same sort.

Hence it is safe to say that, while 'the great black letter volume' which Macaulay saw chained to the reading desk in church and longed to get his young hands on may have been a seventeenth- or even a sixteenth-century copy of the original work, the thing known as 'Fox's Book of Martyrs', which in the memory of persons still living was kept for Sunday reading in many pious households, was as likely as not a later, much altered version of the book, perhaps bought by subscription at sixpence the number. Hence too the book came to be associated in many minds with the prejudices, best forgotten, of a less enlightened age.

INDEX

Index

Canterbury, 25, 108, 165
Cartwright, Thomas, 104–5, 139
Cattley, S. R., 24n., 251
Caxton, William, 146
Chambers, E. K., 234n.
Charles I, 227–9, 232
Cheke, John, 184
Clement, Pope, 173
Cochlaeus, 167
Coilus, King, 137, 150–1
Cole, Henry, 90–4, 114
Commodus, Emperor, 150
Constance, Council of, 164, 167
Constantine the Great, 124, 130, 137–8, 141, 143, 153, 157, 171
Cooper, Thomas, 146, 159
'Copus, Alanus', 166n.
Cotton, Sir Robert, 229, 233
Courtney, William, 163–4
Coverdale, Miles, 51, 54, 73, 200, 208, 214
Cox, Richard, 48, 82
Cranmer, Thomas, 25, 49, 51, 54–6, 63, 76, 176–7, 184, 185, 197; in the Tower, 27–36, 122, 188; at Oxford, 36, 122, 188; condemned as a heretic, 39, 123, 188; execution of, 43–4, 72, 83, 90–1, 189–93; recantation of, 91, 194; illustration of, in Book of Martyrs, 173
Cresme, Nicholas, 162
Crespin, Jean, 65, 69, 160
Cromwell, Thomas, 59, 121, 173, 176–7, 185
Crowley, Thomas, 146
Cuningham, William, 114, 116–17, 118

Damian, 151
Dante, 162
Darcie, Abraham, 229
Davies, W. T., 59n.
Day, John, prints Latimer's sermons, 27, 134; and 'An Harborowe,' 87; and Bullinger's sermons, 90; and Book of Martyrs, 110, 118, 127, 158, 189; career as publisher and printer, 112–18, 221; with Foxe as editor, 114; death, 223
De Heretico Comburendo, 43, 181
Dobbe, Thomas, 184
Doran, Madeleine, 234n.
Drake, Sir Francis, 221, 223
Driver, Alice, 218
Dudley, Sir Robert, 114, 144
Duff, E. G., 148n.

Edward II, 177
Edward III, 141, 153, 157, 161–2
Edward IV, 167, 169
Edward VI, will of, 25; repeal of De Heretico Comburendo under, 43; Latimer's

sermons before, 116; Foxe on, 122, 125, 183; development of printing under, 146; Camden on, 230
Egbert, King, 141
Elder, John, 19n.
Eleutherius, Bishop of Rome, 151, 225
Elizabeth I, religion under, 14–18, 20, 69, 75, 82–109, 225, 242–50; use of Latin under, 51; character of, 84; coronation of, 86; Aylmer on, 87–8; concern over successor to, 119–20; Foxe on, 124–7, 130, 140, 153, 174, 188, 195, 220, 250; Camden on, 230–2; Speed on, 232–4; Heywood on, 234–5; Sanderson on, 235–6; Burges on, 238
Ellis, Sir Henry, 143n.
Erasmus, 23, 56
Eusebius, 65–8, 124, 130, 133, 137, 211

Fabyan, Robert, 138, 146, 150, 157–9, 178
Fagius, 123, 194
Fasciculi Zizaniorum, 62, 164, 166
Fisher, Bishop, 76, 173
Fitzralph, Archbishop, 162
Flacius Illyricus, Matthias, 64–5, 69, 133, 138, 141, 160, 162, 167
Folkes, Elizabeth, 218
Foxe, John, early career, 55–6; meeting with Bale, 56, 70–1; meeting with Grindal, 56; pleads for heretics, 56–7; importance of his work, 57–8; comments on his book, 72; Good Friday sermon preached by (1570), 99–102; on printing, 110; joins forces with Day, 110; pensioned and ordained, 117; burial place, 118; prepares English version of Book of Martyrs, 120; death, 223. See also Book of Martyrs, Foxe's
Frankfurt, 41, 49, 53–4, 56
Frederick, Emperor, 155, 172
Frith, John, 138
Fugatius, 151
Fuller, Thomas, 124n.

Gardiner, Stephen, 22, 25, 27, 45, 54, 62, 101, 113, 126, 176–7, 178, 181, 189, 199, 203–7, 211; imprisons Philpot, 28; defends royal supremacy, 46, 77; character of, 59; Foxe on, 121, 184–6, 195; examines Marbeck, 180; death, 193
De vera Obedientia, 112
Geneva, 49, 65, 73, 78–9, 174
Geoffrey of Monmouth, 138, 142, 144, 150
Gildas, 138, 142, 146, 150, 152
Glastonbury, 150
Glover, George, 228
Goodman, Christopher, 78–9, 82
Goodman, Godfrey, 236

256

Index

Index

Index